ₛtle was born in the old West Riding of York-
ᵤefore the outbreak of the Second World War. He
started collecting antiques at an early age, hoarding his treasures
in a disused hen house, known ever after as the 'junk hut'.

After National Service and a brief period working for an
engineering company, Max and his family heard the call of the
Yorkshire Dales, where they bought a cottage, hung out their
sign – Bullpen Antiques – and made a happy living for many
years.

Max and his family now live in Leyburn, North Yorkshire,
with two dogs, two ponies, a goat named Elspeth and an ever-
fluctuating population of hens, ducks and pigeons. His only
regret is that he no longer has the contents of his treasured
'junk hut'.

TALES FROM THE DALES

The Luck of a Countryman

MAX HARDCASTLE

sphere

SPHERE

First published in Great Britain in 1992 by Little, Brown and Company
First published in paperback in 1993 by Warner Books
This paperback edition published in 2011 by Sphere

A CIP catalogue for this book
is available from the British Library.

ISBN 978-0-7515-4424-4

Typeset in Baskerville by M Rules
Printed and bound in Great Britain by
Clays Ltd, St Ives plc

Papers used by Sphere are from well-managed forests
and other responsible sources.

MIX
Paper from
responsible sources
FSC® C104740

Sphere
An imprint of
Little, Brown Book Group
100 Victoria Embankment
London EC4Y 0DY

An Hachette UK Company
www.hachette.co.uk

www.littlebrown.co.uk

For Adrian and Jonathan

Prelude

The purchase, at auction, of a derelict farmhouse with out-buildings standing in two acres of land gave Max and Vicky Hardcastle the chance to opt for a better way of life for themselves and their children and to relocate their antiques business to the heart of the Yorkshire Dales. It brought them into contact with a whole range of highly entertaining and memorable characters: farmer Ted the next-door neighbour; Baz the village handyman, Jack of all trades and master of most; Rabbit Joe, the third generation poacher, and Mrs Smythe-Robinson, snobbish wife of the local quarry owner.

The village had its shop, pub and school. The latter staffed by the mousy but much loved Miss Wells.

Every Thursday, Thievin' Jack the travelling butcher pulls his van on to the green and Mrs Lewis at the shop moves aside the packets of soap powder so she can keep an eye on him.

The Dales network of part-time dealers includes Long John, the semi-recluse distiller of the potent Swaledale Lightning and Canary Mary, self-styled Queen of the Fleamarkets, eccentric and obsessed with the colour yellow. They, along with Drunken Sam the auctioneer, the diminutive Fiery Frank with Little Petal his mountainous biscuit-addicted wife and the aristocratic de Traffords are all part of the rich fabric of the Dales antique scene. Saleroom battles against the Ring, led by the noxious Fatty Batty, bring many fruitless days and some moments of sweet victory, and summer evenings spent leaning on the wall absorbing horse-lore from the affable gypsy Apple Tom are not, as Vicky thinks, completely wasted.

Chapter 1

Thievin' Jack squatted on the banking, lit a cigarette, blew out a lazy plume of smoke, and stared sadly at his van. 'I ought to wring her bloody neck,' he said quietly.

His van stood in the middle of Tinker's Pond up to its wheel arches in water. A thin skin of ice covered the pond except for halos of clear water around the van and the clumps of brown sweet flag. I leaned against Ted's Fergie, Baz and Rabbit sat in the link box; we were all deep in thought. The night before in the taproom it had all seemed so easy – get the travelling butcher's van out of the pond and we could share between us half a stone of the best sausage in Yorkshire.

As in a lot of enterprises the theory was impeccable. A thorough reconnaissance had proved the water too deep for mere Wellingtons but not impassable in waders. Vigorous probings had established a firm bottom below the layer of mud and the rope had been measured and tested.

Ted and I would be responsible for the logistics, Baz would provide the verve and dash.

At the mention of sausage, Rabbit, the local poacher, had drawn his buffet up and joined our little group. 'What time have I to be up there then?'

We looked at each other not without a little concern, for half a stone of sausage split four ways is nowhere near as desirable as half a stone of sausage split three ways.

Ted had given Rabbit a hard unfriendly stare. 'We've enough. I'm bringing the tractor, he's getting the stuff and Baz is going in.'

Rabbit had cocked his head to one side and given us a wide yellow-toothed grin. 'Ah, but you'll be needing a rope man. I'm good wi' ropes.'

A rope man? Did we need a rope man? Ropes, especially thick sisal ropes, are unfriendly things, they swell when they get wet, knots become Gordian ones, thick and unyielding, and they tend, as of old, to get cut. It was my rope and a good one so I proposed we took Rabbit on as rope man.

My two fellow van rescuers seemed less than taken with the idea, but we all knew that Rabbit would turn up anyway so they had reluctantly nodded their agreement.

There had been a hitch. I had searched high and low but I had only managed to find one wader. The van was at least seven yards from the banking, and the depth of the water, not to mention the bottom mud, precluded hopping. Was Baz willing to suffer one wet leg? 'Too bloody cold,' he had responded curtly, and so we stared glumly at the rope, the wader and the van.

Thievin' was getting very agitated. He threw the stub of his cigarette to sizzle out on the ice and put on his wheedling voice. 'Come on lads, let's have it out – I'm losing money.'

Ted scrubbed his chin. 'When your Ivy drove it in, how did she get from the van to the bank?'

Thievin' turned his head and looked steadily at him. 'She waded!'

'Ah,' said Rabbit raising a thick forefinger, 'so, she got both legs wet.'

'Course she did. Both legs and a bit more; she isn't that tall is she?'

Rabbit kept his finger elevated then curled it slowly down until it was no more than a handspan from Baz's nose. 'This woman, this young fragile woman got both legs wet and you,' here his voice dropped and his finger stabbed nearer to Baz's nose, 'you, daren't get one wet.'

Baz looked indignant, he grabbed Rabbit's finger and pulled it down, and with his free hand pointed to Thievin'. 'Ask him! Ask him where she is now!'

Thievin' pulled out another cigarette. 'She's in bed wi' a touch o' flu and wi' a bit o' luck it'll turn to bloody pneumonia.' He got to his feet and walked up to the tractor. 'Come on lads, you said you'd get it out.'

Ted flipped the throttle on the Fergie, punching a ball of black smoke into the air. 'Don't worry. Get the rope on an' I'll have her out in two ticks.'

Thievin' leaned on the rear wheel and smiled down at our inert man of action. 'It's only one leg Baz, it wouldn't take long. Just loop the rope around the back step and we'll have her out.'

Baz dropped his chin on to his knees. 'No, it's too bloody cold! You sure you can't find the other wader?' he said, giving me a none too friendly look.

'Positive Baz, looked high and low.'

'Well, I'm not going in! When I agreed I thought there was two waders.' Thievin' turned his back on the wheel and all five of us stared at the sorry-looking van.

Rabbit's terriers plunged through the brittle sweet flag sending a pair of mallard slithering and squawking across the pond. Ted pointed to the ducks. 'That's it! Saw it in a book – duck shooting in Eye-tally. What they do is sink barrels into the water and squat in 'em till the ducks come over. What we need is barrels.'

Barrels; we all considered barrels. It could work. We mentally spaced the barrels from bank to van, five at least, but Baz was not enthusiastic. 'How the hell do I get one leg out of a barrel and over into t'next when they're that far apart!' He held his arms wide.

Ted leaned down from the tractor. 'Little planks in between 'em.'

Baz was not happy. 'And how do we stop these barrels floating?'

His question silenced us again. How did we stop the barrels floating? Stones? Half fill them with water? We applied ourselves to the problem; five razor-sharp minds concentrating on one single issue, brows furrowed and knuckles chewed. Several times we heard a 'Couldn't we . . . ' then a pause and a sad 'no'. An idea, brilliant and original, but fatally flawed had stirred in one of our little group. I suspected Rabbit of faking these aborted ideas for he huddled back in the link box, warm and comfortable with corn sacks pulled around his knees and watched his terriers work in the long hedge at the top of the maypole field.

It was getting colder. Thievin' stamped his feet and shook his head. 'Hey, I shall have to get some right men in, I'm losing money.'

Ted was assuring him that he already had the right men when we heard the Colonel's Bentley draw up.

He walked around the pond followed by his Labrador, stopping to survey Thievin's van from various angles then stationed himself in front of us. 'Problem! Van to dry land – right?'

Ted leaned his body over the steering wheel and sunk his head on his hands. 'By, he's sharp this bugger.'

The Colonel ignored him and turned to me. 'Brief me.'

I told him how we'd decided on waders but, when we could only find one, our volunteer had declined to suffer a wet leg.

The Colonel paced the banking, his hands slapping together behind his back. Rabbit pulled himself up and wrapped a sack around his shoulders. 'I'll have to watch this fine military brain at work,' he muttered.

The Colonel stopped and swung around. 'Problem is one functional leg, one non-functional leg; make both legs functional – problem solved. What we need is a barrel.'

This pleased us all enormously, for here was a trained military mind, honed to perfection by years of high command and it had reached the same conclusion as we had. Well nearly, he'd actually said 'barrel', but then all those initiative tests he'd been subjected to in his cadet years must give him the edge on us.

The Colonel's plan was simple: Baz would don the wader and placing his unprotected leg in the barrel work one and then the other until he had made his way across to the van; he would attach the rope, climb into the van, then drag the barrel in after him.

The Colonel sat in the Bentley and charged his pipe whilst we climbed on to the link box and rocked down to the village in search of a barrel.

Baz is a tall man but every barrel we found proved untenable. It was the top lip of the barrel which caused the problem, for the chamfered edge and the iron hoop dug into the young bachelor's groin in an alarming way.

We were on the point of abandoning the search when I remembered I had an old zinc peggy-tub in the yard. We measured it anxiously; it would be a near thing, but Baz pronounced it comfortable so we bore it back to the pond in triumph. The Colonel insisted on a dry run and paced out seven yards along the bank as Baz donned the wader and loosely tied the rope around his waist. We had never established how Baz was going to get the rope around the submerged step but the Colonel brushed the problem aside. 'The man will use his initiative when he is on site, so to speak, and has contributed so much to the operation that he's reluctant to accept failure. He'll do it, you watch.' He tapped my chest and gave a little smile. 'Man management.'

Rabbit was warming his hands on the tractor's exhaust pipe. He called me to him, bent his head to my ear and pointed to the Colonel. 'He's not joining in on the sausage.'

'Quite right Rabbit, he's only here in an advisory capacity.'

Rabbit nodded his head sagely. 'That's it. Them as is advisory don't qualify.'

Baz insisted on testing the tub for leaks before he did the dry run, so we pushed it deep into the water and crowded round to peer into it. 'Dry as a bone,' we chorused.

Satisfied, Baz heaved his unprotected leg into it and on the Colonel's command shuffled along the bank.

'Leg, tub, leg, tub,' we called in unison.

Baz gained more ground with the leg than with the tub, causing him to advance in an arc. The Colonel was quick to

8

spot this and when we launched Baz out into the pond it was, on the military man's direction, at a considerable angle to the van. All went well. The chant of 'leg, tub' was slower, but the progress was good, tub and wader splintering the ice and raising a swirling cloud of brown mud in their wake. The angle of approach had been chosen with such care we all knew Baz was going to land up right over the step. The Colonel is a handy man to have around. When Baz reached the van he took off his jacket and stuffed it in the tub, then rolled up his sleeves and holding on to the handle to steady himself he gingerly lowered his arm into the water, fed the rope through the back step then tied a very workmanlike knot.

We raised a cheer and Baz clenched his hands over his head and punched them to the sky like a victorious boxer.

That triumphant gesture was to be his undoing, for the Colonel's Labrador, excited by the general goings-on, took it as an invitation to join in and plunged into the pond sending a wave lapping over the edge of the tub. Baz bent to retrieve his jacket and in doing so put an inadvisable amount of pressure on the tub which settled into the mud until the rim was an inch below the water level. The tub began to fill rapidly.

'Into the van,' shouted the Colonel.

Baz jagged and tore at the handle. 'It's bloody locked,' he shouted.

Thievin' bit his lower lip thoughtfully. 'Aye, it will be.'

Baz turned and glared at us as the tub filled with a sudden inrush which sent icy brown water lapping up to his crotch. He withdrew his leg from the barrel and waded to the bank, his teeth chattering and his whole body vibrating with the cold. He paused and with much finger wagging told Thievin' and Ted what they could do with their vehicles, the Colonel and Rabbit what they could do with their ideas. Then he slopped off down the lane, the Colonel's dog trotting at his heels.

I was congratulating myself that at least my logistics had not been at fault when he stopped and turned to wag the angry finger at me. ' . . . an' this bloody wader leaks,' he shouted, shaking the offending boot from his leg and throwing it in a high arc into the maypole field.

The Colonel paced the banking again with much hand slapping and humming until the dejected figure of Baz, still followed by the dog, turned into his cottage gate. He then picked his way through the gorse to his car and drove quietly away without a word.

Rabbit tied the rope to the tractor bar with an unnecessarily complex knot and stepped back grinning from ear to ear, 'You could tow t' *Queen Mary* wi' that.'

The Fergie revved and shook and then inched forward. Rabbit's knot tightened, the rope stretched alarmingly and then slowly the van was drawn from the pond crushing my tub into a shapeless mass. We left the van draining on to the road until Thievin' had poked under the bonnet and probed through the cab with much head shaking and clicking of the tongue, coupled with many threats to 'do our Ivy'.

We towed the van backwards up the lane and into Ted's farmyard. The light was failing so Thievin' strung a cable from the milk house then started to work on the engine.

Rabbit picked at the wet knots in vain, his big fingers plucked and prised, he cursed and grunted but to no avail.

'Oh dear, we shall have to cut 'em,' he announced with what I thought was mock concern.

I was having a bad day. I'd lost a good peggy-tub, a decent wader, and now my best rope was going to be hacked about. I bent down and looked carefully at the knots. 'Rabbit, you were taken on as rope man, you ought to undo 'em.'

Rabbit held his hands up to my face. 'It's me pandies; screwmatics,' he whined. I was more than a little annoyed. I pulled and yanked at the knots until my finger ends were raw, then on Ted's advice I worked a six-inch nail into the folds and made my fingers ache with pulling at the cold steel.

Rabbit stood behind me with a bill hook and waited until I'd finished. He shrugged his shoulders and tested the edge of the hook with his thumb as I got to my feet and stretched an aching back. 'Go on cut the bugger.'

Ted had brought the cows in to milk. He slapped the last black and white rump through the door and beckoned to me and Rabbit. 'We'll have to nail him about the sausage, he'll wriggle out of it if he can.' We agreed to 'nail' Thievin'.

The little butcher was kneeling on the mudguard, his head and shoulders buried in the engine compartment, as we surrounded him silently. Ted is a natural spokesman: he's forceful, comes straight to the point, and when money is concerned can be downright pig ignorant.

'Thievin', we'll be in the taproom tonight, we want the sausage before nine o'clock or this van goes back in t'pond.'

Thievin' raised his head in alarm, 'Nay lads, have a heart, I want her back on t'road tomorrow, I'm losing money.'

Ted sniffed. 'Nine o'clock.'

We turned and walked silently into the cow house as Thievin' dropped his head over the engine and tapped a spanner on the injectors. 'I'll wring her bloody neck.'

*

Wives need to be told, especially wives who have spent a dull February afternoon struggling single-handed with two boisterous children and looking after an antique shop.

I crept, a little sheepishly, into the warm kitchen and stood with my back to the fire. The dogs emerged from under the table and nuzzled wet noses into my dangling hands and a lovely smell of meat and potato pie rose from the oven. I heard the shop bell clang behind a customer and Vicky's heels click down the passageway. She frowned at me. 'I've been run off my feet.'

'Run off your feet this afternoon?'

'Yes, I don't know where they've come from.' She listed all the items she had sold. It had been a good afternoon, better than many we'd had in the height of summer.

I'd felt morally obliged to help Thievin' get his van out and even without the added incentive of the sausage I would have joined the rescue team for it had been after our combined housewarming and 'thanks to Baz' party that the butcher's wife, on her own admission a little 'squiffy', had taken the keys from his pocket and driven off, ditching his van in the pond. I told Vicky of our successful effort, making light of Baz's unfortunate plight for I felt it would be wise to omit, for the time being, telling her of the lost wader, the crushed peggy-tub and the shortened rope, because set against the value of the sausage we were, as Rabbit would have said, 'on a loser'.

She pushed a hot cup of coffee into my hands and opened the oven door. The gorgeous smell of pie, borne out into the room on a billow of hot air, made my mouth water.

Vicky folded a hessian towel, pulled the pie to the front of the oven, sawed through the crust with a fork and lifted a section of it, sending a feathering of steam curling up the front of the range.

'That's ready. You can take some up to Baz, he must have been chilled to the bone,' she said, stuffing the towel into my free hand.

The brown pie dish has one of its lug handles missing and its glazing is crazed but it's one of my favourite things in the kitchen for it makes superb pies. I eased it on to the table, the heat just creeping through the towel.

Vicky's little thumbs had indented the crust over the thick lip of the dish, making an annulus of lapping waves of delicious pastry, their crests tinged sienna, their troughs a honey brown. She had snipped bird beaks into the gently swelling golden mound and wisps of steam floated from them and the jagged cut the fork had made. I bent over the pie. It warmed the face and bathed the nostrils in a heavenly aroma; it was a good pie. I knew before the serving spoon plunged into it and turned a pile of potato, carrot, meat and crust into an enamel basin that it was a good pie.

I watched the spoon rise and tilt, then started to peel my coat off, but to my concern Vicky inverted a plate over the basin and wrapped it in the towel. 'You can keep that coat on and take this up to poor Baz.'

'Poor Baz! I'm cold, wet, tired and hungry, never mind Baz.'

'You and him over there,' she nodded towards Ted's farm, 'are like two big kids. Go on; the sooner you're back the sooner you get yours.'

I knocked at the cottage door and pushed it open. Baz was sitting bare-legged in front of a roaring fire, an ex-army greatcoat draped around his shoulders. He scowled up at me as I pushed the basin into his hands. 'Share up in the pub nine o'clock,' I called over my shoulder as I slammed the door behind me.

Ted and Rabbit were already in the taproom when I stuck my head around the door.

'No Baz?'

Rabbit crossed his legs and looked up at the ceiling. 'No Thievin' either.'

Ted was staring into the fire. 'Aye, an' if he's not here by nine that van's going back in. He slithers out of everything, that bugger, he's like an eel in a bucket of snot.' I glanced back at the lounge clock; it was a quarter to.

At the stroke of nine Thievin' and Baz walked through the door. Baz slumped down on a buffet and ignored Rabbit and Ted's enquiries after his health and, when I asked him if the pie had been all right, I got no more than a cursory nod.

Thievin' flopped his parcel on to the table. 'There it is lads, the best there is.'

Ted took charge, unveiling the sausage and slowly counting the links. 'Forty three. We assume, nay, nay, trust,' there was a lot of emphasis on the word trust, 'that there is half a stone here.'

Thievin' snorted, walked over to the fire, and turned his back to us. 'Well,' said Ted, 'that looks like ten apiece and three left over.'

I proposed that we gave these three to Baz as he'd played the greatest part. Baz smiled, Ted agreed, but Rabbit shook his head. 'Let's toss for 'em.'

Baz pulled his stool up to the table and eyed Rabbit angrily. 'You shouldn't have any, you did sod all.'

Rabbit put on his hurt look again and Ted flicked his worn pocket knife open and divided the sausage up, dumping the extra three on to Baz's pile. 'Justice,' he smiled.

Rabbit gathered his portion grumpily and thrust it into his overcoat, where it slithered through the torn pocket to come to rest amongst pheasant feathers, bits of string and lengths of wire which gather in the lining of every old poacher's coat. His terriers eased themselves from under the bench and sniffed around the hem of the coat.

Thievin' pushed his empty glass through the hatch and after nodding in our direction quietly closed the door behind him.

Soon we were going over the events of the day. Rabbit tried to make much of his part in the proceedings but we would have none of it; Baz was the hero. Ted and I slapped him on the back and told him he was 'a real 'un'. The extra sausage and the acclaim brought him round and soon he had us laughing as he cursed the Colonel, his dog, and my wader. Frothy pints were pushed through the hatch into the warm taproom and nobody knew nor cared that the wind had veered and was now salting the green with snowflakes.

Baz was into his third telling of his epic wade from van to shore when I noticed that Rabbit's terriers had chewed through the lining of his coat and were drawing the sausage out link by link. I kicked Baz and Ted under the table and dropped my eyes to the dogs. Both men smiled. Baz leaned back out of Rabbit's view and mouthed the word 'justice'.

The snow had set in by the time we turned out of the pub. It covered the green and the track, up to the washfold, but the road was still shiny tarmac.

Rabbit shouted his good nights and trudged off down Mill Lane, his two terriers, their bellies swollen and tight with sausage, plodding after him. Baz watched him turn the corner then raised his sausage high above his head. 'Justice.'

Ted and I returned the salute. 'Justice,' we shouted in unison.

Thievin' was still working on his van. The naked light bulb cast his huge shadow on to the cow house wall as his numb fingers tried in vain to screw the tiny injector home. It fell, tinkled through the engine, and disappeared into the thick mud. He put his head back, closed his eyes and gripped the spanner in a trembling fist. 'I'll wring her bloody neck.'

Chapter 2

Winter can be a trying time for us. There are little unexpected flushes of business but many a day the doorbell never rings. Clear sunny weather will encourage people to get out their car and turn its nose up one of the dales, and days like this will see several vehicles parked by the washfold. Well-dressed, well-mannered couples browse through our stock, comment in a subdued way, thank us politely and close the door gently behind them. They are the 'carpet dirtiers', for at the end of a long day the till is still hungry, we are tired, and the carpet is a little dirtier.

During these doldrum days we tighten our belts, ingratiate ourselves with the bank manager, tell each other we are in the buying and selling trade and sally forth to do what we can.

The auction sales are a general barometer of the trade's state, no wild swinging of the pointer, but there are clearly defined peaks and troughs so we buy in the troughs and fool ourselves that we will wax fat on the peaks.

Snow is the prison mantle of the Dales. A good fall and we

battle our way to the auction hall, confident that there will be a sparse gathering and fat pickings, but the crowded car park tells us we are wrong. The world and his wife are there. The Ring stamp their feet and nod in a sour way and the stewards blow on cold fingers and watch the clock.

Ted tapped on the kitchen window and flattened his nose against the glass. 'Canary Mary wants you to give her a lift. Her car is in dock.' I groaned and screwed the top on the flask, and laid my Wellingtons to the fire to warm. It meant a detour of four miles along narrow snow-covered lanes, and although the Queen of the Fleamarkets is good company, she, like every sovereign, exacts tribute. No doubt I would end up carting boxes of junk down to her store for her, my only reward a charming smile and a chunk of 'yellow peril'.

Mary stood out against the snow-covered village green, her yellow macintosh, Wellingtons and sou'wester providing the only splash of colour in the tiny hamlet. She pushed her bags and basket into the van and with a few grunts and groans hauled herself up beside me. 'I suppose we'll have to wade through all that magician's stuff, there'll be nothing for me,' she groaned.

The sale promised to be more interesting than lucrative for it was a mixed sale and contained the effects of the late Fantastic Frederico – a magician who had trodden the boards with some success.

There was a good turnout. The Ring had gathered around the only functioning radiator and Canary Mary bustled her way through them to arrange her bags on a sideboard.

The sale had a slow start. Unlotted carpets and white goods generate little enthusiasm so the dealers gathered in small groups and continually told each other that times were slow.

Long John stamped the snow from his boots, stroked his beard into shape, hustled the Ring off a corner of the radiator and laid his red hands across it. 'See yon fella.' He nodded towards a thin bent man in a long gabardine. 'He's the Great Gordini. An' him over there, he's the Great Briani.' He rolled his eyes. 'Having a few words at the viewing they were.'

'Here for the magician's stuff I suppose,' I said half-heartedly.

'Aye, apparently he was a top notcher, some of them tricks is going to fetch money,' he said pointing to the three tables which were packed high with a jumble of flashy props and fabrics. It looked like junk to me.

Long John must have established some relationship with the Great Briani at the previous day's viewing because the fat man edged his way through the crowd to join us, giving me a friendly nod. He then addressed himself to Long John. 'He's here, you see, miserable old sod. You watch me make him pay.'

Long John winked at me. 'Some good stuff is there?'

The great Briani straightened his back and gave a series of little nods. 'Oh aye, there's some good stuff. He was a first rater, the Fantastic Frederico. Topped the bill at the leading theatres in the land. Best exponent of the French drop I've ever seen.' He half turned from us and eyed the tables full of props. 'There's stuff there that's unique. He had one trick – the egg and balloon – which nobody has ever fathomed.'

He turned to me and held out his hand. 'I'm the Great Briani by the way.' I shook a soft white hand and told him how magicians never failed to impress me. Briani gave a broad grin. 'You'd've been impressed by Frederico. I tell you nobody could fathom that egg and balloon trick. I once watched him through four performances at the Dewsbury Empire but I couldn't get it. How he got the egg into that balloon – fantastic.'

The Ring had been listening intently to Briani. Fatty leaned forward and gave a little smile. 'Perhaps he had a very clever hen.'

George threw back his head and laughed. 'It must have been a clever hen 'cos it was a duck egg.'

Briani glared at them. Fatty pulled his lower lip and looked thoughtful. 'I don't think it was an egg at all. I think it was a little white oval balloon he used.'

Briani snorted and rocked back on his heels. 'It was an egg!' he said angrily. ''Cos he used to shake the balloon so the egg bounced inside it, then after the trick he always broke the egg into a basin. It was an egg!' He turned back to us and shook his head sadly. 'It'll be lost for ever that trick, died with him, lost to the profession.'

The auctioneer had dispensed with the household goods and now turned his attention to the effects of the late Frederico.

'There's been a great deal of interest in these lots,' he announced. 'You will see from the accompanying playbills that the late gentleman was an acknowledged master of his craft.'

Briani smiled and nodded his agreement. 'Master of his craft, aye, you can say that again.' The latent antagonism between Gordini and Briani soon flared into open hostility as they glared fiercely at each other across the saleroom.

'Lot twenty-nine – Indian vase trick.'

The steward had hardly time to hold it up before Gordini shouted, 'Twenty pounds.'

'Twenty-five,' countered Briani.

Gordini bit his lip and called, 'Thirty!'

Briani smiled. 'Let him have it.' He turned back to us, leaned forward and whispered, 'All it has is a little rubber ball inside which traps the rope.' He stopped and sucked his lower lip thoughtfully. 'I probably shouldn't have told you that.'

Gordini paid forty pounds for the blossoming rose tree and twenty-five for the three bottle trick. Once again Briani turned to us. 'They're just three hollow tin bottles – you hold 'em with your fingers.' He screwed his mouth up, then pushed his lips out. 'I probably shouldn't have told you that.'

Briani gave us the secret of every trick that Gordini bought, and every time he ended his little treachery with a doubtful 'I probably shouldn't have told you that'.

Someone at the viewing had carelessly mixed up several tricks and whilst the stewards sorted things out, Briani continued to lambast Gordini. 'Disgrace to the profession, that man,' he said finally and turned to face the auctioneer.

There was obviously something deeper than mere professional jealousy here, and Fatty, realising this, did a little probing. 'Bit of poaching goes on in the profession does it?'

'Poaching! I'll say there's poaching. Sods like him can't keep their hands off owt.'

Fatty lowered his head and looked at Briani through half-closed eyes. 'No profession is safe. Why amongst ourselves even, sometimes one appears who is less than honest. They do irreparable damage these people.'

Briani snorted, turned round and beckoned us closer. In spite of the clammy coldness of the saleroom his cheeks glowed red. 'I'll tell you some irreparable damage that bugger did to me.' He paused, looked over his shoulder, then leaned forward and lowered his voice. 'Withernsea Hippodrome 1948. No, no, I tell a lie – 1949. I had this assistant, the Lovely

Marlene, what a grand lass. We worked together a treat. She had a natural aptitude for the profession, you know, a bit of showmanship. I'd worked up a real trick, I had two boxes, about this square.' Briani held his white hands two feet apart. 'Marlene used to get in the blue box at one side of the stage and I'd transpose her to the red one at the other side. Well, when I say transpose, really there were two trap doors in the stage.' He stopped and, raising his head, stared at his reflection in a dressing table mirror for two or three seconds. Then his mouth drooped a little. 'I probably shouldn't have told you that.' We looked at each other, then back at Briani, our faces innocent of all expression. We were, we felt, on the brink of something.

'Anyway I put Marlene in the blue box, said me piece and moved to the red box. Did a bit of cloak swishing and wand tapping. You have to give 'em time you see. I always do these things with – er – with –'

Fatty leaned forward and smiled. 'Panache?'

'That's it, that's it – panache.' Briani smiled around at us and gave Canary Mary a friendly wink. 'I've always had panache.' The smile went from his face and his tone became serious again. 'I opened the box – no Marlene. My mind raced; maybe the trap doors had stuck. Slowly I walked back to the red box and opened that – no Marlene. Did I panic? I panicked. Wednesday matinee, 140 folk in and no bloody Marlene.' His thumb jerked towards the Great Gordini. 'That sod had been seeing her on the side. Down thru' the undercroft she'd gone and out to old Soddo who had a taxi waiting for them, an' all this time my laundry bill is increasing.' He stopped and looked up at Canary Mary. 'Sorry, luv.' His hands dropped to his sides and he half turned towards Gordini, a pale and steady hatred in his eyes. 'Ditched her the following summer at Bournemouth. Going to marry her he was. Poor lass was left destitute. I heard, through the profession like, that she wanted to come back to me, but every time I thought of Withernsea I said no – I just couldn't. The worst moment of my professional career – Withernsea. Anyway, after a year or so old Frederico, him what's just gone, took her on, married her and made an honest woman of her.'

Briani's eyes filled with tears, his pudgy hands pressed into their sockets, then with a sob he turned away to face the auctioneer.

Long John drew a bottle from his inside pocket and filled a paper cup to the brim and held it out. Briani took it and drank silently, pulling in his lips and slowly shaking his head. 'I'll make the bugger pay.'

Briani now started the bidding on every lot and the more he drank the more exuberant he got.

Lot forty saw him advancing down the aisle, cup in hand.

'Twenty pounds!' he shouted.

The auctioneer, never a man to be ruffled, banged the gavel down. 'Flags of all nations to Mr Briani, twenty pounds.'

Briani staggered back to us, his greasy black hair straggling across his forehead and his overcoat open revealing a substantial pot belly.

Long John refilled the paper cup. Briani took a long drink, sniffed, and leaned heavily on a chair. 'I'll make the bugger pay.'

As every lot was announced Briani advanced down the aisle and shouted a bid whilst Gordini eased himself against the pillar and grinned.

When the forest of flowers trick came up Briani was back

with Long John getting his cup replenished with Swaledale Lightning. He took a drink and smiled at Long John. 'By, this is good stuff, old lad. Do you make it yourself?'

Gordini, taking advantage of Briani's lapse, bought the trick for ten pounds and turned to smirk at the wall. Briani returned to the fray as the steward held up the next lot: the costume of the Lovely Marlene. The gold sequinned costume, frayed around the leg arches, had generous gussets let into it around the back and under the bust to accommodate the Lovely Marlene as she had grown over the years.

A pale wintery sunshine leached through the grimy skylight and flecked it with points of fire. Tears welled into Briani's eyes. 'Marlene, Marlene,' he sobbed as he staggered down the aisle. 'One hundred pounds,' he sighed as he sank to his knees in front of the auctioneer's rostrum.

The auctioneer was about to bring down his gavel when Canary Mary pushed her way through us and brandishing her yellow umbrella charged the rostrum. 'No, no, the man is besotted, you can't take that bid.'

A chalky face peered over the rostrum. 'Besotted or not madam, we are here to act on behalf of the vendor.'

Canary Mary brought the umbrella down on his head with a satisfying thud. 'Five pounds!' she yelled. 'That's all he's bidding – five pounds.'

The auctioneer grimaced, raised a hand to his head, and gingerly lowered the gavel. 'Mr Briani, five pounds.'

Canary Mary knelt and pulled Briani's head to her bosom. 'You poor man.' She helped him to his feet, half carried him to the back of the hall, sat him on a mirror back sideboard, and thrust a huge piece of 'yellow peril' into his hand.

With the sale of Fantastic Frederico's professional props

completed, the stewards brought up his furniture and household effects. The Ring began to show interest in the framed playbills and the good quality art deco furnishings and it suddenly became a very pricey sale.

All I managed to buy was a tea-chest full of Fantastic Frederico's books for a pound. Canary Mary had bought several tray lots and a steward started marshalling them together for her as soon as the sale finished.

Gordini commandeered two stewards and under his arrogant direction they scrunched through the crisp snow carrying his purchases out to his smart estate car.

I lugged my tea-chest out to the van and waited for Canary Mary to finish packing her stuff.

Briani sat slumped on the sideboard, the half-eaten cake in his hand. 'Marlene, Marlene,' he whispered as I eased him off the sideboard and pulling an arm over my shoulder walked him to the cashier.

'Come on old son, the hour of reckoning is here.'

'Hour of reckoning, hour of reckoning,' mumbled Briani as he wrote out the cheque in a very shaky and spidery hand.

A steward brought him Marlene's costume and the flags of all nations. Briani stuffed the costume under his coat then slowly and deliberately twisted the flags of Peru, Equador and Liechtenstein into a very serviceable-looking rope. 'The hour of reckoning,' he shouted as he lurched out into the yard, the flags of the spurned nations trailing each side of him.

Small, acerbic, determined men in crombie overcoats are difficult to restrain. Three paces from the door my foot landed on the trailing flag of Haiti and I crashed to the ground.

Gordini was hunched over the back of the estate car carefully packing his tricks. Briani looped the flag rope around his neck and sank to his knees pulling Gordini down with him. 'The hour of reckoning,' he yelled.

Gordini clutched at the bumper bar with one hand and tried to drag the rope from his neck with the other.

'Get him off! Get him off! He's a bloody lunatic,' he shrieked.

'Withernsea, '49,' Briani gasped. 'The hour of reckoning.'

I slithered across the yard, dropped to my knees beside the two struggling men and tried to pull the rope from Briani's grip. 'Briani, Briani, for God's sake man, you're killing him.'

'Withernsea, '49,' he sobbed in my ear.

Gordini's eyes were bulging, his lips were drawn back over his big white teeth and peculiar rasping noises were coming from his throat. He released his grip on the bumper, stabbed his hand into the car and seizing the Indian vase he swung it viciously over his head.

There was a sick thud. Briani let go of the flag rope and with a low moan dropped sideways on to the snow.

Long John and I picked him up and carried him back to the saleroom.

Canary Mary brought a chair from the cashier's office and ran one of her little cream handkerchiefs under the cold tap. Briani winced as she pressed it to the huge lump which had risen smooth and egg-like in the centre of his head. He opened his eyes and, slowly raising them to look Mary in the face, he smiled weakly. 'Marlene? Marlene?'

Mary chewed a finger and looked worried. 'Oh dear.'

Briani pulled the crumpled costume from under his coat. 'Marlene let's give it another try.' He pressed the costume against Mary. 'We can let it out a bit luv. Then we'll tread the boards together again Marlene, just like old times.'

The saleroom was empty, the stewards clattered mugs in the little kitchen and the cashier bent her blonde head over the adding machine.

Long John straightened his back and scrubbed his fingers in his beard. 'We have a problem here old lad. Where does he come from?' Nobody knew. I thought we ought to get a doctor but at the mention of it Briani grew restless.

'No, no doctors. I'm fine.' He struggled to his feet and made for the door still clutching the costume and the flags of all nations.

The cold air seemed to revive him as he leaned against the wall and closed his eyes. 'I'll be all right. Just rest here a bit,' he whispered. We stood in front of him, a protective semi-circle, and looked at each other. What could we do? We couldn't just leave the man.

Long John started to walk up and down the yard, his boots slipping and slithering on the packed snow. He stood for a while looking down the lane. Then he stamped his feet and blew on his hands, turned, and called us.

'I think you ought to ring Charlie up and see if you can get him in at The Ship for tonight. Has he any money?'

Mary's motherly hands pulled Briani's coat together.

'Have you any money luv?'

'Oh, aye, plenty money.'

Charlie was a bit dubious. 'You're not saddling me with a nut are you?'

I assured him I wasn't. 'Fella's all right. Just had a blow on the head and wants to put off travelling till tomorrow.' Charlie didn't seem convinced. 'Ah right, but owt funny an' he's out.'

Although it was bitterly cold I wound both van windows

down and angled the quarter light to direct a flow of icy air on to Briani's face. He sat slumped in his seat, silent.

Mary chattered on as if he wasn't there. 'Poor man, fancy taking me for some Thespian. I wouldn't be seen dead in a costume like that. Not decent it isn't.'

I carried Mary's boxes into the house for her and refused the offer of coffee. I wanted to get home; it had been a long unprofitable day and it wasn't over yet.

Briani was coming round a bit. 'Where are we going?'

I explained I'd got him a room for the night at The Ship and that I would run him into Lalbeck in the morning. He furrowed his brow, then relaxed. 'Aye, that'll be all right,' his voice trailed away, 'the egg and balloon lost for ever.'

Charlie looked at Briani with suspicion – an entertainer with no luggage. But Briani had spent half a lifetime dealing with landlords and landladies and knew how to turn the situation.

'What a super place you have old boy,' he said in a good clipped accent. The accent and the well-cut crombie did the trick. Charlie shrugged. 'Come on I'll show you your room.'

'Pick you up about ten,' I called as they disappeared up the stairs.

Vicky looked at the tea-chest of books in disgust. 'That's all you got?'

'Well there's a good set of encyclopedias in there,' I answered defensively. The children emptied the books out on to the rug and set the encyclopedias in order.

'One missing,' Peter announced cheerfully.

I reached for my pipe, inched the broad-arm Windsor around to face the fire and turned my back on the world.

*

The morning was beautiful, the air was crisp and fresh and a lemon sun caught the snow-covered fells and washed them the palest of creams. Elspeth cantered around the yard picking her hooves high and blowing plumes of vapour from her nostrils. She eyed the rolling, softly growling dogs with disdain, then turned sharply and clattered back to the goat house. The hens trod the snow carefully, their eyes cocked for the grains of wheat I'd scattered; but the ducks, the brave stupid ducks, plunged into the beck and with much quacking and head dipping, rained icy water over themselves.

It is a good part of the day this letting out and feeding of stock; this milking and watching. A good breakfast frying on the griddle, thick slices of home baked bread toasting, a brisk walk down Drover's Lane with the dogs to feed the pony and slap her round flanks, to lean on the lower door and watch her fuss about her hay, the big soft eyes watching me before she turns and arches her neck over my shoulder to have it stroked and to be told how beautiful she is.

Sometimes I linger when I shouldn't. The cares of the day lie waiting at the top of the lane and I cheat them of as many minutes as I dare before I call the dogs to heel.

Vicky forked the bacon from the griddle. 'Where've you been?'

Sometimes we can achieve more with a smile than we can with an apology. It was a morning for smiles.

We are not a tidy household and the contents of the tea-chest were still scattered about the floor, the incomplete set of encyclopedias, old-fashioned looking novels, a dictionary and several guide books. Not good. Sally and Peter were shouted to come downstairs; they tottered sleepy-eyed across to the fire and squatted down with their bowls of cornflakes. Sally sat cross-legged with a small black book on her knees. It was a leather-bound notebook filled with tight writing.

'Where did you get this?' I asked picking it up.

'It was with that lot,' she replied.

The flyleaf was printed with a bold legend. 'PRIVATE. The property of Fred Flowers.' Then in brackets. 'The Fantastic Frederico.' I flicked through the book. It listed all Frederico's tricks giving minute descriptions of the props and their manipulation together with stage directions.

Half-way through was a well-thumbed page and underlined in red was, 'Trick 151, The Egg and Balloon.'

I raced across the village green to the pub. Charlie stood at the back door, his muscular arms under his cellarman's apron, a cigarette stuck firmly between his lips.

'Where is he? Where is he?' I called, waving the book. 'I've got the egg and balloon trick.'

Charlie blew a cloud of smoke out into the chill air. 'Your magician?' He nodded to a line of footprints which led from a fallpipe to the garden gate.

'He's disappeared.'

Chapter 3

Baz shuffled his feet and sniffed, he looked into the tall Cantonese vases and, pushing his nose up to the barometer, tapped it gently and stared at the pointer. He then walked over to the French mantle clock and listened to its steady tick. 'How's things?' he asked at last.

'Bit slow for the time of the year,' I replied.

'You – er, gettin' much from clearances?'

'Not a lot Baz, they don't die fast enough up here – must be the air.'

Baz smiled. 'Aye, its grand this mornin', just thought I'd pop in. I've a bit of wallin' on.' He sauntered back to the vases and peered into them again. The French clock gathered, clearing its throat before announcing the time. Baz waited until it had finished its strike then lifted his gaze from the depths of a vase to the ceiling. 'You got any beds – er, double beds?'

Beds are a nuisance to the trade. People will happily stay in a hotel or bed and breakfast place and sleep in a bed that thousands have slept in. But a second-hand bed? The mattress is gone over minutely and the most innocent stain brings instant rejection. They are better tipped, and tip them we usually do, but if I could muster a pound or two from one, so much the better.

'No, nothing at the moment, Baz.' I watched him rise on his heels and twist his hands behind his back. He was a little embarrassed. Miss Denholm was spending every weekend at his cottage and the charm of the ex-army cot must be wearing thin. 'You in a hurry for this bed, Baz?'

He sniffed again and walked to the desk. 'No, no hurry at all, just thought ... '

The whole village was watching the romance between Baz and the shy Miss Denholm with a warm interest. They were made for each other – everybody said so; it was just a matter of time – everybody said that too. Baz buying a double bed, it looked as if that time was approaching. Should I tell Vicky? She'd be straight to the village shop, a dozen receptive ears would cock, half a dozen slow smiles and knowing nods; half an hour the village would know – half a day and the dale would know. I resisted the temptation to wink.

'Leave it to me Baz. Anything else?'

Once again Baz found something fascinating in one of the Cantonese vases. 'There is one thing.'

I pushed the daybook away from me and folded my arms. Perhaps the not-so-young bachelor wanted advice; guidance even. The steady tick of the clock pecked away at the silence as Baz shifted his attention from one vase to its neighbour.

'It's just that, well, I've never met Susan's folk and they want to come over. My place is a bit – er, small.'

Small wasn't the first adjective to spring to my mind. It

was a tip, a smelly bachelor's den of sunken chairs and holey rugs.

He turned and leaned on the counter. 'Thing is I, that is, we, wondered if we could meet them here, at your place. It would be good if I could show 'em I know folk like you.' He smiled a slow guileful smile, the smile a gypsy employs when she knocks at your door, and thrusts her basket of wares towards you.

'Folks like us? Aye, I can see your point there, Baz.'

Baz had worked wonders for us on the house. He'd laboured long and hard on it, he had rifled through his contacts, done a little bullying and called in a few favours to find the materials we needed. Without Baz, the jack of all trades and master of most, we would never have got the house liveable and the byre converted into a shop in the time we did. Of course he could invite them to our house.

'When would it be Baz?'

He breathed in sharply and grinned. 'Tomorrow afternoon. There'll be me and Susan, her mam and dad, Cousin Leopold, Belgiana, and me Aunt Dot. Don't worry about the grub. Belgiana is doing the sandwiches and Mucky Marion is making us some buns.' He had a last peer into the vases. 'We're calling the banns this Sunday,' he said shyly.

I nursed my mug of coffee and leaned back in the broad-arm. Vicky was baking. Floury arms thumped and kneaded the dough, making the baking bowl clack on the table. She stopped and, pushing her lower lip out, blew a blonde curl from her forehead. 'Come on, you're dying to tell me something.'

Baz hadn't intended the news as a secret but I had hoarded

33

it jealously. For a precious hour I'd held it like a miser holds a gold coin: tight and close. She dropped on to my knee and threatened me with powdery white hands. 'Come on, out with it.'

There is a time for hoarding and a time for largesse. A warm kitchen, the smell of baking, a pretty wife being impish, it was a time for largesse.

'Baz and Susan, Miss Denholm that is, have named the day. First banns this Sunday.' There was a squeal of delight, powdery hands behind my neck, soft powdery forearms along my cheeks and a powdery kiss.

Vicky immediately found she was short of sugar and although a full bag sat in the cupboard she flung a scarf around her head and set off for the shop.

The children were at the Martins so I knocked out my pipe and took myself off to see Ted.

'Ah! Cousin Leopold and the notorious Belgiana,' he said, as I eased myself on to the cornbin and watched him carefully wash the fat pink udders. 'Baz's cousins on his mother's side. You're honoured. It isn't often they come down off the tops.'

'Bit of a character is she, this Belgiana?'

'They both are – more than a bit.'

There were suckings and a twitching of tails as Ted wiped a broad hand across the milking machine cups then offered them up to the teats. He stood straight and watched until the milk spurted past the transparent panel in the pipeline, then turned to face me.

'Both are – their mother was. Frying-Pan Annie, she was known as. Big woman, short fuse. Belgiana takes after her. If she likes yer – yer all right.'

'Unusual name, Belgiana.'

34

'Aye, they're twins.'

Ted took a shovel and started to scrape it along the dung passage. The cows turned their heads, rattling their tethering chains, their thick wet rubbery mouths chewing slowly, strings of saliva drooping from their jaws. Ted grunted as the shovel caught in the uneven floor. 'When Frying Pan wor expecting she wor diddling about in the attic and came across this newspaper from t' First World War. "Brave little Belgium" the headline said.' He stopped and pushed his cap back on his head for although it was a cold night it was warm in the cow house. 'Well, you know how women are when they're in that condition – very susceptible, very susceptible. She couldn't get it out of her head, "Brave little Belgium".' The shovel pawed at a tenacious bit. 'Well, she decided if it wor a lad she'd call it Leopold after the new King o' the Belgians. When owd Dr Nichols told her there was two, she had a bit of a think and came up with this name for a lass, Belgiana. She wor right 'cos there was one of each – a lad an' a flat cock.'

The shovel was laid aside and the heavy yard brush started to hiss over the concrete. 'Yer honoured.'

Canary Mary is very fond of the children and readily agreed to take them for the afternoon and we managed to keep them out of the lounge with a series of threats and bribes until the little yellow Citroën of their adored Aunt Mary pulled up to the washfold.

Mucky Marion puffed and blew as she wrestled the old pram across the village green. She banged the front knocker loudly and swivelled the pram around ready to haul it over the front step. I turned the key, drew the bolts and swung the heavy oak door open to see a wizened brown face peering up at me. 'Like bloody Fort Knox,' she panted as she dragged the pram into the lounge and taking off her ragged mittens started unloading its contents on to the table. 'Cup o' tea would be nice luv.'

With a Yorkshire range, water is never far from the boil, the black kettle sits on the hob, a whisper of vapour floating from its spout. Ease its black body on to the coals and the lid soon starts to dance. I grabbed the teapot, flung a handful of tea in and slopped the boiling water after it.

Mucky Marion had filled the table with a breathtaking array of canapés, gâteaux and flans. She was obviously highly skilled, for the tracery across the flans was meticulous, the icing on the gâteaux perfect and the canapés intricate and colourful.

She had pulled the scroll arm carver from the top of the table and lay back in it, her feet on the pram. She was wearing a blue balaclava, an old tweed overcoat, and on her feet were a pair of dirty tennis shoes which had ragged oval holes cut in them to relieve pressure on her bunions. A pair of black and red banded rugby stockings were pulled up to her knees and where these showed through the bunion holes, the black scored one, the red two.

Marion leaned forward as I poured the tea, her toothless mouth worked and she wagged a thin hand at the cup. 'Prissy little things. 'Aven't you a bloody pot.'

I found the biggest coffee mug we had and streamed tea into it making Marion smile. 'Ar, good and black, just as it ought to be.' She held the mug to her face with both hands and rocked the springs of the pram with her feet. 'Well! What do you think?'

'Beautiful, Marion, just beautiful.'

'It's me trade. Crowned heads of Europe has eaten my stuff. I learned it all in France. Five years I lived and worked there before I came back to look after our George.' She dropped her feet to the carpet and eased herself forward in the chair. 'You gets any Frenchies in here, send for me – I'll tell you what they're saying.'

The pram joggled down the front step; Marion pulled her stockings up and grasped the handle firmly. 'Be back tomorrow for me stands an' things.'

Vicky brought a canteen of cutlery out of the shop and started to set the table. Crockery presented a problem for we had no fancy tea-sets in stock and as we are not very good with china we could only muster three matching cups and saucers. Mrs Lewis at the shop came to the rescue. Her china cabinet was denuded of its precious gold-rimmed Victorian tea-set and Vicky, with a set expression, washed them very, very carefully in lukewarm water. The shop was raided again, this time for two comports to await Belgiana's sandwiches and a vase for the pheasant-eye narcissi Dolly had brought across from the Colonel's.

I lit the fire, filled the log baskets and wound the longcase clock whilst Vicky primed two teapots and stood them in the hearth to warm. We were ready.

Baz stood with his back to the fire and surveyed the table. 'It looks grand,' he smiled, 'doesn't it Aunty?'

He was wearing his plus fours and a very smart shirt and tie, and there was yellow lint from a duster stuck to the caps of his brogue shoes. Miss Denholm was obviously doing a bit of gentle moulding, for it was the first time anybody had seen him wear a tie. His aunt, sitting straight backed in the scroll arm carver, nodded her agreement. She looked old and frail, but there was a firm set to her mouth and her eyes were bright with interest whilst her thin age-spotted hands continually massaged the arms of the chair. She saw Miss Denholm as the saviour of the family and she was most anxious that nothing should go wrong. Baz happily married and weaned away from the tap-room lot was something she prayed for nightly. She'd been in service when the boy had been orphaned and felt a deep guilt that he had ended up being brought up in an orphanage. Nothing like that had ever happened in the family before, they had always taken care of their own.

She had dressed in her very best and had prepared, with much care a little statement. Her hands massaged and plucked – nothing must go wrong. She had asked Baz to send Cousin Leopold and Belgiana to her as soon as they arrived and when he had promised this and assured her again that everything would be all right, we walked out into the yard together.

It was a cold day, still, and mist hung. We watched the goat for a few minutes, then, as we walked across to the barn, there came the faint hum of an engine from the fell. Baz stopped and cocked his head. 'They're here.'

The old Land-rover squealed to a halt at the bottom of the common. Cousin Leopold hooked a butter basket over his arm and after opening the door for Belgiana called his lurcher to heel. As we strolled past the washfold to meet them, Baz explained, 'He'll have to leave the motor there 'cos there'll be nowt on it.'

'Nowt on it?'

'Nowt! No tax, no insurance, no test. It's one he bought off Long John years ago.'

A small group of worshippers was turning out of the chapel. They waved and called greetings across the green as Baz introduced me to his cousins, who shook hands warmly. Taking the butter basket from Cousin Leopold and passing it to me he hurried his cousins into the house and steered them down the hall, into the lounge, and, with a satisfied smile, brought them to rest in front of Aunt Dot.

'Leopold, Belgiana, this is a very important afternoon for our Basil and we are in a friend's house. There will be no swearing, ribald stories ... just good manners and,' she stopped and scowled at the lurcher, 'get that dog out.' The chastened cousins had just arranged their sandwiches on the comports when the Denholms' car pulled up to the front door.

Baz went out to greet them. Shyly kissing Susan on the cheek, he shook hands with the parents and ushered them into the lounge.

Vicky brought the heavy teapots in and, after a little desultory conversation about the weather, the little party settled around the table. The confections and gâteaux received much praise and the canapés began to disappear.

Mr and Mrs Denholm sat with their backs to the window, opposite Cousin Leopold and Belgiana; the old aunt sat at the top of the table with Baz and Susan. Cousin Leopold took the vase of flowers and leaning back in his chair slid it on to the sideboard. Then he smiled across at Mr Denholm. 'I like to see folk when I talk to 'em.' Aunt Dot nodded her approval.

Leopold leaned forward. 'Now I suppose with this lass of yours wanting to be in the family, you'll want to know a bit about us?' Belgiana nodded and smiled. Susan looked at her parents then back to Baz, a worried look on her pretty face.

They had expected her 'to do better', but as she squeezed Baz's hand under the table, she knew she could do no better.

Her parents were quiet, sitting bolt upright they smiled a lot and listened politely to all that was said. Leopold glanced at his aunt, then continued. 'We're one of the oldest families in the dale. Me and me sister here farm up at Goose Pastures. There've been Kidsons there for as long as time itself. We're simple folk, farm our land, run a dog or two and keep a clean doorstep.' Belgiana nodded her agreement and Leopold's voice grew more confident. 'We've put khaki on when needed to and allus paid our dues. We're not strong church but whenever they've come a'asking they've never gone away empty handed. I'm not saying we've all been angels, we've had one or two rum 'uns.' Aunt Dot coughed and hardened her eyes and Leopold feeling her hard eyes on him lowered his voice. 'Well most families have a rum 'un somewhere.'

Mr Denholm's polite smile faded for a moment. 'Yes, that's, er, true, yes.' He turned his pale face to his wife, and said 'yes' once more.

The Denholms offered no family vignettes. Their background was dragged out of them word by word by Leopold who took easily to the role of interrogator.

'You run any dogs?'

'Keep any ferrets?'

'Have you much land?' The string of negative answers puzzled Leopold and pleased Aunt Dot. They were a perfectly ordinary respectable couple and they had produced, in her eyes, a perfectly ordinary respectable daughter. Vicky and I plied them with the tea and good things Marion had made.

It wasn't that Mucky Marion was dirty about her person: scruffy perhaps, but not dirty. It was her cottage that earned her the sobriquet. She kept too many pets. When she was baking she threw her back door open and a tribe of dogs and cats paraded in and out, several cage birds rocked their little prisons, filling the kitchen with a shrill trilling, and a monkey, which was reputed to do unspeakable things in the sugar bowl, bounded about at the end of Marion's clothes-line.

Tempting as the beautiful gâteaux were, Vicky and I stuck to the sandwiches.

Leopold kept up his questioning. As he was unlikely to marry and Belgiana was past child bearing age, the continuity of the family rested solely in Baz's loins and as the breeder of the finest long dogs in the Dales he knew how important the blood was on the dam's side. Steady stuff he was looking for and steady stuff sat opposite him.

The cross-examination showed the Denholms to be low church, semi-detached dwellers with conservative views on all subjects. They owned a Yorkshire Terrier and Albert Denholm was a season-ticket holder at Headingley.

Cousin Leopold nodded and smiled at Aunt Dot. The room was warm but I put more logs on the fire and pushed round the laggard hand of the clock, making it take back its carelessly lost minutes, as Vicky fussed around the teapots and sandwiches.

Leopold had finished his questioning and leaned back contented. 'Any issue of the union will come into quite a bit o' brass one day, so we have to be careful about the distaff side,' he explained.

Susan blushed at the word 'issue', Baz smiled and squeezed her hand, the Denholms looked at each other.

Aunt Dot nodded happily. 'And now I have a bit to say. I'm making Basil's cottage over to him together with the wheel-wright's shop.'

Baz looked embarrassed, his voice was hardly audible. 'Thanks Aunty.'

The noble gâteaux were ravished, the comports were laid bare, and tea cups clattered as the conversation got under way. A common ailment is a great bond between women and a love of cricket an even greater one amongst men. Belgiana and Mrs Denholm were martyrs to rheumatism and Cousin Leopold and Albert followed the fortunes of Yorkshire.

Baz and Susan pressed their shoulders together and squeezed hands under the table. They had reached that stage in their relationship where silences were no longer awkward and for them the world had changed its axis; it now ran parallel to the longcase clock and four feet from its lancet door. Aunt Dot smiled and massaged the arms of the chair.

The Denholms were escorted to their car. There was much handshaking and thanking and then we waved until they were out of sight.

Cousin Leopold whistled the lurcher from its straw nest in the barn and hooked the empty butter basket high on his arm. The dog slunk through the gate and stood at his side, its sad brown eyes watching Leopold's face intelligently. It wasn't the type of dog you felt a need to stroke. It was a one man dog, a killing machine. Thin, painfully thin, wiry grey fur stretched over a skeleton frame, long jaws designed to bite and slash into soft bellies. Leopold gazed at it with pride.

'You could pull her through a wedding ring. Just as they should be.' He handed Belgiana into the Land-rover and pushed the basket in beside her. 'You drive back Belgiana, me and this lass'll walk over the top and see if we can put up one of them long eared 'uns.'

Cousin Leopold and the dog had disappeared over the

skyline before Belgiana had turned the Land-rover around and started up the track. The Colonel crossed the green and joined us watching the old Series One groan and jolt its way up the common and when the grey sky had swallowed the vehicle he turned and shook his walking stick towards The Ship where Charlie was nailing a 'Bed and Breakfast' sign on to a window box.

'Don't like that,' he snapped. 'Could bring some funny characters into the village.'

Chapter 4

February often gives us a handful of springlike days. A maundering west wind takes playful dips over the delves of snow which still lie on the tops before warming itself in the soft sun as it slides down the scree and tumbles over the heather. It skips into the village, gently buffets our hair and brings the pink to our cheeks. Unlike its boisterous brothers from the north it doesn't make us sink our heads turtle-like into our collars and thrust our fingers deep into pockets, and for a week the dale fools itself that winter is over.

Birds, sleeker now, sing in hedgerows pricked with pale green, new lambs scamper from ewe to ewe, tails twitching and soft-toy mouths bleating a playground clamour. The snow has washed the grass a fresh green on the inbye land, and under the blackthorns, where it is drawn and thin, a slanting sun makes it almost luminous. Safe below a tangle of briar a hedgepig stirs, black glass eyes peer at a velvet brown molehill and a black raisin nose turns brittle, fuscous leaves.

Ted throws his greatcoat on to the cornbin and shouldering

a draining spit takes himself off to his bottom land. 'Best done when it's still ploshy,' he tells us.

His wife is ashamed of his ragged sweater trailing grey worms of wool from the elbows and she has told him a hundred times, 'You look a right joskin in that', and a hundred times she has had the same little smile and tilt of the head in reply.

Our ducks come into lay and the hens start to leave four or five eggs a day in the nest boxes, the goat's udder is fuller at the morning milking and the winter coat starts combing out of Topic the pony.

The shop bell rings more often and a dealer or two will pack a picnic lunch and combine business with pleasure on a day out in the Dales.

We start to approach the auctions with a firmer resolve for there are mouths to feed and corn bills to be paid. No more chatting with the Ring, no more half-hearted viewing. We start to advertise again and bend our backs to the task of making a living. The public are getting better educated about antiques. The family knives come out and carve the best bits from the deceased estate. We view the remains, do our sums, and buy what we can. A promising household yields little and then a most unlikely clearance produces something really worthwhile.

We carry a mental list of people's requirements and often save the day financially by acquiring mundane things like a television set or a vacuum cleaner.

Ticker Duckworth had battled long and hard with the planning authorities. There had been several site meetings, applications and refusals enough to fill his old briefcase, and then, finally, a successful appeal to the powers in Whitehall.

He stood in his orchard and smiled happily at the railway carriage. The deep tracks left by the low loader were still scored across the turf and the gap in the quickthorn hedge had been hurriedly fenced across with slabwood.

Ticker ran his tongue thoughtfully round his teeth. 'By, she took some getting in, but I was determined to have her there, between the two plums.' We walked across to the carriage and climbed the makeshift stairs.

Ticker had spent all his working life on the railways. Cleaner and fireman with the LNER, then taking the controls of his first engine, just as the old livery was painted out and the BR decals were stuck on the tenders. Ticker hadn't been on duty when the last steamer had thundered across the Pennines but he had ridden its footplate with an old friend. He had leaned out of the cab letting the billows of acrid smoke buffet and blacken his face, he'd drawn the delicious hot oil smell into his nostrils and felt the living kick and joggle of the footplate under his boots. He'd kept out of the way of the fireman and listened to the scrape of his shovel; three to the left, three to the right, then three up the middle. It had been a night train, a goods express to Liverpool Exchange. The open firebox had washed the three men with a pink glow. The urgent speeding pulse of the cylinders, the white billows of steam snatched away by the wind, the balls of smoke punched from the smokestack as they hammered the gradient. He'd closed his eyes and burned them all into his memory. They had fried bacon on the back of a shovel for the last time, and they had toasted the end of a powerful and majestic lady in tepid tea out of enamel mugs whose rims were hot from the heat of the firebox. He'd left her in Bradford Low Moor and walked away from her without looking back after he'd patted her grimed smokebox.

The passing of steam had saddened Ticker but he'd continued to be a good railwayman until he'd taken early retirement and turned his hobby into his livelihood. Ticker deals in clocks. He doesn't just deal in them, he collects them, lives and breathes them, and worships them.

Ticker's wife is a tough little woman. War years spent driving an ambulance in North Africa have forged a steel core within her and she supports Ticker completely.

Every holiday time she dragoons one of their daughters into looking after their home and their pets, packs the caravanette with a military zeal and drives Ticker on a round of the museums which contain gems of the clockmaker's art. She's older than Ticker and she worries about him, so when their second daughter married and Ticker suggested selling their house and moving into a railway carriage in the orchard she had agreed with him. Smaller, more manageable place, lower overheads and money in the bank. 'Good thinking, Ticker,' she'd said, kissing his bald patch.

The partitioning of the carriage reflected the Duckworth priorities: a minute kitchen, a slightly more generous bedroom and the rest of the space given happily over to what can best be described as a sales lounge. Two easy chairs pointed down the axis of this lounge, a small coffee table and a portable television formed an easy barrier; then the clocks.

Ticker isn't a clock snob; a good movement with a mediocre case is always welcome to a place in his stock. Superb second-empire clock garnitures rub shoulders with heavy Victorian slate-cased mantle clocks. Delicate boudoir timepieces studded with brilliants sit cheek by jowl with American gingerbread horrors. An elegant Vienna regulator hangs happily alongside a basic schoolroom clock whose leaden hands have been watched despairingly by generations of children. At the far end of the carriage a well has been cut into the floor so even the tallest of longcases can be accommodated, and four good specimens stand solemnly to attention, their superior faces staring haughtily over lesser colleagues.

Ticker showed me quickly around his stock then with a flick of his hand marshalled me out of the carriage. 'Come on, the stuffs up in the house, we have to be out by next week.'

It was nearly all clean second-hand stuff. An Edwardian hall-stand, a bureau centre cabinet to delight Fiery Frank and, best of all, a bed: a big solid one with a padded headboard. Mrs Duckworth pulled back the bed tick to show the electric blue mattress. 'Like new. I won't tell you what it cost.'

I pulled a face. 'It doesn't matter Mrs D. Hard to move – even the best –'

Ticker nodded in agreement. 'Aye, I've seen 'em in sales. Fetch nowt.' He spent a lot of his time at auctions and knew the going rate for most things. I offered a blanket price for the lot. Ticker sighed, curled his lip and nodded his acceptance. 'By the way, have you had an owd woman round selling war medals? She has 'em in an old OXO tin. Don't touch 'em, they're bent. She's not as old as she looks and I have it she drives a Porsche.'

I set the bed up in the apple house and sent Peter and Sally to tell Baz. It was nearly nine o'clock before he poked his unshaven face through the kitchen door. 'You've found me one?' he asked happily.

I bunched my fists and thumped the bed all over. 'Look at that, look at that Baz, not a squeak in it, a completely squeakless bed.' Vicky had followed us across the yard and stood in the doorway biting her lower lip to suppress a giggle.

Baz stared over my head, his face impassive. 'How much?'

'Well Baz, a completely squeakless bed can't be cheap, being squeakless is an enormous advantage, you see any –'

Baz cut me off. 'How much?'

'A fiver.'

'Four quid.'

'No, but I'll tell you what,' I started thumping the bed again, 'if I can find a squeak you can have it for four quid.' Baz quickly dropped a crumpled fiver on to the mattress, and nodded a goodnight.

Vicky folded her arms and gave me a piercing look. 'You're wicked, you were embarrassing him.'

'And you're inobservant. Did you see where he went? Straight home; no taproom. That character is reformed.'

The most beautiful cat in the world jumped up on to the bed, curled his front paws under his chest and went to sleep.

The last time we had seen Little Petal she had been heavily pregnant. Fiery was delighted they were going to have a child. He steered her, as a tug steers an ocean-going liner, past hazards, and into safe berths. He fussed around her incessantly, worried about what she ate and how much rest she had. She was forbidden to lift any furniture and he monitored carefully the time she spent on her feet. Little Petal revelled in this attention. Whenever Fiery handled her in and out of the van or wrapped a blanket around her big shoulders she had taken to giving a little bow of the head and what she knew to be a sweet smile.

Fiery became a little less flamboyant. Several gold rings disappeared from his fingers but the bold hunting-pink waistcoat was still slashed across by the heavy gold watchchain. The cowboy boots gave way to sober black shoes and more often than not his greasy black hair was hidden under a quite ordinary flat cap. He confided in me that he was very worried about Little Petal developing varicose veins for he'd heard that the extra weight a pregnant woman carries can play havoc with the legs.

'She's some good legs, guv. Shame to have 'em spoiled. I've left her at home with her feet up.'

I tried to do a mental calculation involving Petal's great weight and the average weight of a healthy baby and as she approached eighteen stones I failed to see how the relatively small increment brought about by pregnancy would ruin her legs.

However I liked the little man's concern for his wife's well-being, and, if there was a superb pair of legs hiding under those caftans, it was only right they should be preserved.

Fiery had become a little harder to deal with. He bargained me down to the last pound over the furniture I'd got from Ticker's then he cheekily held out his hand. 'Bit o'luck money guv.'

I pushed a pound back and led him to the kitchen. 'Coffee's twenty pence a mug,' I told him jokingly.

He thrust his hands into his pockets and grinned at Vicky. 'I'll just have a cup of warm water then, luv.'

Vicky pulled a face at me and settled Fiery into my chair with his mug of coffee. 'How long is it now, Fiery?'

'Another month luv, before Fiery junior steps on to the world stage. With my looks and her style, little bugger's a winner before he's here.'

Vicky gave a giggle and hugged him around the shoulders. 'Why do men always think it's going to be a boy?'

50

Fiery grinned and shook his head from side to side slowly. 'Life gets better, guv, life gets better.'

I collected the eggs from the hen house and went into the pantry to make up the dozen from the cast iron rack – Little Petal would need protein. A brace of pheasants tied high at the neck with billy band hung from a bacon hook. The iridescent feathers of the cock were varnished with light from the small window, pale straw-coloured legs dangled from tight plump bodies, clawed feet gripped at the air like tiny arthritic hands. The scales of the legs were small and smooth and there were no spurs on the cock. They were young birds from the last shoot; hung less than a fortnight.

The billy band cut into my crooked finger as I carried them into the kitchen. Fiery's delight when I dropped them into his lap gave way to a frown and he looked up at me apologetically. 'Thanks guv, but I don't know how to fettle 'em.'

I split two paper feed sacks, spread them over the rug, and ordered Fiery to the milking stool. 'You townies would die of starvation, left to yourselves.' I showed him how to pluck them from the neck down, licking the outside of the thumb and stroking the feathers off. Fiery was slow, he picked out the feathers one by one and dropped them at arm's length on to his sack, watched from under the table by the owl-eyed cat.

I finished my bird and took his on to my knee. Relieved of the tedious work he thrust out his legs and laying a green neck feather from the cock on to his open palm he blew it into the air. The cat's front paws gathered, gently treading the carpet, its head dipped and rose, then it leapt. Stretched paws trapped then clawed the feather from table height. Then the taut, curving body of the cat dropped on to the heap of feathers at my feet, billowing them up to my knees. Fiery threw back his head and laughed as the cat raised itself on to its haunches and cupping its paws boxed the feathers over the hearth and carpet. Vicky squealed and picked up the cat. 'You're a little devil,' she told it as she slammed the door behind its flicking tail.

With both birds plucked, I lit a taper and singed the long hairs from them. The hairs cringed away from the flame, curling rapidly back on to the bodies and leaving little brown-black toffee blobs. I brushed the blobs away with my hand and slapped the birds on to the draining board. 'Now Fiery, a bit of judicious work with the knife.' I slit both vents pulling the skin back. The entrails were cold and firm. 'Come on Fiery, let's see you do your stuff: everything out, liver and kidneys back in.'

Fiery blew his generous lips out and shook his head, 'I couldn't guv.'

The cat jumped on to the sill and watched me through the window, its convex glassy eyes following my hand as I chopped heads and legs and eviscerated the birds. I opened the crops and washed bright fresh-looking grain from their ridged folds.

Fiery had retreated to the milking stool. 'Plucking I don't mind, but ... '

Vicky fetched two good onions from the pantry and brushing the outer crinkly skin from them she set them alongside the pheasants. Fiery was given his instructions, important points emphasised with the wag of a finger. 'Fry the breadcrumbs in butter, lay two rashers of fat bacon across each bird, roll the onions in black pepper ... ' Fiery nodded at each finger wag.

The initial thought had been to send Little Petal a dozen eggs; now it had grown. I got a stout cardboard box and layered the bottom with potatoes, each one carefully turned in hand and inspected for spade cuts and wire worm holes; these were topped with sprouts and leeks and finally the brace of pheasants laid in state; the shiny onions packed between and a border of cocoa brown eggs set gently around them.

'There you are Fiery, food parcels for the rich.'

Fiery laughed. 'I like it, guv, I like it.'

Feathers get everywhere. They were curled into the loops of the hooky rug, they wafted about the hearth and they were stuck to the wet noses of the dogs.

Before we bank up the fire for the night we pull our chairs up to it and have the last cup of tea. I time it to coincide with the last pipe of the day and I tell myself that these are old men's habits, but it is nice to sit there side by side, the children asleep upstairs, all the stock safely locked away, the cat between us blinking into the fire, the dogs asleep under the table and the napping gate propped.

The taper flared and shrunk as I drew on my pipe and the red glow spread across the bowl as I eased myself back into the Windsor ready for the best part of the day.

The back door shook.

Ted's great fist was banging a demanding tattoo which set the dogs barking and the cat's fur bristling. I drew the bolts and let him in.

'I've been draining today, an' you get to thinking when you're draining. You've got a set of encyclopedias gathering dust in your shop. How much for 'em?' he said.

'Gathering dust! They haven't been there that long.'

'Well how much?'

'A fiver.'

Ted made what his wife calls his 'mumpy mouth'. He presses his lips together and pushes them forward. He makes it when

53

the Colonel thwarts him at the parish council meetings and he makes it at Lalbeck cattle market when he thinks an old milk beast could have fetched a bit more.

'Give thee four,' he offered.

I make the same mistake every time with Ted, I never put on any 'talking money'. Put a quid on, knock a quid off – he's happy. Well, I thought as I piled the books into Ted's outstretched arms, Fiery had got his quid in luck money.

Ted's mumpy mouth melted into a grin. 'All the world's knowledge here; all the world's knowledge written down.'

Vicky poured more tea as we pulled up to the fire again. 'They were cheap,' she muttered.

'Aye, well he's only got nine tenths of the world's knowledge because there's one missing.'

Chapter 5

I propped the silver-edged wedding invitation against the egg money teapot. Floating ribbons from angled bells threaded around our name and a happy cherub, his belly tickled by cauliflower clouds, ballooned his cheeks and blew a silent fanfare over the embossed lettering. We replied with haste, Peter and Sally running hand in hand to the post-box.

Sally was to be a bridesmaid and Gwen Radford was to make the dress.

Peach. I heard the word four score times in one week. The shiny square of satin that Susan sent was turned in the light, rubbed between numerous fingers and thumbs, held against Sally's cheeks, and pressed, by the girl herself, over a thin thigh. It was the most handled, most talked about piece of fabric in the dale; its quality, its finish, its depth of colour were discussed and marvelled at. Neighbours came to look at it, relatives of Baz, some we'd never heard of, came to look at it. It was like having a piece of the golden fleece.

The attached note told us that it was available at Brindley

and Fellows, so the following Saturday afternoon, Vicky, Gwen and a very excited Sally took themselves off to Brindley and Fellows.

Peter and I bent our backs to a more masculine task. We put the chain traces on Topic and pulled the two poultry arks into the orchard.

A lot of ponies don't work satisfactorily in chains. They miss the reassuring feel of the shafts, get a leg over a trace and panic. We'd had Topic drag a log around the garth for hours, Ted and I walking each side of her, talking to her and pushing each side of her fat rump when she stopped, to keep her square. She'd been easy to train, this quiet, sturdy Dales mare.

Topic took the slack out of the traces, leaned into her collar and the ark crept forward steadily. Then, when I put my hand gently on her muzzle and whispered 'whoa', she stopped and, leaning back, dropped the swingletree gently on to the grass.

We cleaned the arks out and after shaking brittle yellow straw across their floors we set a wire netting fence between them because the Barnevelders were due.

It is good to have a little project in hand, something to plan and muse over when the last pipe of the night is drawing well. Our current project was to keep a rare breed of poultry, to get two independent strains established so we could make up and sell breeding trios: two pullets with an unrelated cockerel.

Arthur, the expert forger of tables, bred Barnevelders and he was to furnish us with a pen of these big, glossy, finely-laced birds. Vicky had shown a little concern when I ordered the pen from Arthur. 'They will be genuine won't they? I mean, an hour out in the rain and they could be a pen of white leghorns.'

I assured her Arthur faked only tables.

All the afternoon we toiled, hammering in posts and stretching wire, the shop bell only disturbing us four or five times. Some customers look askance at my stained corduroys and baggy sweater but most accept that we are a small country shop and these things are to be expected.

We trooped down to the Radfords' three times for fittings of the dress. Sally stood on a footstool and allowed herself to be pulled and pushed around without protest. Mumbled words from pin-bristling mouths bidding her to lift this arm then the other, turn this way, then back, and all the time the little girl smiled and chattered away.

I put my arm around my son and steered him across the yard to Richard's workshop: a sawdust-strewn haven of sanity and warm smells, a place of preciseness. For here, scriber and gauge rule, not the finger-plucked irregularity of ruche and pleat.

Peter hoisted himself on to the bench alongside me and swung his legs. They had wanted him to be a page boy in satin blue breeches, but the look of sheer horror on the boy's face had sent me straight to his defence, for I remembered as a child being forced to a village carnival fancy dress in a pink rabbit outfit, and the ammunition the resulting group photograph had been in the hands of an evil cousin.

'No! Definitely no. The boy is too old.' We had joined forces, father and son, and stood resolutely against the petticoat squadron. 'Too old. Definitely. The boy would never live it down.'

The dress was finished and we, mere males, were denied a look at it. Bo-Peep style we were told, absolutely gorgeous. It was laid in the guest bedroom shrouded in tissue paper and more than one night Vicky and I smiled at each other as we heard the pad of tiny feet across the landing and the rustle of tissue.

The wedding present list was circulated, containing very modest requirements, mainly for the kitchen. We squandered our half-day off in Lalbeck, feeling guilty lunching in a pub so near home, and we bought them a set of pans, sending the assistant scurrying into the window after the best we could afford.

With the present bought and the dress made we returned to our spring tasks. The new hens arrived, deep bodied with yellow legs and bold eyes and beetle green sickles. The cocks strutted their new territories, marshalled their charges then threw out their breasts and crowed, after the Colonel's Maran cock had put back his head and issued a challenge. It was something we hadn't thought of, a dawn duel across the village green, so we cut squares of old carpet and made makeshift blinds for the hen house windows. Cocks don't crow in the dark, so in the dark they would be kept until breakfast time.

The week before the wedding it snowed. Flurries of small flakes soon blotted out the fells and laid a white sheet over the village.

'Looks like it's going to be a white wedding,' everybody told Baz, for as the day drew near the whole village talked of little else.

Once again every female in the village traipsed through our kitchen, this time to gasp in admiration at the dress and nod approvingly at the pans.

Ted was to be best man. He took his duty seriously and spirited Baz away from his bachelors' party as soon as his eyes began to glaze.

'Bright and perky for tomorrow lad,' he'd said pulling him to his feet and gently pushing him through the door.

Rabbit clicked his tongue. 'It's started already; a ruined man.'

Thievin' Jack swilled his pint glass around. 'She's a bonny enough lass, but it's a hard price to pay.'

As a party it was a flop. We didn't even drink until closing time, for with Baz gone the atmosphere went too and one by one we drank up and left.

Ted's wife looked up at the clock as he bumbled through the door. 'You all right?'

'Dead as a graveyard over there,' he told her.

Charlie banged the empty glasses on to the bar. 'Is it a wedding or a wake we're having?'

The morning of the wedding we were up early. Sally was like a cat on hot bricks, her dress was laid out in the lounge along with her new shoes, and Vicky had to call her back to the breakfast table twice. Peter showed little interest. For him, he assured us, it was going to be a boring day, a day of polished shoes, collar and tie and combed hair.

'What time will we get away?' was his only question.

I washed the van then ran upstairs to change as Vicky fussed over the children. 'We'll be late,' she wailed. Peter was scrubbed pink, bullied into his clothes, had the specks that only a mother can see picked off him and invisible hairs plucked and brushed from his collar.

Then Vicky did a very unfair thing. Her finger tapped on my chest. 'See he keeps clean. I'm holding you responsible.' She disappeared into the lounge where Dolly and Gwen fussed over Sally's clothes. The three women then started to dress the girl who had been shampooed and brushed, bathed and manicured and now stood shivering, but uncomplaining, in shift and pants on the footstool.

The net underskirts bounced around her little calves and then the dress, the gorgeous shiny, peach dress was lowered over her head. Six hands pulled and plumped, tugged and straightened and a small girl shook her head to loosen golden curls and bring a lump to her father's throat. She looked beautiful.

Weak March sunshine poured into the room gilding a lovely young girl in her first very special dress, and sent fingers of light darting across the folds of fabric as Sally gave excited little hops. The three women stepped back, crossed their hands, tilted their heads, and smiled.

The Colonel was taking Vicky and Sally to the church in his Bentley. Peter and I were to have less prestigious passengers. We put three armchairs and a bench in the back of the van. Nellie May, Thievin' Jack and Ivy, Cousin Leopold and Belgiana were coming with us.

Things are never as impellent as women would have us believe, so once the impromptu seating was in the van, Peter and I went to have a look at the new poultry. They were doing well, their combs had reddened and their plumage had a tightness and gloss to it which made them stand out against the new growth of grass. Peter flushed them from under the trees, the cocks flicking their heads, setting their wattles joggling as they clucked reassuringly to the hens and took up the rearguard. We had divided them into two breeding pens, the naturally antagonistic cocks separated by wire netting.

Peter noticed it first. 'Look Dad! It's been bleeding,' he cried. One of the cocks had a piece the size of a pea torn out of its comb. The blood had dried and cracked around the hole which had a rim of scab but still looked raw and angry. It called for a good dollop of Stockholm tar.

I shouldn't have let Peter go into the run to catch the bird for it was too big for the boy. He closed his eyes and grimaced as the wings buffeted his face.

'Get its legs! Get its legs!' I shouted.

The boy groped blindly for its legs, staggered backwards, then fell flat on his back alongside the water trough. The back of his new blazer and trousers were caked in mud. I got him to his feet just before Vicky called from the yard. 'The flowers have come. We're off now, don't be late.'

I gave a wave and a thumbs up then hurried the boy into the kitchen and played Vicky's hairdryer over his back.

Cousin Leopold tapped on the window and pulled his watch from his waistcoat. We hurried out to find Belgiana waiting for us at the van, on her head a vintage cartwheel hat, trimmed with bunches of red and yellow cherries and at her feet, the grey lurcher.

I backed the van up to Nellie May's and half lifted the old gypsy into it. We settled the ladies into two of the armchairs with the lurcher between them. Then Leopold, after much pulling at his jacket and hitching at his trouser knees, sank into the third. Ivy and Thievin' Jack were waiting outside the shop. The butcher's wife climbed into the cab with me whilst Thievin', with a jolly 'fares please', slid along the bench and pretended to eat the cherries from Belgiana's hat, making Peter bend double with laughter and expose his mud-caked back. Thievin' looked serious then rolled his eyes. 'Your mother'll kill you when she sees that.'

Peter with the easy treachery of a child grinned and pointed at me. 'It was his fault.'

'Oh! She'll give it to him in the old ... ' Thievin's finger stabbed at his neck. 'There's something about these do's that can put the fight of a butcher's dog into a woman. A wedding, lad, handled correctly, can be more fun than a funeral.'

The Colonel ushered us to our pews. He had realised that the vast majority of the congregation was on Baz's side, so after the immediate family were seated and with an eye to symmetry he had started filling each side of the church equally.

Belgiana ignored the Colonel's outstretched arm bidding her take a place on what she firmly called the 'wrong side'. She half bowled the dapper man over as she stomped down the aisle.

'Cousins!' she cried with a firm set to her jaw and her cherries aquiver. Cousin Leopold followed her sedately, bowing to acquaintances with the dignity of an old world courtier.

Baz and Ted stood out in front, Ted the more nervous of the two for Baz had repeatedly told him, 'Look after that ring, I'd to sell me double-barrelled four-ten to buy that.'

Ted's fingers worked like a bird's beak in the waistcoat pocket of his 'gentleman's suit' plucking at, then shuffling the ring. He knew how much Baz had thought of that four-ten: it was the best little rabbit gun in the dale.

Susan and her parents had stayed the night in a hotel in Lalbeck and Billy Potts was bringing the bride and her father to the church in his vintage Rolls-Royce. Vicky stayed at the church door with an excited Sally until the bride's car came into view. Even the Colonel's love of symmetry couldn't be allowed to keep married couples apart, so she bumbled and apologised her way along the pews to my side.

I had put Peter alongside a stone pillar with strict instructions not to turn his back to his mother.

Lalbeck Church is small. Its limewashed walls carry brass plaques to commemorate the sons of local families fallen in battle, Gothic letters deep graven and black filled, Inkerman and Sebastopol, Orange Free State and Transvaal, a steady milking of young blood until the watershed of the First World War fills a plaque the size of a card table. A stone flagged floor and plain-pitch pine pews give the church an austere look, until one raises one's eyes to the stained glass. 'Early seventeenth-century, probably made in York,' the Reverend Sidney had told us. The reds are full and deep, as if they would bleed if we scratched them; and the blues, pure cobalt blues have a richness that holds the eye and feeds it. I sat and gazed at the windows.

An engineering background ruins a man. Amidst all this warmth and happiness I wanted to tell Peter that glass is a fluid and, as such, it flows continually, that the top of the panels will be appreciably thinner than the bottoms but Miss Wells' thin legs began to pump the organ faster, her hands moved over the keyboard with definite stabs. 'Here comes the bride . . . '

All brides look lovely. There is something ethereal about them. For the most of us marriage is life's greatest ceremony and the bride is the hub of it. A wild extravagance, the most ornate and costly dress she will ever possess and she wears it for perhaps a quarter of a day. She will never be so cosseted, pampered, looked at or admired again. A once in a lifetime butterfly day.

Susan was slightly taller than her father. As they moved down the aisle, slowly, heads turned towards them and many smiles were smiled.

As she passed our pew I could see her face under the veil. She had taken her glasses off and her hair, normally pulled back in a severe way, lay across her cheeks in soft waves. Her father pressed her arm into his side and stared straight ahead. It was a very emotional time for him; they had always been close, but if he had doubts about Baz, his daughter didn't. Down the length of the church she never took her eyes off her husband-to-be.

Sally walked sedately behind them, her back straight and her arms out wide holding the bride's train, smiling shyly in response to the little fluttering waves she got from each side of the church.

The couple made their vows in strong voices and we all stood to sing 'The Lord is my Shepherd', to the tune of Crimmond.

Miss Wells pumped enthusiastically but a hundred voices drowned the little organ. Taking up the challenge she threw her head back and worked her legs furiously, making the organ inch slowly across the stone floor. One massive stone flag then another fed itself relentlessly under the instrument, Miss Wells hitching her stool along in pursuit. Her worried look gave way to one of gratitude as Cousin Leopold stuck out his leg and wedged a well polished toecap under the runaway organ.

The photographer bounded about the gravelled triangle outside the church door. 'Best light I've had this year,' he called cheerfully, as he formed and then dissolved group after group in front of the massive oak door.

Mrs Denholm, immaculate in powder blue, raised a delicate lace-edged handkerchief and dabbed her eyes. Ted unbuttoned his jacket and thrust it wide to display his heavy watch-chain and leaned his red face close to Mrs Denholm's ear. Her eyes widened then she turned from him and burst into tears.

Ted's big hand shook her shoulder in a reassuring way, then

he gathered Mr Denholm to him and hustled him down the path to where the underkeepers had tied the lychgate with billy band. 'Old Dales tradition,' he explained to the timid man, 'bride's father has to come up with "gate openings".'

Mr Denholm sadly poked two five pound notes through the gate and turned to be caught by the shoulders again. Ted gave him a friendly shake. 'Cheer up, I've just been telling your missus, he can be a twine-arsed sod can Baz, but he'll look after her.'

Chapter 6

I steered Peter sometimes physically and sometimes with eye contact so that he constantly presented his front elevation to his mother. The mud had dried to an even light khaki, a scrub between the hands and a stiff brush and soon all would be well.

Nellie May's legs were aching so I walked her back to the van, sat her in her armchair and tucked a blanket around her. She was beginning to look really old, her mouth sagged open most of the time and her skin drooped in loose yellow folds across her cheeks; the eyes were still bright but she looked stick thin and brittle.

The bride and groom were gently buoyed down the path and through the gates, the generosity of Mr Denholm having caused them to be thrown wide.

Sally still clung loyally to Susan's train, as she shrieked with laughter and bent her head against the flurries of rice and confetti. Thinly gloved hands, powder blue and lilac, beige and white, scrabbled into little boxes then flung the tiny pink horseshoes, stars and bells over the happy couple.

Billy Potts stood by his Rolls-Royce. He'd tied white ribbons to the elegant mascot and put a small bunch of freesias into the plated florette. His trousers were pulled over his Wellingtons, the toes of which he'd polished with black lead, his tie with its squeezed knot was away, and the collar points of his shirt were folded into gull wings, but nobody looked at Billy. The bride and the car commandeered all the attention.

The Rolls was a 1929 Phantom and had been specially bodied by Park Ward for a slightly eccentric mill owner. The passenger doors were wider than normal for he'd been a very bulky man; all the padding in the seats was pure wool and a spare wheel sat on each running board giving the car an older look.

When Baz and his wife were on board, Billy beckoned Peter to climb in beside him, then with several honks of the horn the car drew silently away, only a slight feathering of blue from its exhaust showing it was under its own power.

The long room above The Ship was already filling up as I half carried Nellie May to her place. A score or so of villagers and friends had for one reason or another forgone the church service and had settled themselves in the pub. Rabbit pulled long at his pint, smacked his lips, then eased the glass on to the narrow shelf above the fireplace. 'T'roof would have fallen in if I'd have gone,' he grinned.

Ivy fussed her way along the tables picking up each name card in turn. 'Hope they haven't sat me next to Billy Potts, I'd enough trouble with him at our Cissie's wedding, bloody hands all over.' She found to her relief she was two places from the amorous Billy, then went in search of Thievin'. 'A wedding reception in a pub is filled with temptation for a man who lacks willpower,' she whispered to herself as she clomped back down the stairs.

Willpower arrived at Thievin's elbow in the shape of the powder-blue Ivy just as Charlie was pushing a froth-lapping pint towards him. 'Steady on that me lad,' she warned, and then in a friendlier voice, 'an' get me a double gin and tonic.'

There was a constant coming and going on the narrow stairs. People bustled along to where Baz and Susan stood by the wedding presents, congratulated them, kissed the bride, found their places, then hurried down to the bar for a quick drink before the formality of a reception set in. Miss Wells shyly thanked Cousin Leopold for stopping the organ's slide across the church floor. Cousin Leopold threw back his head and laughed. 'When I saw the owd kist-o-whistle slithering off I thought you were leaving us for pastures new.'

I saw, over the crowded bar, Vicky standing on the tip of her toes and signalling to me. She had one hand on Peter's shoulder and her mouth seemed to be saying, 'What's this?' I signalled back that I would let the dogs out for a minute and closed the pub door behind me with a sigh of relief.

On the village green stood a large crate containing three geese who snaked their long necks through the slats and hissed at me as I read the luggage label tacked on top. 'From Couson Leopold and Belgiana – much hapiness.'

I laughed as I let the bouncing dogs out into the yards. The spelling wasn't good but the gift I thought was first-class.

Cousin Leopold's white head bobbed over the wall. 'See yer on the same job as me,' he said, nodding to where his lurcher scythed through the bracken.

'They're grand geese, Cousin Leopold.'

'Early layers, they'll bring off gozzers that'll make a fair size by Michaelmas.' He eased his wide brimmed hat forward on his head and spat. 'Nowt like green goose.'

When I got back to the reception Canary Mary had soothed Vicky down. 'It's nothing,' she'd told her, raising clouds of dust from the boy's back. 'No bones broken. Worse things happen at sea, don't they luv?' She squeezed the boy hard then threw a yellow bag on to a yellow arm and crooked a finger at me. 'An' you can get me a drink because I've something in my little motor for you.'

In the long room people were taking their seats. Ivy found to her consternation that Billy Potts had changed the place settings around and raised her eyes heavenwards and sighed as he dropped into the chair next to hers.

'Fate, luv, fate,' he whispered beerily into her ear.

'It wasn't fate, Billy Potts, you changed 'em around.'

'Top level decision, luv. It was decided to put all the beautiful people together.'

Ivy failed to suppress a smile as Billy leaned back and folded his arms.

We lost our daughter for the day, she'd become a willing body slave to Susan. A dropped handkerchief was dived for instantly, the flowing train was scooped up from under chair legs and insensitive adults were firmly eased away from its folds. 'The guardian of the dress,' I whispered to Vicky.

'Peter was claimed by Canary Mary. Unlike most of us she doesn't talk down to children: she listens to their opinions, encourages them to expand their ideas, and she shows infinite patience. Peter's finger drew an innocent line on her knee as he explained our latest project to her. 'We've put a fence from that apple tree down here to . . . '

Everybody moved the name cards to suit themselves so

Vicky and I found ourselves sitting next to Cousin Leopold. 'I'll sit down here wi' you then I can bring t'long dog in. Gets very nervous on her own,' he explained.

There was stand pie and roast ham, turkey breast, and glistening wet lettuce, tomatoes cut in a fancy way, and cheese; mountains of cheese.

Mucky Marion was waiting-on with Elsie. As Marion edged between us and clattered the plates on to the table she smelled faintly of gin, for like the physicians of old she's a great believer in 'a little and often'.

The Reverend Sidney said a clear and professional grace and then there was much scraping of chairs and to-ing and fro-ing of plates. Hors d'oeuvre dishes heaped with a variety of pickles hovered over the tables, then were thrust under noses. 'Pickled walnuts Ted? Red cabbage Rabbit?'

Cousin Leopold's lurcher laid its chin on the table and swivelled liquid brown eyes from plate to plate. 'Nervous dog: best 'uns allus are a bit nervy,' Leopold smiled, patting the dog's ribcage.

On the top table Belgiana maintained the family position. The heavily cherried hat dipped politely as she engaged her near neighbours in conversation, whilst Aunt Dot worked steadily at the roast ham, cutting it into tiny pieces. She was happy, her best cameo brooch was at her throat and a married nephew at her side.

Thievin' leaned his thin body over the table and questioned all within earshot, 'What do you think of the pie? It's one of mine.'

Cousin Leopold doesn't approve of Thievin', he looks with a jaundiced eye at the butcher's easy and familiar way with women. 'Man ought to 'ave more respect for the female kind,' he said, taking a piece of pie and pushing it against the lurcher's nose knowing the dog wouldn't touch it until he said it could. 'He doesn't think much of it,' Leopold called up the table.

Thievin' sniffed. 'That brute'll only eat meat if it's raw an' still bleeding.'

Cousin Leopold smiled happily. 'Set!' he hissed at the dog. The ragged jaws snapped and the pie disappeared with a 'shlop'.

Baz and Susan, heads bent together, hardly ate at all. Mr Denholm explored the pie with his knife whilst his wife sat staring, first this way then that, like someone who has blundered into a weird ritual and is making a very calculated and disciplined effort to remember everything that happens.

Two tables away we could hear Canary Mary bargaining with Peter. She was swopping him her trifle for his cheese. It was a highly acceptable deal to the boy but Mary was having him on, loading the bargain. '... and two toffee apples, three bars of chocolate, four bottles of pop, and at Easter I'll give you the biggest marzipan chicken you've ever seen. Oh, and a kiss.' Peter dropped his head on to his hands and his body shook with laughter.

Aunt Dot was still cutting away at the roast ham. She was happy, but puzzled. The vicar had told her that Baz was the village Benedict. 'From Shakespeare you know,' he'd added.

'Benedict? Benedict?' The old lady whispered to herself, 'There's no Benedict in the family. There's a Benjamin on his dad's side, Reverend must mean him.'

A fat aluminium teapot appeared, steam curling from its spout, as Mucky Marion dipped it over cup after cup. 'It's Earl Grey,' she told us in a hushed voice.

71

Long John had not been idle, his innocent lemonade bottle had glugged a sparkling fill-up into many a glass. Mr Denholm smiled and raised his half pint of vintage cider to the light. 'We must buy some of this my dear – a very refreshing drink,' he told his sphinx-like wife.

It became a time of plates. They were passed from table to table, clunked together, gently argued over, chipped here and there, stacked in fat tiers, passed out and called back. It was trifle time. Mucky Marion took the large baking bowl from Elsie's arms. 'Here I'll do it luv. Yer frittin' abart.' Big spoonfuls of trifle were turned on to the plates.

Ted had bounced about in his seat for half an hour; his speech was safely in his waistcoat pocket and he was dying to take the stage. 'A better gathering than the Parish Council,' he muttered as he pulled his watch out and flicked open the cover. 'Another hour an' I'll loose 'em.' The room was noisy with laughter and the clatter of cutlery.

The trifle was distributed with an evenness and fairness that left nobody at odds. Big creamy yellow eggs of custard with plinths of rich soggy cake lay curled on virgin white plates; spoons were raised, poised ready to plunge, then Ted banged on the table with a beer bottle.

'Ladies and gentlemen.' The spoons dropped to the tablecloth and everybody stared at their trifle as Ted started his speech.

Mrs Denholm gazed in wonder at the happy orator as he read every verse and dedication on every single card the couple had received. Unbelievable was the word that kept coming to her mind.

Ted's wife sat opposite him, her eyes never leaving his face; she'd never known a time when he'd failed to make a fool of himself.

Ted's voice was strong and confident. He'd rehearsed well – every cow in his herd having been treated to the puns, the painful jokes, and the innuendo. 'I must be gettin' old,' he joked, grinning around the room, 'it's the first weddin' I've been to where I've fancied the bride's mother more than the bride.'

Mrs Denholm coloured slightly and averted her gaze. Mr Denholm lolled back in his chair and grinned. He wasn't allowed to loll normally, so he revelled in the loll, rocking his chair back near to the point of no return, reckless carefree lolling. He wiped the cider glass along his lips. 'Not bad, not bad at all.'

Dolly glared at Ted and thrust a leg out under the table, but try as she could her sensible country brogue failed to make contact with her husband's shins. The plates of trifle lay untouched as the farmer orator warmed to his task.

Cousin Leopold snorted in exasperation and getting his long legs from under the table with some difficulty stood up. 'Watch me dog,' he said in a loud whisper.

Ted turned towards him and grinned. 'Where are you going?'

Cousin Leopold's reply was slow, measured and had great dignity. 'Hi am going to hattend to a call of nature.'

Rabbit and Billy Potts were conscientiously collecting up unwanted wedges of stand pie, Rabbit carefully wrapping his pieces in paper napkins and stowing them in the inside pocket of his overcoat.

His favourite ferret, a cream coloured gill, rudely expelled from her favourite place, worked her way through the lining of the coat into one of its outer pockets. She poked a bright eyed little face from under the pocket flap and peered up at Mrs Denholm.

The good woman's body went rigid, her eyes half-closed and

73

her well-manicured hands clenched on the tablecloth and, after a sharp intake of breath, she silently implored her maker to tell her that it wasn't true.

Peter came and stood between Vicky and me, he swung on our shoulders and whispered first into his mother's ear then mine. The boy wanted money. 'Here watch this,' I said, taking a piece of pie and laying it in front of the dog's nose.

'Set!' I hissed as Leopold had done but there was no 'shlop', the pie didn't disappear. Instead the lurcher leapt up on the table and made straight for the ferret.

The tablecloth bunched and slewed as the dog's claws fought for grip; plates of trifle, some impressed with a huge pawprint, were sent flying; cutlery and cups were flung into laps; wine glasses to the floor and the flower arrangements spun from their beer bottle vases.

Three massive bounds and the dog had its muzzle thrust into Rabbit's overcoat. The ferret had retreated into the labyrinthine lining whilst its unruffled owner calmly thwacked the lurcher's head with his flat cap. 'Ger-out-yer-blo-dy-an-i-mile.' Every syllable was accompanied by a thwack, but it was to no avail: the highly trained lurcher was not to be put off her quarry. A menacing, rattling growl came from her throat as its raggy tail swept to and fro under the nose of the terrified Mrs Denholm.

Cousin Leopold's command was obeyed instantly, the dog padding back up the table and dropping to the floor at his feet. It laid its head on the now bare table and turned liquid brown eyes to me.

Many hands pushed and pulled the cloth back into place, fresh wine glasses were fetched, and sprays of flowers spiked back into the beer bottles. Cousin Leopold was not pleased with me. 'All that glass about, she could have cut her pads,' he complained.

Ted had completely lost his audience. He prattled on for a while then made his mumpy mouth and sat down. I started to clap and drew bewildered stares from every quarter but soon the clapping caught on and Ted rose to his feet again to thunderous applause and shouts of 'more'.

He grinned around the room then gave us his old-fashioned look. 'Yer not having me on are you? Well I'll be brief.' This brought more applause until he threw back his head and laughed. 'All right! All right! I do go on a bit – but it's me only fault.'

Dolly made round eyes and pulled a derisory face.

'On to your feet then, an' I give you the toast. Bride and groom.'

There was much clinking of glasses, then, when we had settled back on to our chairs, Ted rounded off with his last treasured anecdote. 'They say the worst things in a man's life is a smoking chimney and a nattering wife. Well I know he's got one. Let's hope he hasn't acquired t'other.'

The cake was cut and distributed, cameras clicked. Mrs Denholm was coming around somewhat, and when Baz got to his feet to thank her and her husband for their lovely daughter she dabbed an eye once again and smiled as he promised he would always take care of her. Formalities over, we traipsed down the stairs to the bar and formed a semi-circle around the television set: Yorkshire were playing at Headingley.

Mrs Denholm had the first gin and tonic of her life. Drink was the devil's tool, she knew that well enough, but Albert had had three of those glasses of cider with a little lemonade and he seemed to be taking things in his stride. The occasion called for it and, with some lanky white-haired man pulling at your elbow and insisting you 'come an' look at the geese', it really was a necessity.

After much arm squeezing and whispering Susan managed to drag herself away from her new husband and, along with Sally and Vicky, made off to change into her going away outfit.

I walked up to Baz's cottage to fetch the little red sports car. It was good to drive, crisp and responsive to the accelerator, and as it was warm for the time of the year I dropped the hood and took a turn around the village before pulling up in front of the pub. Lenticular cloud banks were stacked above the fell and a sun that foretold of a touch of frost edged each one with a thin ribbon of red.

Canary Mary wrote 'just married' across the rear window as Peter tied a balloon to the aerial and the Colonel, with his usual preciseness, attached a pair of old boots to the bumper. Billy Potts turned the boots over in his hands and studied them carefully. 'Damned good boots. Would you mind if I swopped 'em for these wellies, Colonel?'

The Colonel gave him the look he used to employ to wither unruly subalterns and waved him away from the car. Billy Potts' wellies dangling behind them was no way for a young couple to start life.

Baz and his wife drove off to honeymoon on the 'West Coast', leaving behind a happy waving throng which, swelled with villagers and a sprinkling of tourists, half-filled the village green.

As I hurried back to Yorkshire at Headingley, Ted's strong hand gripped my elbow. 'Give us a lift with these geese on to t'link box.'

They were not particularly heavy, and when we pushed them

to the back of the link box I jumped up to tie the crate with billy band. The red car, tiny now, climbed to the top of Robin Bank and turned left. Must be going up the dale, I thought, the long way round. Nice evening, quiet romantic meal at some country pub.

Wind-combed clouds, heavy with a winter's greyness, were turned to molten lead, then pencilled around with gold and streaked with a pure and rich vermilion as the sun sank.

Dolly plodded across the green in her slippers to winkle Ted out of the pub. 'Come on, it's past milking time, them beasts is fair mithered,' she told him angrily. Ted was loath to leave, he was watching a card game closely. Thievin' was winning, his thin raw butcher's hands have an affinity with coins. They were pushed, grudgingly, across the table to him to join the neat stacks.

Mrs Denholm and Belgiana had made camp at the posher end of the lounge and the bride's mother, having had two or three gin and tonics, now felt quite composed – happy even.

Nellie May was hard asleep, her little head sunk to her breast, her hands in her lap holding a small white box of cake. Rabbit and Long John with an assortment of underkeepers had opened up the taproom and pulled their buffets up to the fire. There was the ten pound 'ale brass' that Mr Denholm had pushed through the lychgate to get through.

Canary Mary, dragging a tired Sally behind her, jammed her bright yellow wedding hat on to her head and directed me out to her car.

She lifted a small, silver, gravy Argyle out of the glove compartment and handed it to me. I twisted it in the light from the pub window; it was indeed silver and mid-Victorian but the maker's mark eluded me.

Gwen Radford had been looking after the shop for us and after taking out her wages I did not have enough to pay Mary for the Argyle. 'Never mind love, I'll pop in for the rest later in the week,' she smiled.

A bright moon had risen into the sky when I called the dogs for their nightly walk.

Baz's cottage showed one bright chink of light between the thick curtains and through the shrunken boards of the barn I could see the glint of chrome. A bluster of wind fretted the balloon which was still anchored to the car's aerial and pawed at the heavy wood smoke that curled from the chimney then fell in a tangled wraith over the stone roof.

Chapter 7

Ted shook his head sadly, the ewe's back humped and fell as she opened her black-lipped mouth and bleated after her lambs. 'She's calling to 'em and her bag's full, but she's not lettin' 'em feed.' The lambs ran around their mother returning her bleats with shrill little ones. They were hungry.

In the kitchen Dolly wrapped her pinny around the pan-handle and poured warm milk into two feeding bottles. Ted thumbed the teats on to the bottles, shook them and then, dabbing some of the milk out on to his hand, he wiped it across the lips of the lambs. Pink tongues fluttered. 'Come on yer' damned nuisances.' The tiny mouths found the teats and then with half-closed eyes and pulsing throats, the lambs sucked greedily away. Ted's face, his mouth pulled back in a flat smile and his eyes twinkling, belied his harsh words.

The lambs were kept in a cardboard box in the hearth and fed three times a day. Peter and Sally soon found these two new attractions; they scampered home from school, snatched a packet of crisps and a bun and tore round to Ted's. The lambs were cuddled, kissed and fed to capacity and much to Ted's pretended dismay, named.

Every day Ted drew the milk from the ewe and carried it to the kitchen. 'Good strong lambs,' he smiled as Sally and Peter lifted the dangling woolly bodies from the box.

Across the green, Charlie rubbed his hands as the guest book filled its first page and started the second with another flattering comment. Bed and breakfast was a good move. Never mind the Colonel and the other fuddy-duddies. There had been some interesting people, cultured people, good spenders.

The visitors were good for the pub and the village shop but the few that crossed the green to us were mainly idlers. We sold them the odd piece of crested ware, and a few pairs of 'scotch hands' went to searchers after things of rural interest, but in the main they peered through the window, commented on the price and reminded each other what they had thrown away.

We filled in the time between breakfast and loading the car with a walk to Tinker's Pond. Vicky suggested we put back our opening time until ten thirty, morning time-wasters were something we did not need. 'If there's something they are really interested in they'll hang around for half an hour,' she said emphatically. The woman was proved right again.

To the relief of the regulars Charlie made very few major changes in the pub. The visitors breakfasted in the lounge but by lunch-time the white cloths and the cruets had disappeared from the tables. Bowls of crisps and nuts were placed on the bar and chic little mats of pulpy paper appeared under glasses. Ethel bullied her husband into wearing a tie when he was behind the bar, and Rabbit and his terriers were banished to the taproom. Ethel in her drive to take the pub upmarket showed a ruthlessness we'd never suspected.

Neatly printed notices were pinned here and there, ordering us to wipe the mud from our boots, keep our dogs off the seats, and, to the disgust of the Colonel, to park 'prettily'.

The crisp and nut bowls were not put out on market day as farmers' fingers quickly emptied them with no apparent increase in the bar receipts.

Ethel found it necessary to take on more help and, to the amusement of the village, Mucky Marion left her pram at the kitchen door four mornings a week and got cracking with the pan and griddle.

'What the eye doesn't see,' Mrs Lewis observed drily.

Ted only paused in the lounge long enough to raid the crisp and nut bowls before joining Rabbit in the taproom for a good grumble. 'How long is this going to last?' they asked each other sadly.

The visitors mostly kept to themselves, but inevitably there were those who thirsted after local colour and descended the steps to the taproom where their presence was tolerated and they were fed a few stories as long as they had the good sense to realise how thirsty old countrymen got.

When the children broke up for the Easter holiday, Vicky and I sat up late one night discussing whether or not we could afford a few days away. We had not had a holiday for two years, renovating the house and getting the business going had drained us financially and taken up all our time, but as we sat in the warm kitchen after a good day and took stock we both felt we deserved a short holiday.

'It's going to be a good summer, isn't it,' we said to ourselves confidently. We would spend some time with the children, then return to the fray refreshed and raring to go.

Baz was cajoled into looking after the stock, Gwen readily agreed to keep shop for us, and Vicky found us accommodation for four days in a small hotel in Whitby.

We had eight rows of potatoes planted and a good bed of shallots poked new green spears at the sky; the poultry were cleaned out, fresh straw spread; the goat and pony were groomed till they shone; and so without a tinge of guilt we were ready for our halcyon days.

I put two easy chairs into the van, stacked the suitcases between them to form a table, and stuffed sacks with straw for the dogs to sleep on.

Flasks and sandwiches, fruit washed and polished, books and pencils hung in net bags from the backs of the chairs; dog food, bottles of water, leads and bowls filled a cardboard box. Our biscuit-tin first-aid kit was stowed under a seat, and a friendly-looking bale of warm clothing was stuffed and thumped into a safe place.

'Don't forget the kitchen sink,' Ted joked as I slammed the back doors shut.

Provisioned and accoutred like an expeditionary force we waved goodbye to our neighbours and turned the van nose down the dale.

Sally poked a sticky finger at my neck. 'No sales, no dealing, that's what mum says, do you hear?'

I heard, but sewn into my inside pocket was a thick fold of banknotes; you never know when you might come across a 'bit of gear', as Fiery puts it.

The opportunity presented itself before we had left the dale, for, as we skirted the green at Middlethwaite, I noticed a billboard outside the village hall. 'Fleamarket and Collectors' Fair.' Vicky raised her eyes and the children groaned as I pulled the van up.

'Here we go already,' they chorused.

'You never know,' I replied defiantly.

Canary Mary had the best pitch. As soon as one mounted the steps of the village hall one could see her sitting in the centre of the little stage, her two cats Amber and Topaz filling her ample lap and her goods laid around her like offerings left by a band of worshipping subjects. Her heavily ringed fingers flowed constantly over the cats us she turned to smile at, and assess, every potential customer. The Lalbeck amateurs were doing *The Pirates of Penzance* and a rugged backdrop of brown cliffs set off her bulky lemon-yellow dress, the hem of which brushed the dusty stage and just failed to hide the toes of her hand-painted egg-yellow shoes. The children ran down the aisle, parted to skip up the steps which flanked the stage, and dashed across it to plant simultaneous kisses on the upturned face of their Aunt Mary.

'Oh, I'm having a terrible day,' she moaned. 'Barely covering my expenses.'

The cats stood, arched their backs, yawned and draped themselves once more over the ample thighs. 'And I'm a bit worried about her over there.' Canary Mary swivelled her eyes towards a thin mean-mouthed woman who stood staring silently at a stall filled with old wood-working tools. 'She boned my ear for a good half an hour about how she suspects her husband is carrying on with his secretary and then she bought a pair of castrating shears.' Mary closely inspected a gold painted fingernail and then pushed it between her front teeth. 'You don't think I'd be liable, do you, if she ...?' Two heavily ringed fingers made a scissors movement.

'Depends Mary, if they were the "Mark Two Improved Humane Castrators", you'll be all right.'

A smile chased the worried look from her face and soon she was heaving with laughter and dabbing her eyes with a tiny lemon handkerchief. 'Couldn't blame her like, he sounded a real pig.'

The children went systematically over Mary's stock. They were developing a dealer's eye and often brought things of interest to our notice. Peter had found a pair of square-foot rummers and like a seasoned fleamarket buyer kept hold of them as he worked his way around the stall. Mary had spotted him out of the corner of her eye and once again she adopted her moany voice and complained about the lack of trade. She didn't want me to ask for trade discount, or at least she wanted me to accept only a nominal reduction in price, and as two can play at that game, I excused myself and went to look around the other stalls but found nothing. I had to come back to Mary and her two square-foot rummers.

She smiled up at me. 'They're really nice aren't they? The boy is learning.' They were good ones. Regency stars cut into chunky bases and a good tulip shape to the bowls. They were quite modestly priced but when dealing is in the blood, bargain we must.

I turned them up and looked at the bases again. 'Best price Mary.'

She knocked the usual ten per cent off. 'Best I've ever had,' she said proudly. 'They're cheap enough and you know it.' They were cheap; so with a theatrical sigh, a bit of eye rolling and a futile attempt to get another pound knocked off, I told her I would always be a poor man and laid the money on the lid of her wooden till.

Vicky called me from an adjoining stall and I left Mary wrapping the two rummers to see what she wanted. She had found some handmade lace, a little discoloured and needing some repair but very fine work.

'Do you think Gwen could do anything with this?' she asked.

There were several collars and cuffs and a yard or so of deep edging; the stallholder edged nearer smiling.

The problem with being a dealer is that the minute you show interest in something, suspicions are aroused: 'Is it undervalued? Is it rare?' The lace was good but the staining devalued it appreciably because some stains are so tenacious their removal virtually denatures the fabric. The collector has to sigh and live with them.

I shook my head. 'Stick to what we know,' and Vicky nodded her agreement.

'Dad! Dad!' Sally called from the edge of the stage. She pointed wildly to the far steps and we were just in time to see the OXO tin woman disappear into the crowd.

Mary was grinning down at us with her 'cat that got the cream' grin. 'See what I've got,' she announced proudly, spreading her hands to show the medals. 'Waterloo that one. Poor old dear –'

'Wanted her tin back.' I finished the sentence for her and reduced her grin to a wary smile. 'Mary, they're fakes. Haven't you heard of her? She's been all around the trade – month or so ago.'

Mary dropped her head to her chest and gave a little groan. We searched her stall and found a few more bits to buy: stone hot water bottles, a decanter with a passable chip and a box of military buttons. Mary was so depressed I hadn't the heart to ask for any trade discount. She never even looked at the money as I dropped it into her hand. 'She looked such a nice white-haired old dear,' she moaned.

'Mary, her hair is as black as a raven's wing and she drives a Porsche.'

Her eyes were filling with tears. 'What can I do with them?'

'Sit on them a bit, then shove them in a sale. She's conned the best Mary, so don't feel too bad about it,' I told her, as the children hugged her and we gathered up our bits and pieces.

Outside the hall several little girls had set up a charity stall. Two card tables were crammed with old books, homemade buns and pieces of knitwear. Alongside them stood a large vase filled with teazles which had been dipped in bright yellow paint. Vicky pulled one out and smiled at me. 'You know who'd like these.' I took half a dozen of what I thought were the best and asked the price causing a huddle of tiny heads; nobody had priced up the teazles. I offered a pound, a slight pause, then a vigorous nodding of heads. I wrapped the teazles in the tissue Mary had favoured the rummers with and sent Peter and Sally off with them.

'And give her another kiss – she needs cheering up.'

'It's all shipping stuff,' Peter exclaimed as we pushed open the bedroom door. The furniture was indeed all 1930s plywood, but the little hotel was clean and cheerful. We threw the windows wide open for although it was a chilly day we found the central heating stifling.

An old Dales farmhouse is an easy place to breathe, the stone flagged floors and thick walls rarely allow a room to become overheated and whenever Vicky shivers and pulls her cardigan around her shoulders I simply tell her how good it is for the complexion.

'See how women in centrally heated houses wrinkle prematurely.' She gives me a wry look and goes to kick the 'sausage' firmly into the gap under the kitchen door.

The beds were prodded and bounced upon and lemonade poured out into tooth glasses. I lay back on the bed, my hands behind my head, and smiled at the ceiling. Four glorious lazy days before us and the bit of trade we'd done already that morning would pay the petrol and more.

Bird-song is evocative, the pipe of the curlew always takes me back to the fell-tops and the shrill caw of the gull always brings to mind the jumble of Whitby and the zest of salt air.

Whitby draws artists like a magnet. The harbour, set about with massive granite walls, and the Esk, such a clear friendly river, refract a light which is almost tangible. The happy chaos of pantile roofs, warm reds and terracottas catch this light and tumble it over a thousand angled planes so that we have a kaleidoscope, not of colours, but of subtle warmths. We bask in this calidity before our eyes find the stark outline of the ruined abbey. It sits in silhouette against the sky like a black vulture, reminding us of the frailty of life and, suitably chastened, we hasten about our business.

I swung myself off the bed. 'Come on it's two hours to dinner, let's get those dogs on to the beach.'

The early evening was chilly and as we raced along the beach a healthy breeze made our cheeks glow, coats were opened and then finally dumped on the sand as a game of football got under way. We spent more time chasing ball-stealing dogs than footballing so when we climbed the steep cliff path back to the hotel we were tired and hungry.

The days passed quickly. In spite of chill breezes we spent the days on the beach, goose-pimpled legs splashed through rock pools, and hands, reddened by wind and wet sand, searched their pebbled bottoms for tiny creatures. We braved the sea up to our knees and then ran with teeth chattering pell-mell back to our little encampment to towel our legs back to life.

The dogs loved it. The sand clung to their wet bodies as they raced endlessly about the beach until fatigue brought them to flop, tongues lolling and chests heaving, at our feet.

Late afternoon would see us, burdened like pack horses, pushing on weary knees as we straggled up the steep setts and under the whalebone arch. The day's haul of shells was sorted, marvelled at again, and packed into a van which now smelled strongly of dogs and seaweed.

After dinner the glittering lights of the amusement arcades drew us like moths to a candle-flame, but the children were careful with their coins, the thrifty ways of the dale had taken root. When Baz had told them not to 'go throwing it about like a man wi' no arms', as he had pushed a fiver into their hands, it had not fallen on deaf ears.

We walked along the cliff-tops in the last light, the tired children lolling against us. Then I saw to the dogs whilst Vicky put the children to bed and we had a precious hour to ourselves. Seated in the bay window, a carafe of wine between us, we watched the lights of the fishing-boats dip and twinkle on a sea of beaten pewter.

On the last day we dragged two complaining children from the beach and after a late lunch we kicked the sand from our shoes and made for home. The children were charged to keep a watch for Penhill, for when the humped outline of the giant's lair breaks over the skyline we feel we are back in the dale; back home.

We drove into the village slowly, looking at it with fresh eyes, as if we had been away for a year. Our ducks were grazing at the top of the green and at the washfold sat Rabbit, a lamb under his arm and two of Ted's sheep curs at his feet. A red Porsche was parked in front of him. Rabbit was making a great show of cuddling the lamb. He pulled it tight up to his frayed overcoat and brushed his bristly chin over its head, as his free hand found the dogs' heads and gently pulled their ears. Across his shoulder lay a crook and out of a torn pocket hung a feeding bottle. He looked the epitome of the good and caring shepherd.

The car window slid down and a banknote swiftly found a new home in the old poacher's waistcoat pocket.

Baz was turning the goat into the orchard as we pulled into the yard. 'You all look as fit as a butcher's dogs,' he laughed as Sally thrust a stick of rock into his hands. 'Everything's OK. She's milked well and Topic's as round as a drum. I've walked her down Mill Lane every morning. Right enjoyed it.'

I nodded to where Rabbit sat. 'What's he doing?'

'Ah! He's on to a good 'un is Rabbit. He's borrowed a lamb and two dogs off Ted, sits there all day letting tourists photograph him, then he gets talking to 'em and spins 'em a right tale about being a poor 'owd man who widn't 'ev put his dogs down when they're too old to work and how they keep him poor.' Baz pointed absent-mindedly towards the washfold. 'We reckon he's makin' ten to fifteen quid a day.'

Gwen is a good saleswoman. She had worked four good days in the shop and eagerly brought the daybook out to show us how much she had taken. Notes pinned to the pages gave a thorough breakdown of each day's events. 'I was just writing one out for you. An old woman has just been in with an old OXO tin full of medals to sell, says she'll pop back in a day or two.'

I dashed to the door, but the Porsche had gone.

Chapter 8

The days of Topic's pregnancy were carefully ticked off the calendar and when she was in her tenth month we brought her up
from Nellie May's field and turned her into the garth behind
the house. The problem we pondered over was whether to let
her foal outside or to bring her in. Native ponies often foal
better outside we were told, but of late she had been showing
a restlessness and an unwillingness to be haltered or led.

'If anything should go wrong with the foaling she'd be better
inside,' I told Vicky.

So we cleaned out the apple house, limewashed the walls
and sluiced the floor with disinfectant. Either way we were prepared; we'd decide nearer the time.

Old Mr Hall came to see the pony every day. He ran his thin
bony hands over her and talked gently to her, 'Yer doin' all right
lass, yer doin' all right.'

Mrs Lewis didn't like her father spending so much time in
the garth, it took him away from his paraffin job and she was
sure he would 'catch his death'.

Whenever I saw the old man hobbling along from the shop I would swing the kettle over the fire and take him out a pot of tea – no milk, just strong black tea with plenty of sugar.

'How it should be,' the old man would smile. 'Thick enough for a mouse to skate on. She's looking well.' He would work his thin arms along the wall to find a comfortable spot and then take a long drink. 'She's doin' all right.'

If work called I would leave him leaning over the wall talking to the mare, his tea going cold, but if I could spare the time I would also set my arms searching for hollows in the coping stones and let my body sag against the wall. 'What d'you think it will be?' I asked him.

A shaky hand stroked his chin; he'd sneaked out unshaven – another defiant act that would set his daughter clicking her tongue and shaking her head.

'Yer can't tell. Some say they can but I don't see it. All I know is they allus carry colts longer than fillies, that I do know – Apple Tom 'ud tell thee that.'

'I think he makes it up a bit at times.'

Mr Hall laughed. 'Aye he knows some stuff, but now and again he talks as t'wind blows.'

The swallows had arrived. They swooped and planed over the garth while I spent happy hours with the old horseman, the gentle May sun on my back. We would be silent for many minutes without a feeling of awkwardness, just watching the pony graze or flick away the first manure flies of the year with her tail. The old man would pat the wall with his hand. 'She's doin' all right.'

Trade began to pick up and a steady flow of cars percolated through the dale. I painted the pony plough we had got from

Apple Tom: a brilliant blue for the frame, red for the wheels, and two coats of aluminium on the coulter. Every morning I pushed it out on to the green to show the world we were open for business. Several weeks passed and then a little note headed 'Ramsthwaite Parish Council' was dropped through the letter box.

Vicky wrinkled her nose. 'The mean old so-and-so's. It's not hurting anything and it looks good out there.'

The official looking note had requested us not to put the plough on the green. It was, we were told, an advertising implement, and as such shouldn't be on the green without permission of the council.

Councillor Ted didn't take it well when I pulled his leg over the matter. 'What's happened to free enterprise Ted? Tommy Lipton could walk a pig around advertising his bacon but I can't wheel a plough on to the green.' I shook my head in mock sorrow and Ted bent his back over the yardbrush.

'Rules and Regs, we all have to comply.'

'But you park your tractor on the green, Thievin' pulls his van up there and Charlie has his bed and breakfast sign on it.'

'Ah! He has permission.'

With tongue in cheek I sat at the kitchen table and penned a long and intricate letter to the parish council. I found an old *Financial Times* wrapped around one of the stone hot-water bottles we had bought from Canary Mary and this yielded phrases that made my pen fly. 'Economic forces, market trends, expected upswing, unexpected downswing.' I used them all but to no avail: the parish council refused permission.

Ted looked furtive when I accused them of being miserable sods. 'Don't blame me,' he cried, pushing his lips out into his mumpy mouth, 'I abstained.' So the plough was manhandled on to the cobbles in front of the shop every morning. That is our bit and we can do what we like there.

Rabbit delighted in the opportunity to bait authority. 'It's them as 'asn't lived 'ere long is making these rules up,' he taunted the Colonel, who, with only twenty-five years' residence in the village, was still, in Rabbit's eyes, a newcomer.

The Colonel sniffed and silently vowed to get Rabbit sacked from his weed-clearing job at the next Drainage Society meeting, but he knew that as no one in the village would dream of usurping Rabbit from this sinecure, he was stuck with him.

The plough incident ruffled the calm waters of the village for a week or so. We were pleased to find that most people were on our side but we had no wish to antagonise anyone so the plough stayed on the cobbles. 'It's better there,' we smiled.

Spring brought sunny days, chilled at night with a westerly breeze and Ted's Fergie was soon buzzing around the village, its link box filled with well-rotted manure for ardent gardeners. He upped the price a little every year and sugared the pill in the same way. 'Marvellous stuff, just like tobacco. Throw yer seeds on that and stand back.' The gardeners grumbled and paid up, for it was still good value.

The house martins repaired their nests under the eaves of the apple house and Topic got rounder and rounder. Fine evenings found us in the garden until dusk or tired limbs drove us inside.

Mr Hall gave us his daily report on Topic: 'She's doin' all right', but we played careful and got the vet, Mr Airey, to give her a thorough examination.

His carefully delivered verdict after half an hour of sound professional attention was predictable: 'She's doing all right.'

Vicky brought out mugs of coffee and after showing Mr

Airey the proposed delivery box we sat on the apple house steps.

'How long has she gone?' he asked.

'305 days,' Vicky told him.

'Well it looks like she'll be early.'

Mr Hall spat refectively into the garth when I told him. 'It'll be a filly then.'

The children spoiled Topic, they hung over the gate; apples, carrots and the occasional mint on their outstretched palms.

Elspeth became jealous, she paced to and fro along the length of the fence that adjoined the garth, bleating for attention. She became very demanding, standing on her back legs, her front feet on the top rail, her bleats getting louder and more raucous until one of the children ran to her with a titbit. But no matter how she clamoured she never got a tenth of the attention that was lavished on Topic.

We had drawn a red circle around the date that marked the full 340-day gestation period and, as our daily ticks grew nearer to it, Vicky and I grew increasingly nervous. Old Mr Hall had told us some horrific tales of difficult foalings and deformed foals.

'Nowt to do but knock 'em on the head with a hammer,' he'd said with a shrug. In spite of his daily progress report, 'She's doin' all right', he had sown a fear into our minds. The children had become so obsessive about Topic's coming foal that we made a gentle attempt to tell them that things did not always turn out well.

'It's Topic's first foal and we don't know how things will go, she might –'

Sally smiled up at me. 'Oh, it's all right Dad, we don't mind if it's a boy foal or a girl foal.' I looked at Vicky and sighed.

Peter knew what I meant; his unmarked forehead wrinkled into a frown, then he said, 'She'll be all right.'

The children had stuck a nameboard up in their nature corner and the list of potential names grew daily. It covered every conceivable feature of the expected foal. There were names for colts and fillies, names for coal-black foals, names for ones with white blazes. I could foresee a problem here; a happy problem, but still a problem.

Every night I walked Topic into the apple house and fed her there, because although she was living out and doing well, I thought I would get her used to the impromptu stable in case we decided to foal her inside. I partitioned off a corner and put in an armchair and an old coffee table. On Mr Airey's advice I bought some two-inch cotton bandages and an antibiotic spray and then I wrote his telephone number behind the door in big bold letters.

The dogs were banished from the garth and we did our level best to keep the hens out of the apple house.

Topic was talked about in the pub and the shop. The children ran home from school accompanied by a bevy of small friends to fuss over her and Ted kept a watchful eye on her over the wall, but it was Mr Hall who took charge.

'I'm seeing to her,' he told everybody in the shop between his stints at the paraffin tank and the potato sacks. 'She's doin' all right. I'll be along to foal her when her time comes.'

His daughter smiled indulgently. 'Given him a new lease of life, but if he thinks he's trotting along there at dead of night he's another thing coming – he's eighty next month you know.'

The old man grunted and padded off down the passage. 'We'll see, we'll see, when her time comes.'

As the time got near the old man came more often. Two or

three times a day I would look out of the kitchen window and see him draped over the wall, his cardigan pockets bulging with pipe and tobacco tin and a khaki balaclava under his flat cap. He talked continually to the mare in a low, soft voice. 'Good girl, me beauty, yer doin' all right.'

I was swinging the kettle over the fire when he rapped frantically at the window. 'Here, come here and look at this.' The old man pointed to the mare's bag. At the end of each teat was a honey-coloured drop. 'There, that's what I've been looking for; she's starting. Not tonight – tomorrow night. How long has she been?'

'330 days exactly.'

'It'll be a filly then, thee watch.'

Several times that night I went into the apple house to look at the pony but she showed no other signs of beginning labour, merely giving a low whinny and pushing her soft muzzle into my hand.

The following morning I walked her gently around the garth and back into the apple house. The cat had found the chair I'd put in there ready for the foaling and lay fast asleep in it. They liked each other's company so I left the cat in with the pony and tacked a sack over the window. I wanted Topic kept as quiet as possible. Then, telling Vicky not to let the children have more than five minutes with Topic at lunch-time, I set off for the saleroom.

Soon the problems of making a living pushed the thought of the pony from my mind. We needed stock, but to start to buy in strongly would have attracted unwanted attention so I made arrangements with Long John and Canary Mary to buy several lots for me and went to join the Ring in a good moan. Things were fairly buoyant and at the end of the sale I was quite pleased with what the little subterfuge had yielded.

The children pleaded to be allowed into the apple house but I kept them out all evening, just allowing them a peep in before bedtime.

As dusk fell Mr Hall shogged into the yard with a huge bundle on his back, making it clear that he'd come for the night. He commandeered my chair, pulled a blanket around his shoulders, shuffled his feet under a pile of straw and went to sleep.

Lalbeck Church gave a sad dong for half past eleven when I opened the apple house door, burdened down with flask, torches, sandwiches and blankets. Mr Hall had strung a storm lantern from a beam and was leaning forward in the chair staring at the pile of straw which hid his feet. 'Nowt yet, but she's doin' all right,' he said without lifting his head.

I looked over the partition at Topic who was stood with her muzzle pressed against the whitewashed wall, then settled myself on the straw. Mr Hall's thin white hand stretched out to take the coffee. 'Another hour or so and she'll start sweating up.'

'You're sure it'll be tonight?'

'Sure as eggs.'

My eyes became accustomed to the light and soon I was comfortably warm in my cocoon of blankets. When the old man had finished his coffee he stuck his empty pipe in his mouth and leaned back. 'By, I wish I'd a pound for every hour I've spent doin' this.'

'Foaled a lot have you?'

'Hundreds. Just after the First War there was nowt doin' in the Dales so I took a job on the wolds – big ploughing farm.

'I've seen fifteen teams led out into that yard and what a

grand sight it wor. Head man used to lead his pair out, then you all took your turn, second horseman and so on right down to the youngest lad.' He opened his coat and interlocked his hands over his chest. 'Has she been round?' He nodded his head towards Nellie May's.

'No. She's finding it hard getting about.'

'Aye, she's a grand old lass but she's some funny ideas. If she wor' here she'd have charms hung all over. Mind you, some of them old horsemen couldn't do without their "little bits" as they called 'em. Best thing to have was the frog bone, an' you were only supposed to have that if you were in the "society" and knew the horseman's word. My brother wor' in the society, but I could never get him to say owt. He wor' like that.' Mr Hall leaned forward, his eyes sparkling, one fist clenched into a tight ball.

'You never got in then?'

'No I'd 'av liked to but it was fading in the '20s. Still strong in the big ploughing areas of Scotland – Ayrshire and there.' He paused, then went on quietly, 'I wish I 'ad 'av been.' He half-closed his eyes and swallowed, then inclined his head towards me. 'You could tell them that wor' in, they had the use of "the stuff". Nobody else knew how to make it.'

'The stuff?'

'Aye yer can stop a horse with it like that.' He clicked his fingers.

Topic started and swung her head over the partition; she gave a low whinny and started to scrub at her flanks. Mr Hall peered through the rails at her. 'She's started to sweat up a bit, we'll see things start to move in an hour or so. What time is it?'

'Half twelve.'

'We'll keep an eye on her now. The foal will be turnin' in her, gettin' ready.'

I looked up at the vet's telephone number chalked behind the door. I had a growing confidence in the old man but my palms were sweaty as I made a note of the time and recalled the vet's words: 'If there's nothing three hours after her bag's broken, call me.'

Mr Hall smiled across at me. 'She's doin' all right.'

'When will her bag break?' I tried to make it sound as if I was calmer and more knowledgeable than I was.

'Within the hour.' With that, the old man inched his chair around and slid his body down in it so he could see the mare between the rails. 'You shut your eyes a bit. I'll watch her.'

I made a pillow of straw and wriggling my head into it closed my eyes. Although I could hear my heart beating quite clearly and I had wiped my sweaty palms along my jeans several times, I was determined to appear calm.

Mr Hall's boot kicked me awake. 'What time is it?'

'Half one.'

'Her bag's gone ten minutes since and she's a coming,' he cried, gleefully pointing through the rails.

Topic was laid on her side, her legs stretched out rigidly, with the foal's head and the forefeet protruding from her. Her flanks rose and fell steadily, then she gave a convulsion which blew the straw from in front of her nostrils and pushed the foal further from her body. I watched, heart pounding, for signs of life in the foal. The head lifted and fell and I could see mucous flickering at the tiny nostrils – it was breathing. Topic made several convulsions pushing the wet foal still further from her, then rested, panting steadily.

I made to get up and lean on the partition but Mr Hall waved me down. 'Don't mither her, she's doin' all right,' he said as I settled back to watch through the rails. Topic gave a great shudder, pawed her legs in the air and with an enormous grunt completely ejected the foal, then turned to lie with her forefeet spread before her. The foal lay wet and slimy, its back still half-covered in a yellowy membrane. Soon Topic curled her body around and started to lick her offspring.

'It's a good 'un, it's a good 'un,' chortled the old man. 'Now all we want from her is a pair of braces and from *her*,' he pointed to the foal, 'the golden apples.'

'So it is a filly?'

'Didn't I tell thee it would be.'

I guessed the 'pair of braces' the old man referred to was the y-shaped afterbirth the mare needed to part with, but the 'golden apples'?

'First droppings of a foal, bright yellow, needs to get shut, summat in 'em.' We both watched the mare licking away at the new arrival.

It was still dark as I crossed the yard and made more coffee.

Mr Hall was climbing through the rails when I returned to the apple house. 'I've tied her off and dustered her, we don't want navel-ill,' he called cheerfully.

In spite of the coffee I dozed off again, and when I awoke Mr Hall was gathering his things together. 'Come on let's leave 'em in peace.'

It was a brilliant clear night; the horizon to the east had the faintest glow of buttermilk yellow over it, but overhead bright stars still twinkled from an ultramarine sky.

The old man looked up at the sky. 'Starlight! That's what we'll call her, Starlight. A star on her head and born by starlight. Couldn't be owt else, could it?'

I threw some oven sticks on the fire and fetched bacon from

the pantry. Vicky pushed open the kitchen door, her dressing gown pulled around her shoulders. 'All right?' she asked timidly.

'Both all right – it's a filly.'

She smiled her relief.

Mr Hall had difficulty with his sandwich. His rapidly-working lips hauled in an errant piece of bacon. 'Aye, they're both all right. We've decided to call it Starlight.'

Vicky looked at the children's nameboard and then back at me. Starlight wasn't on the board.

Years of antique dealing haven't necessarily honed my brain to a fine edge but there are times, even at four o'clock in the morning, when I can think on my feet. 'We've decided on three names,' I lied. 'Mr Hall's, then one each from the children.'

Vicky shrugged her shoulders and padded off back to bed.

The children were too excited to eat breakfast. They ran across the yard in pyjamas and climbed the rails to gasp in delight at the foal. They accepted the three name ploy without trouble; Starlight, they thought, was good. Sally was quick with her name. 'Beauty,' she cried. 'She's such a beauty.'

Peter deliberated at length. It had, he explained, to be a meaningful name. He wasn't going to be hurried, and two days later he chose his name.

When I led the mare and her foal out into the garth for the first time, Ted's head appeared over the wall. 'And what's this then?'

'This,' I proudly told him, 'is Starlight Ramsthwaite Beauty.'

He lifted his cap, scratched his head and grinned. 'That's a big name for a little hoss.'

Chapter 9

The trade was buzzing with the news, Martin de Trafford and Oriental Otto had fallen out. The de Traffords had enjoyed a special relationship with the rich eccentric widower for nearly a quarter of a century, buying in for him all over the North.

The cause of the rupture was reputed to be a fine, rectangular jade vase with twenty-four rings carved into its four faces. Martin had acquired it from a country house where it had been on view to the public for a number of years. Otto had seen it and coveted it: jade was his weakness. The de Traffords were no laggards when it came to appreciating a fine piece of Oriental workmanship and the vase found a new home in the Louis XVI vitrine they reserved for their very best pieces.

Otto pestered them for it in vain. 'I taught you all you know about jade. Now you do naughty trick to me,' he yelled at them down the telephone. 'I finish you, I get other man.' He cut the photograph of the vase out of the country house brochure and stuck it over his desk. 'Otto don't like naughty trick,' he muttered as he fiercely thumbed on the sellotape.

I was trimming the goat's hooves when Vicky rapped at the kitchen window waving the phone in front of her. I was none too pleased; this was going to be one of my 'stolen' days. Unshaven and dressed in my roughest clothes, my green Wellingtons stained with creosote, I took the receiver she poked through the window and barked a none too pleasant, 'Hello!'

'This is Otto Denck. You know me?'

'Yes I've heard of you, Mr Denck.'

'You come now to see me.'

'I can't make it this afternoon –'

Otto's voice cut in. 'You come now OK.'

The phone slammed down. I handed the receiver back to Vicky, anger welling up in me.

We are an independent breed we antique dealers. Couple that to the liberalism of the Dalesman I now felt myself to be, and you can have a very prickly man.

'Sod him, arrogant bugger,' I snorted as I marched back to the orchard and Elspeth's feet.

Vicky was soon at my side. 'It was Otto, wasn't it?'

'So what?'

'Well he's looking for a new buyer now he's fallen out with Martin.'

'Let him find one,' I snapped, the clippers sending a little crescent of hoof spinning through the air.

Vicky sat on the milking platform, cupped her face in her hands, and smiled at me. 'Suppose he picks Fatty Batty or another of that crew?'

The thought of the Ring getting their clutches on Otto sent me hurrying across the yard to the van.

'Aren't you going to get . . . ?' Vicky called as I slammed the door and sent the ducks flying.

Otto lives in some splendour. The late-Victorian mansion is screened by plantations of spruce and larch, but its roof peeps incongruous welsh-blue slates and terracotta crestings above them. The grounds are well kept and as the visitor negotiates the last bend of the asphalt drive he is made deliberately aware of Otto's financial standing. The coach-house, its doors now fitted with bevelled glass panels, can be seen to house two gleaming Rolls-Royces and an immaculate 1935 Duesenberg Roadster, which must be the most beautiful car in the world.

A Chinese maid opened the door and showed me into a dimly lit hall, floored with harlequin tiles and smelling heavily of incense. Bronzes and lacquered furniture lined each wall. 'You wait here,' she said eyeing me warily.

Otto is a big man, but he swept down the staircase with the grace of a model. Gold dragons contested every fold of the royal blue kimono which reached to his feet and on his shaven head sat a heavily embroidered smoking cap, its gold tassel dancing as he advanced towards me. He held a long nephrite cheroot holder in one hand, while the other heavily beringed hand was extended in greeting. His smile was broad and guileless and exposed an astonishing array of gold teeth. 'My boy, you came,' he greeted me happily.

Otto led me into a large room where a *pietra dura* topped table sat in a bay window. Its top was covered with small jade objects. There was jade everywhere. Cabinets were filled with it, it stood on the mantlepiece, and in the hearth.

Otto grinned. 'This is jade room and this,' he pointed at a huge Old English Mastiff which raised its head from the Khotan rug and stared cold-eyed at me, 'is Cerberus.' Round the dog's neck was a thick collar which had three bronze masks of Japanese fighting dogs set in it. 'You touch – Cerberus tell you no!' Otto laughed.

He stood in the window, his back to me, and drew deeply on his cheroot. 'You know this man de Trafford?' He didn't wait for an answer but continued. 'He and I no longer friends. He do naughty trick on Otto, naughty trick.' To my relief the dog lowered its huge head back to its paws.

'Well I want someone I can trust to buy for me.' Otto swung around to face me and stabbed his cheroot into the air. 'You I can trust?' he asked, his face set and serious.

'Yes you can trust me to buy for you, Mr Denck.'

'Otto, please, call me Otto.' He pulled a bell-cord and, brandishing the cheroot holder high, smiled. 'You English, fine people. Otto live here thirty-five years and Otto know you are fine and noble people.'

I drew myself up straight, tried to look fine and noble, and wished I'd had a shave. He looked down at my stained Wellingtons and then marched across to his desk and pointed at the photograph of the jade vase with rings. 'But there is always bad egg in the curate's barrel, yes?'

I nodded my agreement.

'So! You buy for Otto?'

'Yes. Be pleased to help you Otto.'

'Good man. Start Friday. Here is what you buy.'

He handed me an envelope on which were written three lot numbers. Against the latter two were marked very healthy prices, but against the first, nothing.

'Lot 142, what do I go to on that?'

Otto's eyes flashed. 'You buy.'

The trade doesn't like open ended bids, things can go seriously wrong. 'No ceiling Otto, no approximate ...?'

Otto replied curtly as the Chinese maid entered and made a little bow. 'You buy and bring to Otto on Saturday – bring your lady wife. Goodbye.'

The saleroom was packed. The bulk of the sale was from the estate of a man who'd lived in the Far East for many years. Cheap bazaar daggers, camphor wood chests, and a hideous carved armchair with glass-eyed serpents forming its arms, sat incongruously amongst the day to day chattels, for this was one of the ordinary weekly sales. In the glass-topped cabinet at the auctioneer's elbow lay the three jade carvings. I'd checked the lot numbers half a dozen times and, as I had a last look, Fatty elbowed his way in. 'What we got here, the crown jewels?'

The auctioneer looked down and smiled, he had several commission bids on the jade.

The sale started, as always, with unlotted goods, bundles of bedding, garden tools, pots and pans, going under the hammer with gratifying speed.

Martin de Trafford walked straight down the aisle and opened the glass-topped cabinet. The auctioneer, pausing briefly to greet his favourite dealer, waved aside an unsold clutter of soft goods.

'Lot one!' he announced after a sip of water.

The Ring pricked up their ears and arranged themselves along two mirror-backed sideboards. Martin was still turning the jade figures in his hands. Long, well-manicured fingers, stroked first the recumbent buffalo, then the brush pot. But time and again he returned to the spinach-green figure. It was unusual for Martin to give his hand away like this but the figure obviously fascinated him. His fingers caressed and probed, but his face was impassive.

Fatty watched him like a hawk. 'Fallen out with Otto,' he said, smiling to himself. 'Wonder who he's buying for now? Or, more to the point, who's buying for Otto?'

I sidled away from the group of dealers and, giving Canary Mary a little smile, I held a forefinger to my lips and, climbing carefully through a jumble of chairs, hid myself at the back of the room. The jade was coming up.

Martin leaned against a table, his arms folded, staring at the ceiling.

'Lot 142. Jade figure of immortal, spinach-green. Beautiful piece. Start the bidding at two hundred pounds.' The auctioneer looked straight at Martin who continued to stare at the ceiling.

'Well, one hundred pounds, one hundred pounds anywhere?'

I never like starting the bidding, but I was keen to let the auctioneer know my whereabouts, so I waved the folded envelope over the top of a wardrobe.

'I have one hundred pounds. Do I hear one hundred and fifty pounds?'

Martin lowered his head and winked at the auctioneer. We were off. My heart beat faster as the bidding rose quickly, but Martin showed no emotion. His arms tightly folded he stared straight ahead, only the slight wrinkling of his eye-corner giving him away. There was a hush in the saleroom as Martin bid one thousand pounds and I, with racing pulse and a deliberate slowness, topped it by fifty pounds. The auctioneer waited, gavel poised. Martin stared ahead for several seconds, then shook his head. The gavel crashed down.

'Denck,' I shouted in a shaky voice. Martin spun round and glared at me. He bought the other two pieces of jade at bids above Otto's limits and, stuffing them into his blazer pockets, he marched from the saleroom.

Long John's head appeared slowly round the wardrobe. 'So we have a new buyer eh? Mr Otto So-many-gold-teeth-he-sleeps-with-his-head-in-a-safe has a new buyer.'

I wrapped the jade figure very carefully, standing it in the centre of a strong cardboard box and packing balls of news-paper around it, then strung sellotape back and forth over the top. With buyer's commission it had cost well over one thou-sand, one hundred pounds and I was terrified of damaging it.

Baz and his wife came down to babysit for us the following evening. I helped Vicky into the van and set the box on her lap. 'Here we come Otto. One out of three and a dear one at that.'

Vicky looked worried. 'Over a thousand,' she whispered, glancing down at the box.

'Well, he said buy it, so I bought it.'

I paused by the old coach-house and pointed out the Deusenburg to her. 'Isn't that just the most beautiful car?'

Vicky laughed and pointed to the yellow Rolls. 'It is, but I bet Mary would prefer that.'

The maid showed us into the jade room giving a little smile along with the bow this time. Vicky clung to me as the huge mastiff lifted his head.

'Not to be afraid little lady. Cerberus know you are friend.'

Otto closed the double doors behind him and grinned. He was wearing a sober grey suit but his fingers still flashed with diamonds as he shook Vicky's hand vigorously. 'You lady wife, very pretty.'

He turned to the box and placing it on the carpet knelt beside it, his big hands tearing at the sellotape. He lifted the figure out carefully and kissed it. 'Come my little beauty, you're back home.' He smiled, setting the figure between two other deities on a Japanese lacquered cabinet.

Vicky looked at me and we each knew what the other was thinking. The figure had been Otto's all the time. He'd set Martin up, making him pay well over the odds for the two mediocre pieces of jade.

Otto turned and laughingly pointed a finger at me. 'You do well, you help Otto smack the wrists of Mr Smartyclogs-Clever pants Trafford.'

'All three pieces were yours Otto?'

The big man giggled and wiped a hand over his shaved head. 'Otto can be naughty boy too. This Trafford man, he taken vase, which is symbol of peace, and turned it to symbol of war. Two can play games, eh! Now I show you Otto's collection.'

He took us round the jade room pointing out pieces of special interest. The colours fascinated Vicky. Mottled grey, grey and black, celadon and russet, lavender and spinach-green. Otto handled each piece lovingly. 'It was my wife, little Katya, who started me collecting jade. When we made money and became rich she say, "Otto, you need hobby", and she buy me first piece of jade, this.' Otto held up a pale celadon and beige vase carved and pierced in a most intricate way. He sighed and carefully put it back on its wooden stand. 'She knew what she do. Now we go look at bronze room.'

The dog padded after us as we went across the hall to

another bay-windowed room. 'These Otto like not as much as jade, but they are nice too.'

The room was more dingy than the hall. The curtains were nearly fully drawn, allowing only a thin path of light to come across the parquet floor. As our eyes grew accustomed to the light we could see several black tables cluttered with wine ewers, koros, chalices and bronze groups. At each side of the fireplace stood black pedestals, each supporting a Benin bronze bust, whilst in the fireplace itself stood a massive Chinese bell covered with dust. Vicky shuddered at the grotesque Benin heads but laughed when Otto showed her a superb Miyao group of a monkey-trainer with his charges prancing around him.

Otto's thick finger jabbed at the group. 'See this little fellow, hand in fruit basket, he pinching.'

He beckoned us to follow him back into the hall where he paused beside an immense statue of Buddha. 'This took ten men to carry in,' he said seriously. 'But now, I show you ivory room.'

Down the hall we went in the wake of the big man, the massive dog still at our heels.

Otto paused before two heavily panelled doors and whispered, 'This ivory room.' Then he threw the doors wide open and waltzed into the centre of the empty room. 'What you think? Otto been burgled? No, when Otto find out what they doing to noble beasts Otto sell all ivory and give the money to protect elephant people. Because this room empty, one, maybe two elephant live. What you think?'

Vicky threw back her head and laughed. 'Otto, it's a beautiful room.'

The big man took our hands as if we were children and led

us, laughingly, back into the hall. He stopped and inclined his head thoughtfully then swung our arms in the air.

'So much money, probably three elephant.' We were still laughing when he showed us into his study and waved us to a vast pale rose sofa. 'Now we have tea.' Otto squatted on the floor and poured the tea into Japanese eggshell cups. 'This was Katya's favourite room. It's so bright, so cheerful; so I make it my study.'

The room was smaller than the others but well proportioned with French windows giving on to a flagged terrace beyond which stood a chinoiserie summer house. The rose marble chimney piece was flanked by white marble columns on which stood busts of Apollo and Seneca. The walls were a delicate mushroom-pink and the window drapes of pale cream were bunched with thick gold ropes. An Irish glass chandelier was not lit but from each corner of the room a soft yellow light was shed from lamps in the form of cherubs. A low red lacquered table held a massive bowl of crimson tulips and around the floor were scattered rugs, not the Chinese one expected, but Herez. Their warm browns and reds a perfect foil to the canopy of light formed by the walls and ceiling. The paintings were in the romantic vein, swains and lovers, young girls with flowers; all perhaps a little overcleaned, but very choice. By the window a writing table held several framed photographs, the largest of which showed a laughing woman with long blonde hair.

Otto handed a cup to Vicky and seeing her looking at the photograph smiled, 'Yes, that's my Katya – she pretty.'

'She's very pretty Otto.'

'She die now ten years,' Otto sighed and tinkled a spoon around in his cup. 'Otto never marry again. We fall in love when sixteen, marry when eighteen,' his voice trailed away.

'Otto never marry again.' He stuck the spoon in the sugar bowl and looked up at us. 'I see her now, come through window, basket on arm and full of flowers, she very pretty, even when older lady, very pretty.' The old man patted the mastiff vigorously. 'Still, we have forty wonderful years Katya and me. We come to England from Germany in '38. No job, no money. When we land at 'Arwich very very cold, we so hungry and so frightened.' He pulled the dog's ears gently. 'But man in uniform come along station; he smiled at us and gave us porky pie and cocoa. When we in train to London, Katya snuggle against Otto and says, "Otto! When man in uniform smile and give you porky pie and cocoa, this must be good country. We be happy here Otto." And I know she right.' He stretched his legs out and grasped his knees with his heavily ringed hands. 'We work hard, all war in munitions, making shells, then after war work hard making money. Otto and Katya have one hotel then two, then three. When we become rich we go all over world, dine here, dine there, Maxim's – all these kind of place. But many times Katya smile and pat Otto's hand. "That was very nice, very nice, but best meal I ever had, Otto, was porky pie and cocoa."'

We drank our tea and talked of jade and paintings, dogs and cars. The wood-pigeons were clattering to their roosts in the trees when Otto playfully pulled the dog to its feet. 'Come on, I show you garden before dark.'

Beside the summer-house was a large formal pool. Emerald plates of water lilies floated on its surface and below them glided fat carp. 'Look, look, come and look,' cried Otto opening the summer-house door. Cut through one side of it was a narrow stone lined channel and when Otto rang a little bell the channel boiled with fish. Otto laughed as he scattered feed. 'Katya think this up, she sit in here and do crochet and feed

113

fish, good eh!' The gold teeth glistened as he beamed like a schoolboy.

The hand of Katya was everywhere in the garden. Bronze fawns peered through banks of irises and bronze cranes stared at their reflections in the pool. A secret arbour was guarded by lead putti and on a Japanese-style bridge a bronze cat waited for mice that never came.

Cerberus padded after us as Otto led us happily around the grounds, finally coming to rest in front of a very ornate cast-iron garden seat. 'Here our favourite place,' he announced.

We sat awhile on the favourite seat listening to the clamour of the pigeons as they found their roosts and the gentle tinkle of water under the Japanese bridge. It was a warm and still evening and the garden was heavy with scent. I saw the maid cross the lawn and lock the summer-house and remembered Baz and Susan.

'We'll have to go Otto. Some friends are looking after the children but we don't want to leave them too long.'

Otto sat in silence awhile deep in thought. 'Yes! yes!' he said, eventually jumping up. 'You wait please,' he called as he walked briskly up to the house with the dog trotting at his heels.

'This for you,' he held a sealed envelope out to me, 'and this for you,' he draped a beautiful crimson kimono worked in gold and silver thread around Vicky's shoulders and then held his hands up to stay her protests.

'No, no. You must have it. It was Katya's. When I saw you get out of van and sun on your hair, Otto's heart stop, you so much like her.'

We thanked him and left him sitting on his favourite seat, the big dog pressed up against his legs.

A full round moon had risen in the cloudless sky by the time we breasted the top of the moor. I turned the van off the narrow metalled strip and stopped on the short sheep-cropped turf.

Vicky turned to me, a puzzled look on her face. 'What are you doing?'

I took hold of the kimono and gently pulled her to me. 'Come here my little Oriental beauty, it's a long time since we had a kiss in the moonlight.'

Chapter 10

Mrs Bunney gets into Lalbeck once a month, she refuses to travel on the bus which passes a hundred yards from her cottage gate but waits for one of her daughter's regular visits to do her business in the little market town. Jane, her businesslike, 'hurrying through life' daughter, sits in her Triumph Spitfire, her foot tapping restlessly on the floor, whilst Mrs Bunney bustles round chemist and grocer, bank and florist.

Mrs Bunney pays no heed to her daughter's agitation. 'Oh, Jane's always been wound up like an eight-day clock,' she laughs.

Unlike her daughter Mrs Bunney rarely gets annoyed or frustrated. Her life is devoted to the furtherance of her late husband's fame; Edward Raphael Bunney was an artist of some renown. His watercolours are greatly sought after and his oils, a medium he never felt truly at home in, are as rare as hens' teeth.

Jane held the door open for her mother who walked up to me with little hesitant steps and a sweet smile. 'Hello,' she said, 'I'm Mrs Edward Raphael Bunney.'

'Mrs Bunney, I'm delighted. Both my wife and I are great admirers of your late husband,' I replied, showing her to a chair.

Jane ambled around the shop continually kneeing her handbag in impatience whilst her mother settled into the chair and slowly peeled off her gloves. 'What I'm looking for, young man, is a chair. One of those with a big hooped back and good strong arms.'

'You mean a Yorkshire broad-arm.' There was a pause, the gloves were laid carefully, one on top of the other.

'Yes, yes, if that's what you call them, broad-arms, quite comfortable.' She smiled up at me. Her face was heavily wrinkled and the colour of putty but her eyes were a lovely periwinkle blue. If there had been a Victorian novelist lurking about the dale looking for a heroine whose sensitive face could be saved from ugliness by a pair of particularly fine eyes, then here she was.

'Not easy to come by Mrs Bunney, they have become very sought after.'

Mrs Bunney's pudgy hands sieved through her enormous handbag. Finally she found a stained and crumpled card which she handed to me with a flourish. 'Should you get one, drop me a line will you?'

Jane sighed and kneed her handbag viciously. 'Mother! I have to get back.'

Mrs Bunney smiled again. 'She's a sweet girl but oh! Rush, rush, rush. You'd think the world was going to end tomorrow.'

The handbag snapped shut and the gloves were carefully drawn on with much splaying of fingers. As I helped her to her feet I saw Fiery Frank's van send the gravel flying in the yard. I led Mrs Bunney to the door. Jane already in the Spitfire, was racing the engine.

The blue eyes looked steadily into mine. 'You see, Edward Raphael Bunney always painted in a chair like that. I've been getting his studio back into shape over the years. His chair disappeared. I had to go away for a little while after he died and when I returned the chair had gone. His sister I think.' She added in a low voice, 'Jane takes after her. All rush and not too particular.' The wrinkled face gave me a knowing nod.

'I'll do my best Mrs Bunney.'

'Mother!' Jane called from the car.

Fiery had brought Little Petal and the new baby and when I got into the kitchen the baby was just being transferred gently into Vicky's arms. Women instinctively know how to hold babies. The crook of their arm is just right to support the tiny head and their hand spreads in the very place that makes the bundle secure. Little Petal sat at the table and watched intently as Vicky carefully fingered the white blanket away from the little pink face. 'He's lovely. What's your name little fellow?'

Fiery stood, with his heels on the fender and his thumbs hooked into his scarlet waistcoat, beaming at the child. 'That's Gunnar. Isn't he a little cracker? Six pound, eight and a half ounce he was.'

Little Petal's fat arms were laid on the table. As Vicky swung the bundle gently from side to side, her blonde head bent well over it, Little Petal raised her arms in sequence as if to take the baby back. Vicky hugged the baby to her in a final sighing cuddle. 'I could eat him he's so lovely,' she said, returning him to Little Petal's outstretched arms. The mother pressed the baby to her and then unbuttoned her blouse and started to feed it.

Fiery watched intently, a wide smile on his generous mouth.

'Sometimes, when it's a bit dark and she's feeding him, it looks as if there's a light inside her.' Little Petal showed no concern at the attention her breast was receiving. The baby, its eyes closed, sucked away, tiny fat hands crooked on to its mother's gleaming white skin.

Vicky hardly took her eyes off the baby as she prepared lunch. The children left their group of friends at the school gate and raced up the village green when they saw Fiery's van. They burst into the kitchen and skidded to a halt in front of Little Petal.

'Well! What do you think of my baby?' she asked. Neither child said anything as they stood and stared at the baby, shuffling their feet, broad smiles on their faces. Sally cupped a gentle hand over the baby's head not daring to touch it. Fiery rocked on his feet clacking the ends of the fender on the hearth and hummed to himself happily.

The children ate their lunch standing at the table near to Little Petal and the baby. Topic and her foal, the rabbits and the goat were all forgotten. Fiery made a great show of playfully kicking their bottoms down the yard when the school bell rang. 'Off you go you rapskallions, back to Miss Wells' College of Knowledge.'

'Will you still be here?' they called from the bottom of the green.

Fiery thumbed his waistcoat again. 'We'll see; depends how much cheap furniture your Dad has.'

Fiery was definitely getting harder to deal with. I'd taken all our shipping goods out of the apple house so Topic could foal in there and it was all sheeted up under the Dutch barn. Fiery seemed to think this cavalier treatment of what to him was 'good gear' somehow devalued it. 'Look at this guv,' he moaned, swishing straw from a marble-topped washstand. 'Nice bit o' gear like this outside and covered in god knows what.' He pulled the big green tarpaulin back and sent a hen scurrying into a nettle bed clucking in alarm. The hen had laid a clutch of eggs on a hideous beech *chaise-longue*.

'Can't take that Fiery, sounds like she'll be sitting soon.' Fiery dropped the tarpaulin and started unravelling a tangle of chairs. 'Any sets?'

'A six and a four and two odds.'

Fiery sorted out the chairs and went back to the *chaise-longue*. 'Can't you move that nest?'

'It'll leave 'em Fiery, I'll lose a few quid.' The hen came out of the nettles and after clucking about our feet, hopped on to the *chaise* and fluffed her body out over the eggs. 'You can buy it now, take it later,' I told him.

'How long?'

'Three weeks at the most.'

He wrinkled his nose and rotated his sovereign ring. 'Give us a price then and bear in mind.'

'Bear in mind what?'

Fiery nodded towards the green where Little Petal had spread a travelling rug and knelt beside the baby.

Vicky beckoned me from the kitchen door, 'There's Duke Brockway in the shop. He has got some stuff to sell.' Duke Brockway was Amby's eldest son and the brother of Rabbit's errant wife. To everyone's relief the Brockways were seldom seen in the village and their infrequent visits to Lalbeck were usually made in order to appear in front of the magistrates or to bring the odd cast cow into the mart. They were banned from every pub in the town and when they felt the need for 'a blow-out', as they put it, the Fighting Cocks was the only threshold they could cross.

When the landlord saw the three brothers coming across the fell in Indian file, he took his precious oil-painting off the wall and moved all the lighter pieces of furniture into the snug for the Brockways were always trouble.

Duke is a big man. His head grows out of massive shoulders without the aid or support of a neck, and his arms, thick at the ball of the shoulder, hardly taper at all to the wrists, then sprout into hands the size of a number nine shovel. He moves slowly and without grace, hunched and scowling. He was wearing stained trousers into which was loosely tucked a khaki shirt open down to his belt showing a matt of ginger hair on his barrel chest. The same curly hair, a shade darker, covers his head and the lower half of his face. His eyes are set close together: glittering, small, unfriendly eyes over which rest bushy eyebrows – a perfect match to the ginger of the chest hairs. His nose is flattened and resembles a small saddle and when he laughs he shows a gummy mouth sparsely set with brown peg teeth. I'm not fond of Duke.

He was leaning his huge body on a Scotch chest, his hands thrust into his belt. 'I 'ave some stuff I might want to sell.'

'If you've got the stuff, I've got the money,' I replied with a jauntiness which surprised me. He eased his body off the chest. 'Come up, now.'

'I've a customer in the yard,' I protested.

Duke fixed me with an unbelieving stare. 'Come up, now!' He ambled out of the shop and hauled his ungainly body on to his tractor.

I apologised to Fiery, told him I'd be an hour and jumping into the van took off after Duke.

*

121

The yard at Sottenghyll was littered with rusting machinery. Two curs, lips curled back over yellow-rooted fangs, hurled themselves from a shanty roofed with plastic fertiliser sacks and snapped and snarled at the van wheels as I pulled up behind Duke's tractor.

Duke beckoned me into the kitchen. Heavy curtains stiff with dirt were only half pulled back making the room dark. The walls were limewashed and the floor was bare flags. A square table was set in the middle of the room, a book jammed under one leg to cater for the unevenness of the floor. It was the table that Rabbit had stood in front of cap in hand as Amby had laid the three half crowns and the cartridge out.

Beside the fire the old man sat slumped in a chair. His eyes were vacant and saliva glistened at the corner of his mouth. His hands dangled in his lap and one leg was twisted back under his chair. Duke raked his foot under the chair and kicked the leg out so it lay in a more natural attitude.

'Starts twitchin' and gets it stuck. Our lads are supposed to watch him when I'm off. Bet the buggers haven't fed him.'

He pawed the back door open and yelled at two men who were sitting on a low wall. 'Here, have you fed him? Come and get him fed.' The two men scowled across towards the house. 'Oi!' Duke shouted stabbing a finger at them. 'Jem get him fed. Aub come and get this stuff out.'

Jem brought a bowl of cold porridge and started spooning it into Amby's mouth. Duke watched four or five awkward spoonings then lashed out with his boot at the reluctant nurse. 'More milk, yer idle sod, yer know he likes it milky.'

Jem, dodging the boot, snarled and pushed brusquely past me to fetch the milk can from the pantry. Aub was filling the kitchen table with an assortment of gin traps, powder flasks, butter markers, horn trainers – all interesting and old items an auctioneer loves to call 'Dales bygones'.

Two wrecked shotguns, hammers broken and barrels split, were laid across the pile, then Aub eased a box of ancient cartridges on to one corner and laid a tin of black powder on top of it.

Duke was still watching the old man being fed. Porridge oozed from the sides of the slowly working mouth, and milk drew a zigzag line down the unshaven chin.

'Look at him, look at him. Used to be the strongest man in the dale. Once carried the anvil from Ramsthwaite smithy and threw it in the washfold for a five pound bet. Look at him.'

Duke turned slowly and folded his arms. 'Now then! There's some good stuff here and I'm tellin' thee what I want for it – two hundred and fifty quid.'

I pulled out my notebook and made a list of the items, writing their value at the side. I added it up twice, each time coming nowhere near Duke's two hundred and fifty pounds.

'Sorry Duke can't do it.'

Duke leaned forward menacingly. 'Two hundred and fifty quid!'

'Can't do it – nowhere near.'

'I need two hundred and fifty quid.' He unfolded his arms, straightened up and put his head back in an attitude which had quietened many a taproom. 'Rosie says she'll wed me if I have me teeth done an' I need two hundred and fifty quid. Come on, you buggers is makin' a fortune, yer sellin' the dale up.' He slammed his fist on the table. 'I need two hundred and fifty quid.'

His two brothers went and stood behind him. All three glared at me, hard unblinking stares that made me swallow and my palms grow sweaty. I breathed in deeply and looked around the kitchen. Ambrose was sitting in a good broad-arm Windsor. I quickly ran my eyes over it looking for missing rails or split arms. 'Tell you what, throw the chair in and I'll give you three hundred pounds.'

Duke's grin was mirrored a second later by both his brothers. 'Get him up,' he said without taking his gaze off me. Jem and Aub lifted the old man on to a couch and Duke snatched the cushion from the chair and threw it after them. 'Here put that under his head.' I picked up the chair and made towards the door. 'Oi! Colour of yer money first, sunshine,' Duke said in a low and menacing voice. I counted the money out on to the table and as I laid the last note down Duke swept it up and fanned his face happily with it. 'Get me teeth done now Rosie my luv, and wed we shall be.' He followed me to the van as I carried the last of the stuff out.

'A hundred acres she has coming to her, an,' he added, leaning his ugly face towards mine, 'she meks damn good meat and tatey pies.'

I slowed down for the cattle grid and looked back at the farmhouse. Ambrose, Marmaduke, Jeremy and Aubrey – fine names for a rough lot.

Fiery was carrying the baby across the village green when I returned. The proud father was off to show his beloved offspring to Nellie May, and Little Petal waddled behind him, switching at imaginary flies with a stalk of ground elder. I was pleased Fiery wasn't there when I unloaded the van. He is straight to deal with, but if he takes to anything he has to buy it, and he has the tenacity of a sheep tick. He'll follow me around, 'Come on guv, give a price', until I weaken.

There were things I wanted for my own collection: horn trainers, a bullet mould, and an unusual horse gag I hung from the kitchen beams. The cartridges and black powder I put into the cool pantry and the rest I laid out on the shop floor, after hiding the Windsor in the lounge; that was for Mrs Bunney.

Fiery shook his head at the shotguns. 'No, no guv. Had enough trouble with the last artillery.'

The memory of Fiery flying up the apple house steps with the shrieking Little Petal after him, her buttocks blackened and smoking, set me laughing. Fiery looked a little downcast and then he too began to laugh. 'By, I thought I'd had it that day guv!' He leaned on the counter his head drooping to his hands, his body shaking. 'I didn't know. I just threw the gun into the van, hells bells, what a bang. She couldn't sit down for a week. No! No more artillery. When we got home she set off after me again waving that Jezail around her head. No kidding guv, I slept in the coal house for two nights.'

'Not to worry Fiery, they're good pub decorators. They'll find a home.'

'Not wi' me they won't,' he laughed.

Fiery backed his van up to the Dutch barn and we loaded it with everything but the *chaise-longue*.

'Can't you move that hen?' he protested.

'No, you can have it in three weeks,' I replied, peering under the tarpaulin to make sure she had returned to her eggs.

I waved the van off and then crossed the green to the Colonel's. He has an eprouvette.

He has been beginning to look tired recently. His daily walk round the village with his Labrador was taking longer than it used to do and he had begun leaving his stool in the pub half an hour before closing time.

'Never used it myself,' he said laying it on his desk. 'It seems OK.'

I thanked him and hurried back to test the black powder.

Screwing the powder measure from the pistol grip I filled it level and poured it into the pan, pulled the frizzen down and cocked the hammer. I was just going to pull the trigger when I remembered that at my feet lay the tin of black powder. Although the lid was firmly pressed on to it I gave a shudder and, laying the eprouvette aside, carried the tin back to the pantry. Seven pounds of black powder would flatten the farm-house. The flint was worn and I had to reset it in the jaws several times before I got a spark, which made my hand kick, sent a ball of black smoke growing out of my fist and made my ears ring. The marker wheel had spun nearly its full register to number ten: it was good stuff.

Ted shook his head. 'No good to me, black powder. It's slow burning, needs long barrels. Anyway it's damned messy,' he added, grinning at my blackened face.

'But them cartridges, I'll have a go at them.' His eyes narrowed. 'That is, if they're cheap enough.'

'They're cheap enough, Ted. You can have 'em for nothing.'

He'd given me two bales of straw to bed Topic down for her foaling and waved my offer of payment aside with an 'It's all right.'

The cartridges were old waxed-cardboard ones, faded to a pale pink. Ted's thumbnail scraped at his front teeth. 'Aye, they'll do to bang the rabbits off. Only man I know who could use that amount of black powder would be Pigeon Pie, an' he hasn't been for a year or two.'

'I don't like having it in the house,' I confessed.

'Safe enough. Just keep it out of the way of the kids.'

I didn't tell him that I'd got it from the Brockways because the mere mention of the name makes him grind his teeth and curse. Amby still owes him for a Swaledale tup and one of his best dogs had been spirited up to Sottenghyll never to be seen again.

We stood at the top of the green watching Baz cut the grass. His motor mower snarled and leapt and sent a spume of daisy heads into the air as he manhandled it over the mounds around the washfold.

'Little fella wor sat out there this afternoon with his wife and bairn.' Ted nodded towards where the beck dropped through the wall of rough hewn stone. 'It's a bonny bairn. Little fella was as happy as a flea on a broody hen.'

I cleaned the eprouvette very carefully and oiled the mechanism lightly before taking it back.

'Worked perfectly, Colonel, number ten on the dial.'

'Good stuff. But I've seen the Pathans make a powder that would blow the wheel off this.' He laid the eprouvette back in the gun cabinet. 'Sit down, sit down.' He poured two huge glasses of whisky and sank back in the library chair. 'You say it came from Sottenghyll? Funny lot the Brockways. When I was on the bench there was one of them up in front of me nearly every week. Their mother died when the children were young and Ambrose just went ... ' He paused and searched for a word. 'Odd,' he added.

'Well, he's in a bad way now.'

The Colonel took a long drink and pursed his lips. 'Stroke! Rabbit married his daughter you know, she disappeared. Had enough I suppose. They have a daughter, a clever girl done well for herself.'

Rabbit spoke of his wife only rarely, referring to her always as that bitch, but a daughter he'd never mentioned. I held my hand over my glass as the Colonel offered the bottle over the desk. One tumblerful of single malt is enough for me. He refilled his glass and found the depths of the chair again. 'Funny! Two rough families, ne'er do wells and poachers, and they produce a girl like that.'

'Clever one is she?'

'Clever! I'll say she is. She's a mathematician. She's the looks of Brigitte Bardot and the brain of Einstein.'

Antique dealers are prone to daydreaming. Idle hours in auction rooms we dream of unearthing treasures or recognising the unprepossessing canvas for its true worth; so our imaginations grow and gain muscle, but, try as I could, I failed to picture this body of Bardot and brain of Einstein calling Rabbit ... 'Dad'.

Chapter 11

It was the second day after Ted broke his leg that I began to regret having sold him the encyclopedias. He sat in the kitchen, his plastered leg on a low stool, the books on a higher one, spectacles at the end of his nose, and read all day.

Baz came down twice a day to milk for him whilst I tended his poultry and kept an unprofessional eye on the sheep.

Every time we went to report to him or passed the kitchen door we were bombarded with unanswerable questions. 'What's the highest mountain in the Himalayas? Largest river in China?' We shook our heads in ignorance and hurried about the business of running the farm. Receiving no satisfactory answers, in fact no answers at all, Ted changed his tactic. He would educate us.

'Do you know ...?' became a phrase that made us groan and roll our eyes. We were lectured on the importance of the grass family to mankind, the life-cycle of the mayfly, the construction of ocean-going liners, heights of skyscrapers and lengths of bridges, kings and presidents, inventors and explorers. Ted absorbed facts and figures as a sponge takes up water, then he squeezed his knowledge over us, a superior smile playing about his mouth.

'I've had enough. Where did he get them damned books?' Baz groaned as he tipped the unit full of milk into the cooling tank.

I skilfully ignored the question and emptied the basket full of eggs on to the wood rack. 'He does go on a bit,' I admitted.

'Go on a bit! He's driving me round the bend.'

Over the next few days Baz evolved a crafty ploy. With a serious face he queried every one of Ted's statements. 'I think you'll find, the Seven Years' War ended in 1764 not 1763,' he said, causing Ted to frown, make his mumpy mouth and return to his encyclopedias.

Later Baz was hailed triumphantly from the milk house door. 'Yer wrong! Yer wrong! I've checked it, 1763 definitely.' Baz looked suitably subdued but, as he pointed out with a smile, we'd had an hour's peace.

I was subjected to some wrinkled-brow questioning. 'What's an *étagère*? What's *chamlevé*?' Some I could answer and some, much to Ted's delight, I couldn't.

Baz was at the farm at the crack of dawn every morning and I, after seeing to my own stock, usually arrived when Ted and Baz were having their elevenses. Over the years Ted's elevenses had crept forward until now they sat at the scrubbed top table, mugs of tea and bacon sandwiches in front of them, well before Lalbeck clock struck ten.

I never intruded on this little morning tête-à-tête, assuming it was heady farming talk of butterfat percentages and conversion ratios. I stuck my head through the door, said good morning, and went about my business.

130

On the fifth day of the broken leg, Baz joined me in the feed house, a half-eaten sandwich in his hand. 'I've had enough. That damned WLA has pounded my ears this morning till me head's throbbin'.'

'WLA?' I asked innocently.

'Aye, World's Leading Authority.'

'What's he the WLA on this morning?'

Baz rattled a bucket of dairy nuts into the feed barrow. 'Every bloody thing.'

Dolly employed the best tactic of all – she completely ignored him. Mottled-pink arms busied themselves over the sink as she stared out of the little square window at the green. Ted countered this with his 'bet yer didn't know – well I'll tell yer' technique, but this soon palled. A WLA needs response. He feeds off widened eyes and puzzled looks, and these he found for a short happy period in the taproom.

Rabbit has a great respect, almost awe, for 'book learning', and if the fount of knowledge can be made to gush forth a pint or two of best bitter – so much the better. And so, those warm still evenings of early summer, Rabbit happily made his way home from The Ship, the terriers tripping at his heels and the intricacies of the Bessemer converter whirling in his head and causing him to steady himself on the Martins' wicket gate.

Ted poured over the books every morning and afternoon. His memory was surprisingly retentive and flushed with new found knowledge he worked his crutches vigorously across the green to the pub every evening.

The taproom gang soon took up Baz's new name for the walking oracle. 'Hey-up, here he comes, the WLA,' they would moan as Ted, resting on his crutches, pushed the door open and grinned at his 'students'. He felt that his newly acquired knowledge was taking him up the social scale a little, so after his taproom tutorial he awkwardly negotiated the two steps up to the lounge to instruct the Colonel and the vicar.

'Where did he get these damned books,' groaned Charlie. I confessed that I had sold them to him and was subjected to several hard and unfriendly stares.

'You'll be glad to know that there's one missing,' I told them encouragingly. One missing or not, nine-tenths of the world's knowledge is still an awful lot of knowledge. There's enough to empty a taproom of all but Rabbit, and enough to make the Colonel blow a strong cloud of pipe smoke across to the optics and wish he was back on the North-West Frontier.

'Man's becoming a damned nuisance,' the military man hissed as he brushed his moustache with the end of his pipe. 'Can't you keep him down there Charlie? Hide his blessed crutches or something.'

The grass in the meadows was hip high and the ground elder brushed Ted's elbows as he rested on his crutches and sniffed the air. 'Time we wor gettin' into it Baz.'

Baz bolted the cutter-bar on to the Fergie and stroked up the blades with a file. 'Thick lushy stuff these meadows, take some getting through,' he explained. 'After we cut the "way-in" I'll show thee what to do.'

The scythes brought a cloud of dust down on us as we hooked them off the rafters. Baz worked the strickle across their blades. 'Ought to be hung outside really. Old timers used to insist they slept the winter with their blades north–south. Said it got a better edge on 'em. I suppose when you were knocking more than an acre a day, owt you thought helped, you'd do.'

'An acre a day?' I felt the weight of the scythe, a hot sun on my back and a full day swinging this. 'Must have been strong men.'

'Aye, them Irish lads that used to come across for hay timing were a tough lot. Me Dad told me he's seen 'em drink all night then sit in the hedge bottom waiting for the dew to go off so they could get stuck in.'

We started to cut the 'way-in' to the five acre. The long straight pole scythe or Lea, as Baz would call it, was an ungainly tool.

'Yankees are the best when you get used to 'em,' Baz panted as he swung his scythe into the grass. 'We'll not cut a right "way-in", nobody does these days. I'll just drop it behind the gate and then we'll go straight at her.'

The scythe with which I had not cut a single blade of grass was exchanged, on Baz's orders, for a pitchfork. 'Follow me,' he said, 'and owt stuck in the fingers, winkle it out, yer'll find mouses' nests the worst, some of 'em are as thick as a bull's ear; they get under the tines and then the cutters run over the grass instead of cutting it. When I stop and back up, summat's stuck. All right?'

'All right.'

Baz started up the field, 'a bar and a half from the wall', as he had been at pains to point out. The grass fell behind the chattering cutter-bar in a wide swathe.

A wave of brown seed-heads speckled with yellow buttercups poured itself into a river of greens. The ground elder, stalky and proud, spun its umbrels and died a dignified death a trembling moment after the common grasses. The air was heady with pollen and sap and as I trudged over the thick matting of grass and weed, my eyes watered and nose itched.

'Herby stuff', Ted called it. I searched through a million stalks with the prongs of the fork: cow parsley, buttercup, nettle and vinegar-grass and under the sycamore at the top of the field, goose-grass and shy periwinkle. Baz stopped the tractor, let it roll back a foot and pointed at the cutter-bar. I hurried up the field feeling guilty at my dereliction of duty. A tangle of brown grass was wedged under the finger bar. Gingerly I inserted a prong and eased it out. It was still recognisable as a nest, a matrix of bleached stalks around a core of moss and ginger fur. I bent low working my hands down the fork shaft peering at the nest looking for bits of pink.

'It's all right, it's empty,' Baz called, shaking his head and waving me back from the cutter he put the tractor in gear and with a clatter went on with the 'knocking down'.

We did two circuits of the field then Baz did a jerky reverse under the sycamore. 'We'll cut the other way now, cut the wheel marks out,' he explained.

I fell in behind the tractor, my handkerchief tied over a streaming nose and my prickly eyes glued to the cutter-bar. More mouse nests, all thankfully empty, and then down the long side, by Alma field, an exasperating run of twigs kept my fork probing between the finger bar.

'It's when he lops the hedge, he doesn't clear 'em up straight off an' t'wind blows 'em in,' Baz shouted. I cursed Ted's bad husbandry as sweat stuck the shirt to my back.

With half the field done Baz stopped the tractor near to the gate. 'Drinkin's,' he yelled gleefully. Then swinging himself down from the tractor, he pulled his shirt outside his trousers and with a stumbling walk made to where Ted leaned on his crutches, an allowance can dangling from each hand. Bacon sandwiches wrapped in newspaper were brought from inside his shirt as Baz and I dropped into the hedge bottom to savage sandwich and cold tea.

Ted turned the grass over with a crutch. 'Lushy stuff – it'll tek a bit o' sun to kill this.' The bit o' sun blazed down from a cloudless sky.

'It's haying already,' Baz mumbled, his mouth full of sandwich.

We finished the five acre at lunch-time. Baz looked around the edges of the field. 'I don't think we'll bother pinking the sides, we'll get on and knock the Alma down this afternoon.'

After a light lunch I stood at the sink, stripped to the waist, and sponged myself with deliciously cool water. My shoulders were beginning to ache and the Alma was a big field.

'Don't forget you've to take that chair up to Mrs Bunney,' Vicky called after me as, shirt in hand, I trudged off to the Alma.

The sun was high in the sky as Baz paced a bar and a half from the wall then paused, spat the stalk of grass from his mouth, and drew a mental line down the field. 'She's a big 'un,' he grinned, setting the cutter-bar clashing.

After two circuits of the big rectangular meadow we stopped to wipe the pollen from our faces and wash the dust from our throats. The water from the aluminium can was warm and tangy but we gulped it greedily, letting it flood across our upturned faces and run in tickling trickles down our bare chests.

Baz lowered his can and belched, then inclined his head to one side and raised a forefinger. 'He's here.'

Over the hedge came the faint, crackly but distant sound of 'Rock of Ages'.

Praying Billy had pulled his black mini-van up to the wash-fold and was leaning into the back of it cranking the handle of an old wooden gramophone.

Stacked alongside the van were plywood placards each beautifully signwritten in Gothic-style script.

The end is nigh. Repent ye sinners. Thy grace is enough for me. Black sombre letters on pristine white.

We stood on the tractor, semi-naked sinners, the sweat of honest toil on our brows and, waving our water cans in tune with the music, sang to the scratchy record.

Billy gave us a friendly wave. 'God is with you brothers.'

'Good,' Baz shouted as he jumped down, 'we could do with another hand.'

My shoulders soon began to burn and I had to drape my shirt cape fashion around them.

The Alma is a flat meadow and has been re-seeded several times so it is not as herby as the five acre and my duties were light. The grass, stalkier and more erect, fell evenly before the blade and circuit after circuit I shogged after the noisy machine with nothing to do but stab my fork idly here and there into the swathes and listen to the invisible skylark.

Billy had left his van and bowler-hatted and sober-suited, was taking his tracts around the cottages.

'Comes every year or so,' Baz told me on one of our water stops. 'Nice old lad, doesn't shove it down yer throat an' doesn't mind his leg pulled a bit.'

'It's a smart set-up he's got. I'd give him a few quid for that gramophone.'

Baz tapped me on a sensitive shoulder. 'Hey! Look at that daft owd sod.' He pointed to the five acre where Ted, his crutches set at a wide angle, slowly swept a scythe into the hedge bottoms. 'Trying to do the piking. Wait till Dolly sees him.'

Dolly saw him just as Praying Billy doffed his bowler at the kitchen door. She brushed past him with a friendly smile. 'Hang on a minute Billy till I get that pillock out of the meadow.'

Vicky brought our teas out to the field. 'Don't forget Mrs Bunney's chair,' she reminded me in a serious way. 'You promised.'

Promise or not I was determined to finish the Alma with Baz so that when he announced in the taproom 'We've knocked down the five acre and the Alma today', I would be a full part of that 'we'. Able to smile around at the nodding and knowl-edgeable heads and to become a thread in the tapestry of village history. Something I could recount in years to come. 'I remember the day me and Baz . . .'

'Don't worry, I'll take Mrs Bunney's chair up this evening,' I told Vicky. She folded her arms and put her head back, a sure sign she wasn't pleased. So I told her the sun was making her hair blonder and that her arms were a lovely brown. She made a wry face but couldn't suppress a tiny smile before she plucked a grass stalk and, with her print frock swinging, she picked her way over the swathes to the gate.

It was milking time when we finished cutting the meadow. I eased my aching body into the chair and plonked my hot feet on the cool hearth as Baz called the beasts into the byre and washed their udders. Dolly took him a can of tea and a bacon sandwich, and whilst he sat on the cornbin she told him in hushed tones of Ted's confrontation with Praying Bill. It appeared there had been 'a right old ding dong'.

The old soldier's trick of holding tired feet under the cold tap works. Refreshed and changed, I loaded Mrs Bunney's chair into the van and winding the windows down set off for the late artist's cottage.

*

With a glass of homemade lemonade in my hand I followed Mrs Bunney into her parlour.

Under the window an architect's table bristled with artist's brushes. Stuck in jam jars, tin cans and even a celery vase were hundreds of brushes: expensive brushes. Mrs Bunney looked at them sadly and stroked a hand over them. 'Edward Raphael loved brushes,' she explained. 'The war years worried him; he couldn't get the brushes he wanted so when they became available again, he just kept buying them.'

Two deep window-sills carried their share of brushes, whilst on the floor, stacked against the uneven walls, were hundreds of unframed watercolours.

'This is where I wanted the chair.' Mrs Bunney chopped the air with her pudgy hands. 'Edward Raphael used to sit here hour after hour watching the light change on the fells. He never tired of it. "Missus" he used to say. Funny he always called me that. "Missus – to me these hills are alive, they're never still."' Mrs Bunney smiled out at Edward Raphael's hills.

'I know what he meant,' I told her. 'I have seen dozens of his paintings of that fell, every one is different, yet every one is true.'

The periwinkle-blue eyes fixed on mine and she smiled. 'He was a truthful painter. If he did anything that didn't feel right to him, no matter how much work he'd put into it, it would end up on that fireback.'

'I've always liked his paintings Mrs Bunney.'

Her smile broadened. 'Come on, I'll show you something.'

Up the narrow stairs we went, Mrs Bunney grunting at every step. 'It's my legs,' she explained flinging open a bedroom door. 'There! Go in.'

I ducked through the low door into a small room whose

ceiling plunged with the roof line leaving the outer wall no taller than waist height. Set in the centre of the wall was a dormer window and before it stood an easel on which rested an unfinished watercolour.

Mrs Bunney's voice was a whisper. 'Edward Raphael was doing that when he died.' On a tall elm stool, of good colour, sat that artist's paintbox and washpots and pushed under the easel was a pair of carpet slippers.

The picture was of the view from the window. The late Mr Bunney had washed in the distant hills with overlapping grey wedges and in the foreground a broken wall and barn were suggested with thin, barely visible lines of the palest grey. Scant as it was, it was obviously the work of a skilled hand.

'It's fading with the sunlight, Mrs Bunney. You ought to put something on the window.'

The old lady tiptoed into the room and peered at the picture. 'Oh dear, I think you're right, what can I do?'

'Either turn it from the window or put a lace curtain up. That should do the trick.' Mrs Bunney chewed a finger. 'I'll put a curtain up. It shouldn't be moved, should it?'

I shook my head in agreement and thought of Mrs Bunney's businesslike daughter. If anything happened to the old lady the painting would be moved along to the saleroom double quick, together with the easel, the stool, the stickback chair and the three hundred other watercolours.

I put the chair where Mrs Bunney had indicated and stood back as she shyly tried it out. 'Yes, it's just like Edward Raphael's. I'll never forgive his sister for taking that chair.' She ran a hand over the back. 'And now I'll show you something else.' She grinned happily, squatted awkwardly on a slipper box and searched carefully through a folio of watercolours. 'Here it is,' she cried, offering it to me on flattened hands. 'Do you recognise it?'

It was a painting of Bullpen Farm, done sometime before it had fallen into disrepair.

The heavy oak-panelled door was the same and there were the very Yorkshire Lights that Baz and I had thrown, rotten, into the yard. The two stone slates were still set tent-fashion on the chimney stacks, but where the Dutch barn now stands stood a low cart shed, pantiled like the cow byre. The apple house was just visible, its eastern wall covered by a plum tree in full leaf.

I laid the picture on the table and, arms behind my back, scrutinised it carefully. 'Looks like he was standing by the wash-fold when he painted this Mrs Bunney.'

'Wherever he was standing dear, it'll be true. Edward Raphael was always a truthful painter.'

'Looks like late summer and, by the way the shadow falls half across the gate, mid-morning.'

Mrs Bunney clapped her hands in delight. 'There, what did I tell you. Edward Raphael only painted mornings and evenings. He wasn't a lover of harsh light.'

'I don't suppose it's for sale Mrs Bunney?'

The artist's widow shook her head. 'No dear, I have my pension now. I've no need to sell any more. Every evening I go through them. It's as if he was still here with me. Every day I swill out his water pots and refill them and draw the pull-ons back on his favourite view. But I will put something at that window as you say. It would be a tragedy to lose Edward Raphael Bunney's last truthful lines.'

*

140

Vicky was in a sour mood when I got home. 'I've hardly seen you all day and now you're off to the pub. The shop doesn't run itself you know.'

I was longing to get into the taproom, to unbutton my shirt to the waist, straddle a stool and hold the pint glass cool against my chest. I would sit next to Baz, two seasoned haytimers together, the men who knocked the five acre and the Alma down in one day. But the tilt of her head and the set of her mouth told me it was not to be.

'All right, I'll give it a miss.'

We sat on the front wall together clacking our heels against the stones. It is rare that we have a tiff and when we do it never lasts long. Soon we were clacking in unison: little smiles and a nudge or two and then we were chatting away happily about the day's events.

Vicky rolled her eyes. 'Ted and Praying Billy had a real heated argument. There were some very unchristian words flying about.'

'Well, the saviour of mankind and the world's leading authority on everything; it's a heavy mixture.'

Vicky laughed and playfully butted her head against my shoulder.

'Now then you two, we'll have none of that in this village of sinners.' Ted leaned his crutches against the wall and folded his arms.

Praying Billy toiled up the green towards his van, *The end is nigh* placard over his shoulder.

'Now this is what I can't understand,' said Ted, easing himself on to the wall. 'He's been coming for twenty years with that same placard. Now, if it was nigh twenty year since, how can it still be nigh? Ask him, go on, ask him.'

141

Ted didn't give us time to ask. He put his hand to his mouth and yelled down at Billy, 'How do yer know it's nigh?'

Billy threw the placard into the back of the van and pointed a trembling finger at Ted. It was a long time before the words came and when they did, they came slowly and with feeling.

'It's damned know-alls like you that'll be the ruination of religion.'

Chapter 12

The day after the meadows were mown we had rain. A gentle steady rain that hummed on the tin roof of the barn and sent the hens squeezing deep into the hedge bottoms. The goat bleated to be taken in and Topic and her foal poked their heads out of the apple house and waited for Mr Hall to totter across the yard, his pockets bulging with contraband carrots. The dogs lay under the table licking their wet legs and the cat sat in the window bottom and blinked out at a quiet sodden world.

'It'll not do much harm,' Ted observed optimistically. 'If we'd have dashed it out it would have been worse, but laid as it is, it'll run off.'

All day it rained, never slackening. The shop did badly; the few who dashed from their cars to jangle the doorbell were in no mood for buying. Charlie stood in the pub doorway and blew a cloud of smoke out into the rain. Baz milked and then, drawing the ragged mac that hung behind the feed house door around his shoulders, trudged off home to saw logs under his lean-to. 'There's nowt else to do,' he told us.

Late afternoon I fed the stock, milked the goat, and hurried across the yard with an armful of kindling wood and shooed a reluctant cat out on to the wet cobbles. No doubt there were gardeners looking out on sodden lawns saying, 'We needed it,' or, 'it'll do good.' Need it we did, for when I had gingerly scraped away the soil from the first earlies I had found to my dismay they were no bigger than marbles. I filled my pipe and stretched my legs in the hearth, and smiled to myself when I thought of Long John leaning over his gate and watching an ominous grey cloud shoulder its way over Penhill.

'More rain, more rest,' he'd said with a wry smile.

The children mooched around the kitchen pestering Vicky. They wanted to paint and draw but as soon as brushes and pencils were found they wanted plasticine, and tiring of that, they knelt on the hearth rug and complained in loud voices that there was nothing to do.

Vicky looked up from her sewing. 'There's a darning mushroom somewhere in the caravan. Now if you were to find that for me I may know where there is some chocolate.'

Wellingtons were thrown out of the cupboard and then pulled on with enthusiasm.

We had towed the old caravan into the garth and jacked it up under the sycamore. It had been our home for many months whilst we had renovated the house and many a rain lashed night we had vowed to burn it when we were finished with it. However, we were continually short of storage room so good sense had prevailed and, gutted of its fittings, the caravan provided a good home for all the things that we acquired which had little value, but enough of it to prevent their being sent on the one way journey to the tip. It housed a variety of plastic containers, aluminium pans, colanders and washing-up bowls.

Boxes of cutlery were laid about the floor and a pair of cast-iron seat ends awaiting new planks stood under the bow-window. It had become a depository for wood which 'might come in useful'. Carved pediments from Victorian wardrobes and their mirrored doors were stacked along with mahogany table leaves and the lids from walnut pianos.

'Retirement jobs' Richard Radford called them as he surveyed his own stack of 'might come in useful' wood.

Someday we'll get around to making that cheval mirror from the wardrobe door and steaming the veneer from that piano front. Our pile had grown steadily. Woodwormed chests were broken down, the pulpy bits consigned to the woodshed and the ones that showed only a scattering of flight holes were stripped of their nails, and joined the stack.

The children were off a long time. 'Must have found something of interest,' I muttered, knocking my pipe out and pulling my Wellingtons on.

Sally was kneeling on the caravan floor sorting through cutlery whilst Peter, his tongue describing a slow arc across his upper lip, painted a large twenty pence sign on the side of a box. 'We've had this idea Dad,' he explained excitedly. 'You've said yourself that people like ruttling through things. Well, we are going to have some ruttle boxes. Boxes full of stuff that people can ruttle through.'

Sally had found a matching set of forks and was binding them together. 'We break up next week. We can put our boxes out and make lots of money.'

Peter stepped back and looked thoughtfully at his signwriting. 'It's all right isn't it, Dad. We can do it?'

I like a bit of enterprise, and so I readily agreed. 'The only thing is,' I told them, 'you'll have to set your stall out on our cobbles. If it's on the green we'll have the Colonel down on us again.'

Sally dropped the bundle of forks elegantly into a thirty pence box and smiled up at me – an innocent sweet child's smile. 'We call him old mouldy balls.'

The ruttle boxes were a success. Mrs Thompson found a worn down carving knife which winkled the weeds out of her nagged path beautifully. Ethel smiled as she fished a pewter napkin ring out of the thirty pence box and Mucky Marion pounced on an enamel pan at twenty pence. ''Ave you any more?' she demanded. Peter led her up to the caravan where she searched until she had found a matching pair. 'Still twenty pence apiece?' she asked, a twinkle in her eye.

'Go on,' Peter replied in a tired and grown-up voice. 'You'll have me in the poorhouse.' Marion threw the pans in her pram and cackled all the way home.

The Ship was doing well. The strategically placed advertising board caught the coach drivers' eyes before they changed out of second gear, the pub looked inviting, and the road up to the washfold provided easy parking. The bed and breakfast rooms were full every night and when Charlie took his sign in and looked over the cars of his guests he was a happy man.

The coach trippers were good box-ruttlers too, and some days the children's biscuit tin had as much money in it as the shop till did.

I borrowed Ted's tractor and cut the land we rented from Nellie May. Vicky followed me with the fork but her duties were light. No mouse nests, no twigs, no bunching of lush grass. It was a scant crop but it was our own. We strewed it with the old Bamford Dasher which, according to the village sages, made the best hay going. Then, with an assortment of rakes and forks, we rowed it up and left it to the wind and the sun.

Ted grunted as he worked his crutches down the lane. Two young sheep curs were tethered to one crutch with billy band. He tied them to the open gate and then leaning heavily on it, he wiped the sweat from his brow, and began to put us right. 'Now, yer say yer not baling it.'

'No Ted, we're having some old-fashioned hay.'

'Right, well, first there is footcocks then jockeys.' He rubbed his unshaven chin and looked at me steadily. 'Yer don't know what I'm on about do yer?' I confessed I didn't.

The rake was taken out of my hand and replaced with a crutch. 'Now, footcocks,' he balanced on his good leg and thrust the plastered one forward, 'pull the hay from each side of yer and over the foot. It's easy, two thatches, one footcock: two foot-cocks one jockey. But footcocks today jockeys tomorrow.'

My tutor made another footcock and gave me the rake. 'Go on, get on with it.'

I got on with it for the rest of the morning under Ted's direc-tion. 'Bit thin there, pull a bit more up. Them's too bunched.' The tutor constantly guided his pupil.

The sun came out full and strong. I peeled off my jumper, but hot and sweaty as I got I dare not doff my shirt as my shoulders were still burned from my earlier haymaking with Baz. I soon got into a rhythm. The wooden rake felt cumber-some at first but I got the knack of spreading the hay across its full width and tilting it over my foot to make an open loose cock. 'Let the wind get through 'em,' Ted shouted from the gate.

When I had covered what I estimated to be half the field I dropped my rake and took my drinkings down to the gate. Ted took the flask top and dropped heavily beside me, spilling most of the tea. 'There won't have been any hay made like this in the village for twenty year,' he laughed.

The sheep curs fought over the scraps I threw to them.

'Ginger one's no good, it'll have to go.' Ted shook his head. 'Don't know why I took it. Should stick to black and whites. It hasn't a strong eye; the old ewe stamps her foot an' it's off. Won't stand to 'em and master 'em. It'll have to go, can't feed it for nowt.' They were both strong healthy dogs, no older than ten or twelve months.

'It seems so young, won't it learn?' I asked him.

'No. If it isn't in 'em, it isn't in 'em. Best get shut.' He eased himself up and arrayed himself with crutches and dogs. 'I'll have to be off, it'll be dinner-time when I get back. I'll be glad when this damned thing's off.'

'Jockeys tomorrow,' I called after him picking up the rake.

Topic and Starlight were doing well. The foal, accustomed to constant handling since birth, ran loose alongside her mother without a head collar. Old Mr Hall ran his hands over the mare. 'A little gentle work won't do her any harm.' There was about an acre hayed up and ready for bringing in. If I worked her across the slope of the field instead of up and down it she could bring the hay in without too much collar and breeching work. I made some simple hay ladders for the coup cart and with the foal cavorting around us we forked the jockeys on to the cart. Loose hay has to be drier than baled we were told, so it had been felt and smelled and tossed in the air until Ted had announced it was 'just right'.

148

The stone barn was soon full to the eaves. The children spread and trod the hay as I forked it through the small square forking hole high on the gable end. With the last load safely in, Sally and Peter peered through the hole. 'How do we get down?'

I stood on the cart and lifted them one at a time on to my shoulders. 'Should have left you in there for a week,' I teased them. 'Your mother and I could have had a bit of peace.'

The bottom of the coup cart was covered in seed. Sally swept it up and carefully filled one of the sandwich bags with it. 'I'll seed the bare patches of the village green with this,' she giggled.

It was well past their bedtime when I closed the gate and they scrambled on to the cart, Sally clutching her bag of seed and Peter taking up the reins.

Pipistrelles fluttered a drunken flight over the hedge tops as we plodded up the lane.

The children went to bed with a glass of milk and as I rubbed Topic down in the yard the summer curtains were drawn in their bedroom windows.

Baz and Susan walked hand in hand across the village green. 'What you need now is a bit of rain to bring the fog up,' he called over the wall.

The rain did not come. The brown stalks of the grass stayed dusty and dry and the fog was slow to put a green haze on the meadows.

Every morning I walked the dogs down the lane to the field and opened the barn door and let the delicious smell of new hay flood around me. I would grab a handful, sniff it, and, smiling, put it back into the pile. Our own hay; not the best, but well-won old-fashioned hay.

*

Long John turned down Ted's offer of the ginger sheep cur. 'Never had owt but black and whites. Don't fancy ginger.'

The bachelor dealer had a pack of curs and terriers running around his isolated farm and one more, ginger or not, wouldn't have made much difference I thought, for Ted had threatened to shoot the timid dog if nobody wanted it. Vicky and I had kept this information from the children because our menagerie was quite large enough. We asked the Radfords, Canary Mary, Fatty Batty and Fiery Frank, almost everyone we knew but nobody wanted a dog.

Ted tied the dog in the yard and fed it grudgingly. 'Eating its head off, useless devil,' he muttered, scowling at the poor creature. 'It'll have to go.' He repeated his threat to shoot it so we redoubled our efforts, making it in our way to visit Arthur the Faker and even calling, a little nervously, on the de Traffords, but it was to no avail.

Mucky Marion considered taking it but finally shook her head. 'No, if I bring another animal into the house the monkey goes mad, flings stuff round in the kitchen. Jealous yer see.'

The dog was doomed.

The children's ruttle boxes were too successful. Not only were they emptying the caravan at an alarming rate but the children had become far too money-orientated. Instead of playing with the other village children they wanted to spend every fine day out on the cobbles making money. Two Post Office savings accounts had been opened and they were very healthy. After a long talk we decided to limit the trading to two days a week. There were long faces for an hour or so but soon they were clambering over the fell with the Martins' two girls, a knapsack heavy with lemonade and a variety of chocolate bars on Peter's back. Fridays and Saturdays we designated as ruttle box days and these mornings would find the children eagerly scanning the sky for clouds because rain ruins the ruttle box trade.

The coach did not stop at the washfold. It crept up the uneven track and stopped with a hiss from the brakes right in front of the shop. The shadow from the cream and chromium monster fell over the children and their wares. They glared at the driver but their glares immediately turned into grins. 'It's Colin,' they shouted gleefully.

Colin jumped lightly from the coach, waved to the children and with ingratiating smiles and whispered words helped a score and a half of middle-aged ladies down the steps. Soon the cobbles, the shop, and the yard, all had their share of cardiganed and blue-rinsed matrons clutching handbags.

Colin swung the laughing children off the ground. 'Where's your beautiful mother and your grumpy old dad?' The beautiful mother was held at arm's length, smiled at and told she was more beautiful than ever and getting younger and younger and I was slapped on the shoulder and asked how on earth I scratched a living in this one-horse place.

Colin hadn't changed. He was still the same daft, feckless, lovable half-rogue who had brought us the auction advertisement for Bullpen Farm two years previously. 'Never thought you'd do it,' he said shaking his head, 'leave that smashing shop and live in the sticks.'

A cardiganed blue rinse appeared at his elbow. 'Oh, by the way, this is the wife.'

We shook hands, introduced ourselves and I ushered Colin and the new Mrs Colin, as the children called her, into the kitchen, whilst Vicky slipped into the shop.

'Doing all right, old boy,' Colin said, stretching his legs and unbuttoning his plum-coloured blazer to reveal a PSV badge pinned over his shirt pocket. 'Got this last year, amusement trade – zilch.' A well-manicured hand slashed the air. 'Me and the missus here – her father has the coaches – run these tours for unattached females.' He pulled a creased card out of the shirt pocket and passed it to me. 'That's me, Considerate Colin's Carefree Coaches. Doing all right. Thought we'd have this trip up the Dales. Delayed honeymoon like.'

The new Mrs Colin smiled shyly. She was in complete contrast to the string of tarty birds Colin had courted over the years. A plump quiet woman with a kindly face, she constantly fiddled with her teacup and handbag. He was a little fuller in the face and slightly tanned but he had lost none of his exuberance.

'Look yer losing trade.' He looked at the children and pointed out to the cobbles where a bevy of women bent well-coiffured heads over the boxes. He turned sharply back to me. 'Got something in your line. We're here to make you rich, aren't we love?' He leaned forward and patted his wife's hand bringing another shy smile to her face. 'We're right as a box o' birds, aren't we love?'

The yard's contingent of blue rinses interspaced with a few virgin greys clustered at the gate and 'ah'ed' at the foal.

Old Mr Hall graciously handed out carrots to the better-looking women and basked in their admiration as he related all the details of the foaling to them. 'I wor a horseman for a forty year, there's nowt you can tell me about hosses. I knew it wor a filly before it foaled,' he told them gleefully.

Colin went across to the pub to renew his acquaintance with Charlie and arrange lunch for his ladies. 'We're staying here for lunch girls,' he announced brightly on his return. 'All right, that OK with everybody?' It seemed OK with everybody.

The ladies soon returned to the shop and ruttle boxes except for one tall, particularly well set-up woman. She had taken an excited Mr Hall to sit on the straw under the Dutch barn. 'Now, you clever man, tell me all about yourself,' she whispered, patting his brown hand.

Colin blew three shrill blasts on a whistle. 'Come on girls din-din time.' He hooked a laughing woman on to each arm and led his giggling and heavily scented pack of cardiganed 'girls' across the green.

'Last one in doesn't get a kiss,' he called. The last one into the long room was the shy new Mrs Colin.

The well set-up woman who had ignored the call to lunch, walked along to the shop, bought two fruit pies, kicked her shoes off, scuffled her feet in the straw and smiled at Mr Hall. 'Blackberry and apple or plum?'

The old man flicked his pocket-knife open and stabbed it into a straw-bale to clean it. 'We'll have half a piece.'

Colin, fed and watered was, he told us, a happy man. The stop in Ramsthwaite had amused his girls. It had saved diesel and he had, as a mark of appreciation from a grateful landlord, a crisp five pound note in his blazer pocket. 'Now son, a bit of business.' He winked and led me to the back of the coach, where with much straining, puffing and blowing, he pulled out an old coal sock that thudded heavily on to the track.

'Cannonballs.' He held a rusty ball in his hand and grinned up at me. 'I have this mate in the Portobello Road. What he does is he puts one at a time in his window with a little sign saying "The last cannonball fired at Waterloo. Definitely not for sale." He sells three a week, at a fiver apiece. What d'ye think?'

I thought fraud, the Trade Descriptions Act, gullibility and finally, 'No!'

Colin frowned. 'Well maybe don't go as far as last one at Waterloo. Maybe . . . ' He paused and clicked his tongue. 'What about Civil War?' I shook my head. 'Battle of the Standard?'

'No, but I'll have a couple off you, just as interest pieces.'

'They come in packs of five old son,' he said, delving happily into his sack and bringing out another four cannonballs.

Colin pushed a copper coal-helmet to one side and draped wine-coloured velvet over the music stool. 'There, it looks a treat. You'll sell that old lad. Put a fiver on it – no six quid, you'll want a bit of talking money. You know the secret of this trade?' He stood in the window, his arms spread like a conductor about to start a major symphony. 'Anything that doesn't sell, you polish it, move it, and put the price up.'

I looked at Vicky who smiled and shrugged her shoulders. Here was Colin, failed antique dealer, telling us the secrets of the trade. I thought of the time we had called on Colin to find his shop empty except for a Doulton jug. He had, as we say in the trade, 'eaten his stock'.

'I'll remember that Colin, very good; polish it, move it and put the price up.'

Colin gave me a wide-eyed look and wagged his head. 'It works.'

He jumped nimbly down from the window and stacked the four remaining cannonballs in the corner. 'You'll wish you'd bought more, I shan't be up for another year.'

His ladies crossed the green in twos and threes and climbed up into the coach. The new Mrs Colin counted them twice – one missing. The well set-up woman gave Mr Hall a quick peck on the cheek and, picking strands of straw from her cardigan, mounted the coach steps to cheers and shouts of 'Well done, Vera. Clicked again Vera.'

Mrs Lewis saw her father through the sighting hole hidden between the washing powders where she watches for Thievin' Jack. She ran along the track. 'Where've you been, yer dinner's cold, we've been worried. Thought you'd had a do.'

Mr Hall turned and waved at the coach as he was led away by his clucking daughter. 'Hey!' he called to me before he was bustled through the shop door. 'That hen on that couch is bringing 'em off, there's five chicks out.'

Vicky was kissed, the children hugged and I was shaken warmly by the hand. 'Be up next year; they've enjoyed it.' Colin sprang up the coach steps. 'Now girls, what do you think of Colin's country cousins?' he laughed into the address system. There were cheers and waves, and blown kisses as the coach crept down the track. Colin gave three long blasts on the horn and waved a plum-coloured arm out of his window. We waved until the coach was swallowed by the green hedgerows. Old Mr Hall stood in the shop doorway and wiped a smear of black-berry and apple from his cheek.

I laughed and shook my head. 'He hasn't changed has he?'

The children chinked money into their biscuit tin, they had done well out of the coach.

I went into the shop to write up the daybook, a nice entry for the accountant to smile over. 'Five cannonballs – ten pounds'. As I slammed the door behind me Colin's little pile collapsed and one ball rumbled an erratic course across the floor towards me. I picked it up and noticed that cast into it was a little car-touche with lettering. I licked my thumb and rubbed until the words became clear. 'Made in Taiwan'.

Chapter 13

I'm not particularly fond of minding the shop. If it's slow times, I can stretch my legs under the desk, lean back with a good book and intersperse the day with slippered trips to the kitchen to refill the teapot, so it's not bad. In winter I direct the fan heater on to my legs and summer sees me opening the small window, which opens into the orchard, to fill the shop with sweet air and the muted sounds of the village.

It was a warm day. Not only was the orchard window wide but I had propped open the door with one of Colin's cannon-balls. They were irregular enough to fulfil this duty. As I felt I would never be able to sell them, idle moments had set my brain searching for alternative uses, and doorstops seemed to be the only viable one.

My book slipped on to my lap, the most beautiful cat in the world sat in the window and licked its paws, a cock crowed from the orchard and a host of admirable bees hovered then plunged, nectar hungry, into the honeysuckle. The cars droned past and up the dale, our ducks settled themselves by the washfold and buried their beaks amongst their back feathers.

A non-ruttle box day, the children, flush with money, had chosen to accompany their mother on a shopping trip. I hadn't pushed the plough out on to the cobbles; the open door would suffice, I told myself as I eased down into the chair and closed my eyes.

'Hey! Hey!' I awoke to find a thin red-haired woman standing over me, poking my shoulder with a very pointed finger. 'You were asleep.'

'Not really, I just closed my eyes a bit. Hayfever. They get a bit prickly this time of the year.'

She stepped back and folded the poking arm on to her hip. 'You were asleep! I rattled the sneck, said 'allo till I felt I was going barmy. I banged that damned gong – you were hard on.'

My sleep-soddened brain was, I felt, unable to cope with such a woman, so I smiled pleasantly and asked if I could help her.

'Yes, that brooch there,' she replied. An abnormally long fingernail tapped at the glass top of the jewellery cabinet. 'The one that says Miriam. That's my name, see, only everybody calls me Mim.' I took the Victorian brooch out of the cabinet and laid it on the glass. Mim, with some cringe-making scratchings of nail on glass, picked it up and turned the price ticket around. 'Gawd almighty. 'Ere do my eyes deceive me? That's the price, or is it a bleedin' catalogue number?'

'That's the price, Madam,' I answered her coldly.

I feel we should be awakened from our dreams by blue-eyed maidens with golden hair as soft as swansdown and gentle, gentle ways, not a stick-thin harridan, pancake make-up plastered on her thin face, hair tight curled like a panscrubber, and nails like the talons of a vulture.

''Ere, yer'll knock a bit off for me, won't yer dear?' A full crimson mouth split into a wide smile showing even but slightly yellowed teeth. Some women are saved by fine eyes, we know that, but many more are saved by their smiles. Mim stared at me steadily, her smile fixed, her long fingers turning the brooch over and over. 'Go on! Yer can knock a bit off for old Mim.'

I reached out and looked at the price ticket. 'Three pounds. Three pounds off for old Mim.'

'Make it four, duck.'

I gazed back into her eyes. They were large eyes, grey with good clear irises and on close inspection she proved to be a rather better looking woman than I had first thought. 'Go on then Mim, four quid off.'

Peter's words, sagely spoken, when Mucky Marion bargained for the pans, came back to me.

'You'll have me in the poorhouse.'

Mim laughed. 'Well, we'll be in together duck, because owt I get, I spend.' The ludicrous fingernails worked into her purse with little result. The notes were difficult but the coins impossible. 'Sod it,' she said finally and tipped the entire contents on the desk top. 'Come on pin it on me duck.' Mim was smaller than I had thought, her heady perfume filling my nostrils as I pinned the brooch on to her gold lamé bolero jacket.

'We're staying at the pub, me and my Joe. Probably see you across there,' she called as she grimaced at the cobbles and then, taking her high heeled shoes off, tiptoed across them to the green, her black skirt pulling tight round her thin thighs.

'Fine-looking woman,' Ted commented with feeling as he opened the gate to the Alma and watched his cows, heads down, plod slowly towards him.

*

The children commandeered the table top, laying out their new toys. A super model lorry for Peter and a big sophisticated doll for Sally. Vicky emptied her shopping bag on to the draining board. 'You've only sold a brooch? Nice day like this, I thought you would have been busy.'

I reversed the lorry between the sugar basin and the doll and answered her half-heartedly. 'Picnic weather, they're all up the dale picnicking.' She gave me a disbelieving look and clattered out to the dairy.

Peter demanded the lorry back so I wandered out into the yard and leaned over the gate. Topic and her foal were doing well. The mare had become very possessive, chasing off the cat and the dogs whenever they strayed into the garth and even the hens were sent scurrying and clucking back under the fence. Mr Hall said it was normal. 'Foal proud. Just handle her and the foal a lot – get 'em used to being handled, that's the secret.' He had left a headcollar on the mare and two or three times a day I led her and the foal into the apple house or out to the Dutch barn, just to keep her used to being led and handled. The foal was still receiving a lot of attention from the children and their friends and was not in the least bit timid. It bounded alongside its mother shaking its head in the air, did a spindly-legged frolic or two then pranced back to press itself against her flank.

Long John's van coughed into the yard and shuddered to a halt. He slammed the door harder than was called for and muttered a few obscenities about scrapyards and engines. He then reached through the open window and brought out a large brown bottle which he thrust into my folded arms. 'Drop of the very best. I think this is, well,' his fingers pinched the air, then his beard, 'it's rather special.'

I looked at the old cider bottle full of Swaledale Lightning. 'If it's any more special than the last, it's lethal.'

'No, you'll like this, it's a bit peaty. Gathered the water from a bit higher up this time; cleaned the still out and got on the best mash I've ever done.' He turned and dropped his arms on to the gate, pausing whilst his eyes ran over the foal. Then he reached out a hand and tapped the bottle. 'That is six months old.'

It was meant to impress, and impress it did, for the product of the little copper still that he kept under the floor of his store-room was usually drunk the same week. A special mash and matured for six months and a big bottle of it. Something was afoot.

'A filly?' he asked.

'Yes John, it's a filly.'

'She's comin' on. Legs like a coffin stool.' He turned towards me and, stretching his hand out, patted Topic's neck. 'How much?'

I winced and closing my eyes I dropped my head on to my hands.

'John. I've been waiting for this, John.' I said his name again to give myself time to marshal the words and make them sound truthful. 'We would like you to have her John because it was you who first got us interested in Dales ponies, but you know the mare came from the Snows?' Long John nodded. 'Well, they've asked for first refusal on the foal. But if they don't want her, we'll talk money.'

I didn't want the foal to go up to Davy Banks. It would be well treated and it would be in knowledgeable hands but it would have a hard life. Vicky and I had seen this problem coming up and we had discussed it at length. She was initially against letting the foal go at all, but we couldn't keep two ponies. I had convinced her of that. There had been times when I felt it ought to go up to Long John's and earn its keep, jagging hay and carting muck; it's what they were bred for, but now, suddenly faced with the problem, I had blurted out a lie. The Snows had never shown any interest in buying the foal.

'Aw, now then,' Long John's fingers went back to his beard. 'If they don't want it I'll have it. It's coming on grand, a good neck and head, an' them legs – grand legs.' We leaned over the gate in silence for a long time, John continually appraising the foal and me considering how I was going to get out of the contrived lie I had told. Suppose John rang them and told them of his interest? I would ring them and offer them the foal cheap: that was the way out.

'Well we can't do any trade, so I'll go and see yon queer fella,' he nodded across the green to where Rabbit was talking to a thick set man in a grey silk suit.

Long John cursed the engine which burst into life on the penultimate obscenity and with a rattle of gravel reversed out of the yard through a cloud of blue fumes. My hand was on the sneck and my mind on where I had put the Snows' phone number when the van erupted back into the yard.

'Here! I'd forgotten to give you this,' said Long John, holding out one of Canary Mary's little primrose notelets. She would, it said, call on us for lunch on Thursday. I looked at the calendar hung behind the pantry door. The derogatory comment about not knowing which day it is often applies to us. Wednesday. I was sure it was Wednesday and Vicky confirmed it as she fished the Snows' number out of the bureau.

'Mary's coming tomorrow,' I told her absent-mindedly.

'I wish she would get her phone put back in. I'm sure she

161

must have forgiven the GPO by now,' Vicky sniffed. 'One yellow phone box wouldn't have hurt and it did look rather good.'

I like to sit on the orchard wall to watch for Mary's bright yellow Citroën, but a grey drizzle sent me upstairs to perch on the bedroom window-seat. Long John's van pulled up outside The Ship. It was unusual for the semi-recluse to be seen in the village two days running and when I saw Rabbit and the silk-suited gentleman hurry, with bent heads, from the taproom door to join him, I knew something was afoot.

The two vehicles passed each other with much honking and waving. Mary pulled up to the bottom of the washfold and I hurried down to greet her.

'You ought to have this bit done.' She waved her hand at the rough track and sent a gathering of bangles leaping up her arm and back. Her yellow shoes were freshly painted and her yellow two piece was pressed to a military sharpness. Her hat, a saffron cloche, had a bunch of cloth primroses arched elegantly over one ear and at the throat of her lemon polo-neck sweater was a huge amethyst brooch. I took the small parcel from her and held a citrine gloved hand as she picked her way up the rain-rutted track.

'You ought to have this done. Isn't that Ted fellow on the council?' My answer was drowned by two shrieking children who hurled themselves, coats flying, out of the shop door to fling their arms around their ample Aunt Mary. 'Keep that parcel away from them till after lunch,' she joked. 'I don't want their mother after me with the yard brush.'

'Fat rascals,' the children called in unison. 'They are, aren't they?'

I lifted the box higher than the four clutching hands and called to them to wipe their feet. When Mary comes to lunch rules are broken. Dogs are fed from the table; the cat pokes a wide eyed face from between Mary's bangled arms and dips its head gracefully to take a titbit from her; the children spread elbows on the table, crowd near to their adopted aunt and stab at their food with a fork.

The pie was a good one. I plied the gravy jug over my plate and watched the rich brown rivulets course between steaming meat and potato and wash an orange boulder of carrot down into a pool whose surface glittered with tiny opals of fat. Let them chatter, I thought, looking around the table as I discarded my knife and refilled my wine glass.

It's no use talking seriously to Canary Mary until the children have had her for an hour so I reached the bottle of wine from the dresser and took advantage of the anarchy by having a third glass. We do not normally have wine with lunch but when Mary comes I'm in need of a little support.

The fat rascals were heated and buttered under the big woman's supervision. Peter, his hands swathed in a towel, swung open the oven door for Mary to sniff and prod at the brown lumps of pastry, and on receiving the go-ahead from the fat-rascal expert he grunted and heaved the hot oven-plate on to the table, Vicky pushing her cutting board under the sizzling metal just in time to save the bleached pine.

Mary had nothing for me; no little treasures in her car for us to haggle over when the chairs were put round the fire for coffee. I lit my pipe and as a concession to our guest, kept my slippers on as my feet found their accustomed spot on the hearth tin.

'Nothing doing Mary? No exciting finds?'

She shrugged her broad shoulders. 'No, things are quiet for

the time of the year.' She looked at her coffee for a long time then gave a little giggle and turned to me with a gleeful look. 'You know those medals I got stuck with? I had a little idea. When you really looked at them they did look a bit new. So I buried them in rabbit droppings for a few weeks and they've improved.' As she leaned towards me the gleeful look turned to a full-faced laugh. 'You should see them now.' Her big bosom heaved as the laughter welled up in her. 'They'll be in the next auction. Pity they're not the Chinese Order of the Ten Million Lilies or something like that – then you could have bought them for your Otto.'

Vicky sponged the spilt coffee from a yellow knee and play-fully dabbed Mary's nose with the cloth. 'How can I bring these kids up right with you two around? Dung-aged medals and last cannonballs fired at Waterloo. What next?'

Sally passed her Aunt Mary another cup of coffee and when she had wiped the laughter tears from her eyes, Mary searched through her handbag and brought out a brown paper bag which she opened and held under her nose. 'Gor, they look authentic now but they don't half pong.'

Peter was up on her knee and reaching for the bag. 'Let's look Aunty.' His serious look turned to a guffaw as he took the bag and peered into it. 'They're lemon drops,' he said in a slow loud voice. Mary threw back her head and sent the coffee spilling once more into the saucer.

'Aunt Mary,' Sally said with mock severity, 'you get worser and worser.'

My pipe was going well, making Sally and Peter wave angry hands into the air to disperse the blue fug which hung around the fireplace, for they were being lectured by Miss Wells on the evils of smoking.

164

Vicky screwed her eyes against the smoke. 'You really ought to smoke that thing outside, it's terrible.'

I broke off a piece of fat rascal, pulled on my Wellingtons and went out into the garden to find all the ducks plucking the tops off the onions. The dogs, in pursuit of some small animal that had wriggled under the chicken netting, had left a hole and the entire flock of ducks had waddled through.

Mouth stuffed with pastry I hissed, cursed and shooed Aylesburys, khaki Campbells and Muscovies back through the fence but not before every onion had been cropped to the bulb.

Ted's red face appeared over the wall.

'Look at this! Every damned onion,' I said with some bitterness.

The WLA on everything pondered for a while, then wagged a finger thoughtfully. 'They might grow again, an' then they might not.'

Vicky, the children and Canary Mary lined the fence and surveyed the damage. 'I'll wring their damned necks,' I threatened. Over 200 plants, calculated to make us self-sufficient in onions, ruined.

Mary drew a deep breath and sighed. 'Never mind love. You won't have to season the ducks when you cook them, they've done it themselves.'

We watched Ted climb the path slowly. He had recently had his plaster off and walked with the aid of a heavy stick, groaning slightly as he thumped it into the hillside. Under his left arm he carried a shotgun and tethered to his belt on a long piece of billy band was the ginger sheep cur.

Canary Mary wiped a piece of butter from the corner of her mouth and pointed to him. 'He's the one that's on the council. Get him to have that road seen to, it's a disgrace.'

'He wants to Mary,' I told her. 'It's the Colonel that thwarts him, says the village is getting too twee.' Ted and the dog disappeared through a green bristle of gorse.

Vicky climbed up on the gate. 'He shouldn't be shooting, he only had the plaster off yesterday.'

'He isn't shooting really, just the dog,' I told her.

Canary Mary's jaw dropped open. 'You mean he's going to shoot that dog?'

Vicky clicked her tongue and the children stared at me with blank faces.

'Aye, it's no good, won't stand to the sheep. We asked you if you wanted it,' I said turning to Mary.

She blew down her nose and flung her arm out. 'Get after him!' she shouted, 'don't let him kill it. You never said it was such a lovely colour.' Before I could move, her finger stabbed me in the chest. 'Go on!' she screamed. 'Run!'

The children were first over the wall, but I caught up to them before they reached the patch of gorse. My lungs were bursting as I breasted the hill and saw Ted tying the dog to a stump. The back of my throat was raw and my strangled cry of 'no!' came too late as Ted flicked the gun closed and put the muzzle to the dog's head. I was a 100 yards away but I distinctly heard the click. I shrieked. Not a discernible word, just a panic-induced shriek. Ted looked around and I waved my hands in front of me. 'No! No!' I cried between pants.

The children ran past me as I staggered through the wet grass. 'No! no!' they shouted in unison. 'Aunty Mary wants it.'

Ted untied the string and handed it to Peter. The children sank to their knees and put their arms around the dog which licked their faces. Ted broke his gun open and took out the dud cartridge. 'Them shells you gave me. I don't know how old they are, but one in three is a dud 'un.' He threw the cartridge to the ground in disgust. I picked it up and put it in my pocket and followed the laughing, skipping children and the dog down the hill.

'I asked you if anybody wanted it,' Ted shouted after us.

The dog was cuddled, patted, kissed and fed, then Mary knelt on the grass and hugged it. 'You're coming to live with Aunty Mary, Amber and Topaz. You're a lovely, lovely dog. I didn't know you were such a lovely dog.' We formed a circle around the dog, smiling down at it and telling each other what a near thing it had been.

Mim tottered into the yard, her arms folded across her thin chest. 'Here, don't you ever open this bleedin' shop?' We told her about the dog, how we had saved it in the nick of time.

'Lor,' she said, bending over and patting the dog, 'you were in a pickle weren't you?' Her friendly face turned to Canary Mary. ''Ere that's a good name for it – Pickle. Yer want to call it Pickle.'

Sally clasped the dog and dropped her forehead on to one ear. 'Pickle, do you hear? That's your name now.'

Canary Mary smiled weakly at the thin woman and eyed her from top to toe. 'Yes, rather appropriate,' she said slowly. There was no conviction in her voice but the children laughed and subjected the dog to another flurry of hugs.

Mim pointed a long fingernail at me but looked at Vicky. 'Yesterday, I went in the shop and there he is fast asleep. I could a' been away with the bleedin' lot.' Vicky's hard look reminded me that the goat needed cleaning out so I threw the dud cartridge into the beck and went to look for a shovel.

Vicky opened the shop for Mim as Mary and the children

167

shepherded the dog into the kitchen. There were fat rascals still in the oven.

Mim is, as a lot of women are, addicted to jewellery. She tried every ring we had on her thin fingers, held every brooch against her thin chest. 'If that husband of mine can waste his money on cards, Mim can have a bit of flash for her fingers. What do you think duck?'

Vicky sold her two rings and was in a far happier frame of mind when I crept back into the kitchen. The dog was still the centre of attention. Our spaniels had been ousted into the yard but the cat sat on the milking stool yawning and ignoring the goings-on.

Mim stood at the pub steps and showed off her new rings to Charlie and Ethel. 'Who's the ball of sunshine?' she asked, pointing across the green as we escorted Canary Mary and the dog back to her car.

'Put the top down for me dear,' Mary said as she stubbed her broad feet into the track. 'This is deplorable.' I rolled the canvas hood back and held open the car door. Pickle was excited, he padded to and fro looking up at the seat before making a leap and landing on Canary Mary, who shrieked with laughter as the dog licked the cloth primroses on her hat.

'Pickle! Pickle, behave,' called the children.

Mary looked across at Mim and then back at us, her mouth twisted into a wry smile. 'I've been thinking about the dog's name. Pickle's a bit common. I'm going to call him Piccalilli!'

Chapter 14

It was a drizzly cold morning for the first of July. Mucky Marion tied a string from the hood of the pram to its handle and draped a sheet of plastic over it. She had some good quiches and a black forest gâteau in it that wouldn't do to get wet and, tucked in between were two old shoe-boxes.

'Here!' she called, handing the boxes through the shop door. ''Av a look at these and see if there's owt worth owt. I'll have to get over there, I'm late. Ethel'll be doin' her nut.'

I put the boxes on the counter and looked at the labels stuck on the ends. Women's shoes, broad and flat heeled with little fussy bows of the 1930s on them.

Well Marion, I thought, the boxes are genuine enough, and, when I laid the pieces of jewellery out on the green baize cloth, so was my delight. There were several ladies' fob watches, their delicate enamel dials sprinkled with flowers; rings galore and bangles and beads enough to equip a whole troupe of belly dancers. Some of the jewellery was bazaar stuff, flashy and poor quality, but there were some nice jade brooches, a couple of good gold bracelets and a beautiful snake ring with ruby eyes and a hollow skull head that flipped open. A poison ring, bringing into my tiny Dales shop on that damp grey morning a little touch of the exotic East.

I weighed gold and silver, tested bangle and bead and laid them across the counter in four long lines. There was one particular ring I kept returning to, a large table-cut diamond set in fourteen carat gold. A little yellow but still impressive. Several times I screwed in my eye glass and lifted the ring to the light: it was flawed, and so, difficult to value. Putting it aside I made a long list of all the other jewellery and wrote an approximate market value against each item. Marion had quite a lot of money in those two shoe-boxes, well over two thousand pounds.

''Ell fire! Are you sure?'

'Sure as eggs Marion and that doesn't include this.' I dropped the diamond ring on to the top box and passed them to her.

'It's flawed. A big impressive diamond in fourteen carat, so it's been mounted on the Continent, but it's flawed. Difficult to value, but worth quite a bit.'

Marion shoved her dogs out of the doorway. 'Come in, come in.'

The kitchen was stifling hot. Two vintage electric ovens, their mottled-green enamel losing a battle with creeping brown staining, stood on legs against the wall. A good fire burned in the old-fashioned grate and before it lay three ranks of loaf tins, their dough rising nicely, like little white buttocks. On the tables and chairs and on a low dresser were wire trays filled with buns and cakes. The dogs milled around our legs then flew under the table as a dark brown monkey leapt from the airing cupboard and landed neatly on the table between a black forest gâteau and a cream sponge.

Marion laughed and poked a finger at the dogs. 'They bugger off under there 'cos he pulls their ears. Don't yer, yer little sod?'

The monkey stood on its back legs and looked at me with tiny jet eyes. 'I'd better have him,' Marion laughed, ''cos if he don't like yer he'll bite yer. Won't you, you little bugger?' She lifted the monkey off the table and cradled it under her arm. It reached out a tiny black hand and took the diamond ring. 'He likes owt that glistens, don't yer?' The monkey wriggled free and bounded from table to chair then back to its den clutching the ring to its little chest.

'Marion, that ring's worth a couple of hundred quid.'

'Aw, it'll be all right, he never loses owt, stores it away up there he does.' She put her mittened hands on to her hips and smiled up at the monkey. 'There's them in the village says he shits in the sugar, but he don't. Come here, I'll show yer where he shits.' She pulled me to the corner between the fireplace and the dresser and pointed to a loaf tin. 'There, I puts a bit of sand in and he shits in there. See he's been this mornin'.'

'Very hygienic Marion.'

She smiled down at the monkey faeces then up at me. 'Yes, that's it – hygienic.'

The kitchen was oppressively hot, so I edged to the door and opened it. 'Get that ring off him, Marion, and hide that other stuff away.'

''Ell, where can I put it?' she muttered, pinching her lower lip between a grubby forefinger and a black rimmed thumbnail. ''Ow much do I owe yer?'

'It's OK Marion, my pleasure.' I put my head out of the door and drank in cool fresh air.

'Just a minute,' Marion called, filling a brown paper bag from one of the trays. 'Here, take them bairns of yours a few buns.'

Later, I crumpled the buns over the chick coup. The broody hen clucked and half spread her wings as the chicks cheeped excitedly and dashed through the grass, pink and yellow icing hanging from their beaks.

Saturday night the children were invited to Tracy Martin's birthday party. 'Could they stay until ten o'clock?' Tracy pleaded. It'll give Vicky and me a chance to go out together I thought as I agreed and ten o'clock on a bright summer's night didn't seem at all late. We both knew that they had started sneaking out of bed on warm summer evenings and sitting in the landing window, where they wriggled their toes, whispered, giggled and watched the village go to bed.

We did not mind as long as it wasn't overdone. We would listen for the creak of the floorboards as they tiptoed back to their bedrooms unaware that their secret and delicious vigil had been monitored by the grandfather clock.

The Ship was full. Charlie had propped open the door and the hubbub and light spilled out on to the village green to greet us. Village throats were dry and dusty from gardening and farming or just sitting and watching the world go by.

The taproom was, for tonight, forbidden territory. We would form part of the smart set – washed and shaved with pressed trousers and neat tie. It was the lounge for us; polite conversation, decorous behaviour, no raucous laughter, no *risqué* jokes.

The visitors tend to favour the tables furthest from the bar. It's either the Colonel's silent back or the way Charlie stands, arms folded, staring at his beams full of horsebrasses, that drives them from the area where the lights are slightly brighter and the carpet a little more worn. They gaze around at the polished brasses and wonder at the horned hare that bares its fierce-looking teeth from over the fireplace.

Charlie keeps us informed of the increasing value of the taxidermist's joke; the man from Birmingham's bid of fifty pounds has been topped by Cockney Joe's. 'Offered seventy-five for it,' says Charlie rolling his eyes.

To show our status as villagers we shuffled our feet on the worn carpet, drinks held close to our chests, until Mim called us from a corner table. She was sitting with Mucky Marion and laid in front of her was my valuation list. 'This tourmaline and ruby, is it really worth forty quid? It looks bugger all to me,' she said, holding out the ring, rubbing it between a forefinger and thumb so the light caught the stones. Mucky Marion's mittened hands were spread over a shoe-box and trapped between two of her fingers was an empty wine glass.

'What you having Marion?' I asked.

Mim never took her eyes off the ring. 'Gin and tonics luv, that's what we're on.' Marion smiled.

Mim bought the next round and, before I could intervene, the round after that. 'Shuv it on the bill duck,' she called to Charlie, as she weaved through the crowd swaying the cluster of glasses in front of her. 'Now, duck, about this ring. Is that an insurance valuation or what?'

'It's "or what",' I told her. 'Basic market value, put another twenty quid on for insurance.'

She blew down her well-formed nose and gave the ring

back to Marion. 'Let's have a look at that emerald cluster again.'

Marion doffed a mitten and brought out the emerald ring.

Mim curled a well-defined lip. 'Emeralds is a bit cold, I'm rubies and diamonds meself.'

Marion scrubbed off the other mitten. 'Here's a diamond for you, luv.' She held out a grubby hand.

The diamond caught the light and splintered it into a hundred intense shards making Mim sigh, 'Oh! That's nice, that is nice.'

Marion grinned and hunched her shoulders. 'It's like me luv, impressive but flawed.'

Mim swivelled the ring on to a bony finger and held her hand out. 'It's nice.'

Marion pulled on her mittens. 'Damned monkey was off with it, but I found it this morning in his loaf tin.'

Mim sighed again. 'How much duck?'

'Not for sale that.' Marion held out her hand for the ring. 'You can buy owt else, but I'm keeping that, 'cos it was given to my mother by an Indian prince, that was.'

There are times, usually in the depths of winter, when talk dies away in the taproom and someone will start the old game of superlatives. 'Who is the tightest man in the dale?' Or if we feel a little capricious, 'Who is the bonniest woman in the dale?' But never, 'Who is the biggest liar in the dale?' We all know it's Marion.

She worked the ring under a mitten and drained her glass. 'Royal blood in these veins, luv.'

Mim arched her brows and without a word pushed the empty glasses in front of me but before I could get up the thick-set man in the silk suit placed a hand on my shoulder. 'I'll get these.'

Mim looked up briefly. 'This is my Joe, or at least I think it is. Been that long since I bleedin' seen him.'

Joe smiled weakly. 'When you're on a lucky run you have to stick with it – you know that, Mim.'

'Make 'em doubles then, if you're bleedin' lucky.'

Joe grunted and spread pudgy fingers to gather up the glasses.

Marion put her shoe-box on the floor between her feet and leaned forward. 'Born in India I was, the mystical East. My mum – international beauty she was.' She paused for effect and screwed her mouth up. 'My mum was the confidante of kings and presidents, she was so beautiful. Ran off to India when she was a young girl with this maharaja, an' that's when I was born, into a palace with servants.' A mittened hand closed around a full glass. She sipped delicately, as becomes one born in splendour. 'Well this maharaja wanted to marry my mum, but she says no. "It won't do Ali," she tells him, "we being of different hues." You see things was different then,' she gave Mim a coy look and then nodded her head emphatically, 'fifty year ago.'

Mim nodded back, her crimson mouth was wide open and her fine eyes stared fixedly into Marion's royal but rheumy ones. 'Your mum wouldn't marry him?'

'No, she could have been a maharajaress if she'd wanted to. Anyway he gives her this ring. "Beautiful but flawed," my mum used to say. Now it's mine and I wouldn't sell it for owt. But the other stuff, luv, you can buy any of that. I haven't rested since he told me how much they was worth. I've hidden 'em 'ere, I've hidden 'em there.'

Mim turned to me sharply. 'How much is that diamond worth then?'

'Well!' I said slowly, 'neglecting its royal origins and taking into account this flaw, it's very difficult to say, but some hundreds.'

Mim's elegant mouth turned down. 'A bit vague, some hundreds, thought you was a bleedin' expert.'

'It's the flaw Mim. It wants a real qualified gemologist to look at it. The diamond is so big it may be possible to cut the flaw out and still have an impressive stone. I don't know.'

'No! No! Nobody's cuttin' the flaw out. It's flaws as makes characters.' Marion slapped her hands on her thighs, laughed, and poked a finger at Mim's gold bolero jacket. 'Don't tell me you ain't got no flaw.'

Mim held her empty glass out towards me. 'Yer, I got a flaw. I married one.' Joe had crept back to the taproom and the card game so I reluctantly pushed my way through to the bar.

When I got back to the table Vicky and Mim had drawn their stools nearer to Marion. ' . . . twenty-five elephants.'

'Elephants? What about elephants?' I asked.

Marion's mitten snaked out and captured another double gin and tonic. 'Just tellin' 'em about my fifteenth birthday party.'

Mim reached out absent-mindedly for her glass and clasped it in heavily ringed fingers. 'An' this other maharaja, he wanted your mother to marry him, and he gave your mother the opal brooch.'

'S'right Mim, they all wanted to marry her. Twenty-five maharajas all on elephants.' Marion hiccoughed. 'All come to propose on the same day. India had never seen the like.' There were two rapid hiccoughs. 'The viceroy, he was a nice chap, he advised my mum to leave India. "You'll be the cause of a civil war Blanche if you stay here," he told her.'

Marion leaned forward and twirled her now empty glass.

176

'She was so beautiful you see. An international beauty.' The women leaned back and smiled at each other and Marion, after a deep breath, continued with her tale. 'Hot season off to Ootacamund we went, Snooty Ooty we called it. Glorious it was, Balls, Balls, Balls.'

I dumped the glasses on the table and left three ladies gowned and tiaraed, genteelly fanning away the heat of an Indian night.

The taproom was full. A blue haze drifted slowly to the burnt sienna ceiling, dominoes clattered on the linoleum-topped tables and conversation was permeated with the clunk of glass on table.

Cockney Joe, Long John and Rabbit sat at a corner table, cards in hand and, judging by the piles of money laid before them, it was a serious game. No one looked up as I leaned against the fireplace and slid my glass on to the mantelpiece. Three set faces stared at the cards. Cockney Joe's pile of money was appreciably larger than the other two's. So much so that several coins had fallen to the floor and lay there untouched.

Long John held out his empty glass. 'See to it for us, would you?' It looked like I was going to spend my night off waiting on other people. I gathered the three pint glasses and tapped on the serving hatch and watched Charlie fill them to overflowing.

'How's it going?' I asked.

'Rabbit's in deep. Too deep if you ask me,' the landlord whispered. Rabbit took his drink without a word, his eyes were riveted on to his cards and a big horny thumb stroked the jack of diamonds.

Cockney Joe looked at his two fellow players, then up at me. 'All right in there is she?'

I told him she was OK. 'Chewing the dust of India, but OK.'

Joe grinned. 'We'll not be late tonight will we lads? It's the hunt tomorrow. Early start, up with the larks.'

'Hunt?' I asked. 'What hunt?'

'Yep, me and the lads here have a licence to take a horned hare.'

'Licence?'

'Yep. Rabbit here got it,' he said, turning his attention back to his hand.

'You, er, got the licence Rabbit?' I enquired gently.

Rabbit sucked his teeth and threw the jack into the centre of the table. 'Aye, it's at home in me safe. You know what them licences cost.'

He gave me a long steady look which was meant to preclude any further questioning, but fortified as I was with a pint or two and being of an inquisitive nature I persisted. 'Where did you get this licence from?'

Rabbit grunted as Cockney Joe threw down a queen and curved his arm around the pot. Joe was happy; he called to Charlie through the serving hatch, 'Give our Mim what she wants and four more here when you've got time.'

Long John threw his cards down and drained his glass, thumping it back on to the table with what I thought was unnecessary force. 'We got it from the estate office, where else?'

Joe tapped his feet and shuffled his cards. 'They don't issue many. Cost me an arm and a leg it did.'

A horned hare hunt; an experience, I thought. 'Would it be all right if I tagged along?'

Rabbit and Long John snapped back in synchronised refusal. 'No!'

'The licence is for two dogs, huntsman, whipper-in and one follower. Ought else will disturb the grouse,' Joe explained.

To the obvious discomfort of the huntsman and whipper-in, I pulled a stool up to the table. 'Not many horned hare about now.'

'No!' Rabbit threw down a card and glared at me.

'Do you think they've been overhunted?' Another card slapped on to the table.

'Aye.'

'They say they run like skoprils.'

'Some do.'

'Is it just the jacks that are horned?'

'Aye.'

'By, lads, I wish I were going with you.'

Long John reached into his coat pocket and brought out an innocent looking bottle and passed it to me. 'Here, have a drink and shut up.'

Joe beamed around the table. 'Something to show the blokes when I get back to the smoke – a horned hare. I've just the place for it, 'cos we have this big random-stone fireplace with little holes in it for Mim's brassware. It'll look a treat between 'er leaping 'orse and 'er peacock with red eyes.'

I poured a measure of Swaledale Lightning into my beer. 'You're privileged Joe, it's not easy to get a licence.'

Rabbit ground his teeth. 'Rare as rocking horse shit,' he grunted.

Joe beamed around again. 'Cost an arm and a leg – but worth it.' He laid his cards on the table with a flourish. Rabbit and Long John shook their heads and reached, simultaneously, for the bottle.

*

Mim had moved closer to Mucky Marion and with her elbows on the table she bent her head attentively towards the old woman. Vicky sat on her hands and rocked her stool; she was laughing a quiet lip-biting laugh as I sat down beside her.

Marion straightened her back and waved a mitten in an elegant way. 'Up at Ooty we was waited on hand and foot, liveried servants to do our all. Me and my mum, we danced every night away in glorious abandon till the sun came up over the Blue Hills.' Marion gave me a nod and the slightest of smiles. 'Just telling 'em about the Balls at Ooty – what a time we had, me and my mum.'

I smiled back at her. 'It must have been nice Marion.'

'It was lovely, all them officers in uniform, starlight nights, soft scented breezes, an' as much booze as you could 'andle.' She pushed another empty glass towards me. The bar was quieter now, so luckily I was back at the table before the train left for Madras. 'Never had to lift a finger. Mind you, the journey back to the plains made you drag yer arse a bit, it was so bloody 'ot.'

Mim massaged cigarettes and a gold lighter out of her bag. Marion blew a cloud of smoke over the table as Mim snapped the lighter shut. 'Thank yer, luv,' she said, wrinkling her eyes. She put her feet up on an empty buffet and clacked them together, studiously avoiding where the rugby socks swelled through the bunion holes. ''Ad to come back to England to finish my education, yer see. Lor, there was a wailing and a lamentin' when it got abroad that me and mum was leavin' for 'ome. A constant stream of officers and dignitaries beggin' mum to stay. "No!" says me mum. "The girl's got royal blood in her veins and heducation's very important when you got royal blood."'

Mim tapped Marion's arm. 'What about your dad, didn't he want you to stay?'

Marion blew smoke down her nose and scrubbed a black fingernail into her hair. 'Didn't I tell yer? He got killed. Naffin' tiger ate 'im just afore he could make a settlement on me and me mum.'

Vicky turned towards me and, biting her knuckles, shook with mirth. Mim was wide-eyed. 'Poor sod.'

'Yer, 'e was a fine man. He'd 'ave made an 'ell of a settlement on us if he'd 'ave lived. Well, you've only to look at the ring, ain't yer. He was no tight-arse, the old maharaja.' Mim stubbed out her cigarette vigorously and reached out and took Marion's mittened hand.

''Ere, let's 'ave another look.' The ring flashed its ice-sharp fire again. 'Ooh! It's gorgeous.'

Marion put her head back and stared up at the beams. 'The quayside was lined with officers and dignitaries when me and mum sailed. Strong men cried, an' women sobbed. An' as for maharajas, there was every bleedin' maharaja in India on that quayside. Some 'ad even put little black bands around their jewelled turbans they was that bleedin' sad. The ship 'ooted all ashore and what do yer think?' She sighed heavily and the empty glass dropped into her lap. 'Mr Gandhi 'imself comes running up the gangplank and gives mum a big hug. I could see tears behind them little funny glasses he used to wear. "Blanche!" he said, his voice tremulous with emotion, "India won't be the same without yer."'

Vicky and Mim each had an arm gripped by mittened hands.

'It was on the voyage home the diamond got flawed. 'Cos it wasn't flawed when the mara ... marar ... me dad gave it to

181

me mum. We was a couple of days out when me mum finds out that one of the stokers is an old pal of hers. Chalky White, a pal from her Stepney days, when she had a grace and favour residence there.'

'Stepney!' Mim clapped her free hand to her forehead. 'Would yer bleedin' believe it. Joe's garage is in Stepney.'

Marion took a long drink, then went back to her tale. 'She was not a snob, me mum, so down she went to see Chalky. Stiflin' hot down there, so she takes off the ring and puts it on a steam pipe for safe keepin'. Didn't want it to drop off her finger an' into them bilges see. Well, her and Chalky's having a good old chin-wag when the diamond explodes, through the heat you see. It went with a rare old crack, sent a shudder through the entire ship. Down the steps comes the captain, his face all ashen and his white gloves fluttering about like a pair of fantail pigeons. "What was that Chalky, 'ave we 'it a hiceberg?" Me old mum always used to laugh when she told this bit. "Hiceberg! Hiceberg! In the middle of the Hindian Hocean," she says. The captain started to laugh, and Chalky started to laugh, and soon me old mum is laughing away too. They laughs till the sweat dripped off their chins. Then the captain slaps his thigh an' says, "Blanche, I got a spare chair at me table, come and plonk yer arse amongst the gentry, where it belongs."'

Marion leaned forward and lowered her voice. '"An' bring yer lovely daughter with yer, we can all utch up a bit." They was 'alfway up the stairs when the captain turned and shouted to Chalky. '"Ere, Chalky, put a bit o' laggin' round that pipe, old son, we can't have himportant passengers gettin' flaws in their jewellery. Not on the Hempress of Hindia, we can't."' Marion's eyes closed and her head dropped on to her chest.

The cool night air did little to revive her. She clutched her shoe-box of treasures to her chest as I walked her back and forth in the pub garden, her plimsolled feet sodden with an early dew stubbing amongst the tussocky grass.

Vicky hurried away to fetch the children as I laid Marion and the shoe-box in her pram.

'Thank yer, Captain,' she said softly. I was promoted every ten yards. It was major as I crossed the green, colonel at the washfold and as I lined up the pram to negotiate her narrow gritstone gateposts she gave a low burbling chuckle. ''Ere we go, General, through the gateway to India.' A mitten reached up and pulled at the overhanging orange blossom. 'Hunder the triumphal harch. Me an' mum, hinternational beauties.'

The dogs barked furiously as I swung open the kitchen door, the caged birds fluttered and the monkey peeked nervously from its den. 'Come in for a choka-peg yer Hexellency,' mumbled the international beauty as I laid her in an armchair and with averted face and wrinkled nose pulled off her soggy and stinking plimsolls. The toes that had twinkled across the French-chalked floors of Ooty wriggled with pleasure.

'That's nice, yer Royal 'ighness, that's nice.'

I put Marion's jewel box into the chair with her and went to fetch the dogs out of the garden.

When I got back to the kitchen the monkey had riffled the box and was squatting over his loaf tin, a look of deep concentration wrinkling his face, one tiny black hand gripping the rolled edge of the tin in support as the other clutched a prince's gift to his little hairy chest.

Marion opened one eye. 'Give us a kiss, your Majesty,' she sighed. Nobility has its obligations and royalty its duties. I took

183

a deep breath and leaning over kissed her lightly on her forehead.

She smiled, turned on her side, yawned, and tucked her mittened hands under her chin. Her voice was sleepy and gentle and far away.

'Us hinternational beauties is 'allus gettin' kissed.'

Chapter 15

'That's nice, that's nice.' Jack the Pat looked thoughtful. He'd patted all the furniture in the shop with a whispered 'that's nice', but for some reason the little oak side-table got two pats and a double rating. 'Nothing in my line? Nothing tucked away?' he asked.

Jack specialises in inlaid furniture: work tables, *bijouterie* tables. 'Anything that'll make a woman sigh,' he'd told us with a wink.

Jack is well-off; well-off enough for Fatty Batty to grudgingly admit that 'he isn't short of a bob or two'. He lives with his widowed mother and several cats in a delightful mews cottage.

Across a flagged yard fringed with flower-packed stone troughs, a converted coach-house is home to Jack's extensive stock. The best pieces are kept upstairs in the old hay loft, now fitted with a large picture window which gives Jack's customers a superb view of Addlebrough. The loft is draped, lighted and furnished in the manner of a nineteenth-century bordello of the better type. Heavy plush curtains track across the massive window at the push of a button; romantic music emanates from somewhere in the region of a life-size statue of Apollo; and a square niche, that in prosaic times housed the stable boy's dartboard, now houses a well-stocked drinks cabinet.

Jack's mother never ventures into the coach-house. 'He knows his business and is best left alone,' she tells her friends at the bridge club. The bordello cum saleroom is cleaned by a taciturn woman from up the dale who twice a week leans her bicycle against the trough full of miniature Cupressus and mounts the stairs slowly in a heavy footed way; for Jack has been known to effect a sale early in the day. She dusts and vacuums and polishes and as she gathers the empty bottle and wine glasses and plumps up the flattened cushions on the Regency sofa she runs her eye over the stock to see which piece is missing. 'Ah, the little inlaid box.' A blonde hair from one of the Berlin wool work cushions is held to the window and smiled at. Must be that little blonde from Lalbeck. A handful of summers past her prime, a meagrely paid job as a seamstress and yet she has one of the finest collections of inlaid work-boxes in England. Our cleaning lady resumes work, for she is very thorough, but there is just the hint of a smile about her rat-trap mouth as she plies the yellow duster.

There are no price tickets on Jack's stock. The turn of the leg that mounts the stairs and the rapport engendered on the Regency sofa, as, glass in hand, he and his customer discuss the place in question, can have a radical effect on the asking price.

Jack's mother worries about him working so hard. 'Out delivering until two o'clock this morning. Came in absolutely fagged out,' she tells the envious postman.

Jack is a puzzle to Canary Mary on two counts. She cannot

understand why he practically gives away some pieces of furniture and 'Why,' she asks the Ring, 'has he never married when he is such a good-looking man?'

The Ring give each other knowing looks and Elly clicks his teeth. 'Got it made has Jack the Pat, got it made.'

The man who had it made stepped back from the side-table and tilted his handsome head. 'You ought to polish it, call it a lowboy instead of a side-table and put the price up fifty quid.' He brushed a speck from his blazer and shot his cuffs. 'Well I'll have to be off, I have a customer coming to look at a rather nice little *bonheur du jour.*'

Jack's advice echoed, to a large degree, that I had got from Colin, so I cleared the top of the lowboy and set to with the beeswax. The best lowboys have cabriole legs and a good drawer arrangement. This one was from the Continent I suspected. It had one large drawer across its width, and plain tapered legs, but it was a good colour and half an hour's hard work resulted in a rewarding effect. The wood came to life under the polishing rag and a little metal polish made the pear-drop handles sparkle. I moved it into the centre of the shop and placed a Sheffield-plated inkwell on top of it.

Vicky fingered the new ticket. 'You've put the price up and called it a lowboy.'

'Psychology,' I beamed. 'The psychology of selling.'

'I suppose it is a lowboy. Could have done with some better legs.'

I scratched my chin and gazed at the horizon where Addlebrough shoved its grey hump into the sky. 'Yes, good legs can speed up a sale no end.'

*

Rabbit banged on the shop window and beckoned to me. 'Bit of stuff to sell,' he whispered, as I poked my head through the door. 'Bit of a crisis in the old financial department.'

After a simple alfresco lunch of cheese and bread in the orchard, I called the dogs and set off for Rabbit's cottage.

Cockney Joe was milking him dry. 'But it's an ill wind,' I mused as I stopped by the mill pond and watched the coot hack their way across the water. The hare hunt was supposed to retrieve the fortunes of the two card players; something had gone wrong.

Rabbit stood in front of the fireplace, his hands clasped behind his back. His baggy corduroys failed to hide his holey grey socks, and his vest, stained with beer and snuff, looped over their waistband between broad ex-army braces. There was a three day growth of silver stubble on his chin.

'I have money coming in 'cos there's some wallin' for the Colonel and a bit of draining to do.' He scrubbed his finger-nails into the stubble and pulled his lips back revealing his huge brown teeth. 'It's just gettin' round to 'em – fittin' 'em in like.'

I nodded in sympathy. Drinking, card playing and poaching are time-consuming occupations.

I sat in the armchair with its cushions stuffed with dogs' hair and worked my body into a fairly comfortable position.

'How did the hare hunt go?'

Rabbit snorted. 'Well enough.'

'Got one did you?'

He turned his back to me and took a horn snuff box out of the powder cupboard. ''Av yer come to look at this stuff or 'av yer come to gab?' he said in a gruff voice. I took the hint. Hare hunts weren't on the list of social chit-chat this afternoon. He

188

drew a thumbnail full of snuff up each nostril and blinked at me. 'Chair – 'ow much?'

'This one?' I said, slapping a greasy arm.

'No! No! Widgeon's chair.'

I was taken aback, for Rabbit had always sworn he wouldn't part with his grandfather's chair. 'That'll be the last thing that goes,' he'd said with vehemence, slapping the table hard enough to make the glasses rattle, when I once asked him about it in The Ship. It looked as if the crisis in the financial department had promoted it rapidly to first place.

'How much?' he grunted.

I knew instantly I was going to buy the chair and I knew I was going to keep it for myself, but looking at it closely it wasn't as good as I remembered. The cow horn stretcher was broken and the arms had been stiffened with metal plates and there was a lug missing from the splat. However, it was Widgeon's chair and in all probability it had never been out of the house in a hundred years. It was nicely worn, nicely patinated, and I wanted it.

Rabbit continued to scrub his chin, whilst I stared at the chair in silence. He was obviously agitated; the snuff came out again, this time to be blown into a khaki handkerchief the size of a small tablecloth. 'Thar' not saying much, doesn't thar want it?'

'Yes, it's all right. It's just the damage makes it – well –'

Rabbit pushed his lower lip out. 'There's folk in this village would give fifty quid for that chair.' I smiled to myself and thought there's folk in this village would give ninety quid for this chair.

'Rabbit,' I said, pulling myself out of the sunken armchair, 'I'm going to be fair with you. I'm going to give you as near your price as I can.'

189

Rabbit rocked back on his stockinged heels and re-tensioned his braces with his thumbs. 'Come on then let's be knowin'.'

I picked the chair up and turned it this way and that looking for woodworm and any other damage. Richard would repair the stretcher easily but the metal plating? Well it had lived with the chair so long, it was now part of it.

'Forty-five quid, best I can do.' I put the chair back in its place on the hooky rug and turned to stare at the rows of mounted heads that filled one wall of the room.

Rabbit released one thumb from his braces and scraped it audibly up his unshaven throat. 'Make it fifty.'

'Can't, too much repair wanted.'

'Split it wi' me then, forty-seven and a half quid.'

'Can't, I've come out with top whack first time round – as a favour.'

The scraping became faster then stopped. 'All right forty-five. It seems a shame it has to go, nice old chair that.'

'Anything else whilst I'm here?'

Rabbit looked thoughtful then wagged a finger at me. 'Come wi' me, there's summat out here might interest thee.' I followed him out to the garden through the lean-to pantry. The glass panes of its roof were bordered with verdigris and its floor of quarry tiles littered with the necessities of Rabbit's life. There were traps of every description: long nets, several draining spits, sticks dressed and sticks awaiting dressing, fishing rods and creels and an assortment of muddy boots and Wellingtons.

Above the draining board of the stone sink hung a huge headless hare.

Rabbit tried to shield it from my view and waved me past

him towards the open door, the dogs, escorted by Rabbit's yapping terriers, trotting after us into the garden.

'Thar' will like this, real old country piece.' Rabbit reached under the pine table that carried his ferret hutches and with much grunting and wheezing pulled a massive copper cheese kettle free of the strangling goose grass. He tipped it sideways spilling out on to the grass a tangled foetid mass of rabbit guts. 'Usually keep me ferret jock in it, but thee have a look over it. Grand cheese kettle that.' He plucked at his vest. 'I'll just pop in and put a jumper on, it's a bit nippy.'

The kettle was a good one. Over two foot wide with massive pan-head rivets down the side seam and a heavy blacksmithed steel handle, but it stank. Maggots crawled through a black ooze that clung to the bottom; rabbit entrails in various stages of decay were stuck to its sides and, unbelievably, it stunk even worse than the ferret cages.

Rabbit tucked the ex-army sweater into his trousers. 'It'll wash out. Damned good kettle – ought to be worth a bob or two.'

'If you clean it out and bring it up to the shop I'll give you forty-five quid for it.'

'Forty-five quid! I'll 'ave it up this afternoon. I looked at it the other day an' thought, ay, me old pal the antique man 'ud like this. Forty-five quid eh. Don't you worry my old pal, it'll be there this aft, clean as an egg. I know just how to get that gunge out of it.'

'Just get rid of the stink and the fisherman's friends, Rabbit.'

When we went back through the pantry the hare had gone, only a dark patch of dried blood on the draining board remained.

*

At the top of the lane I put the chair against the pinfold wall and sat awaiting the dogs who had put up a rabbit and had streaked off across the meadow in yelping pursuit. The sound of a healthy splash from the mill pond brought me to my feet.

Rabbit stood on the banking surrounded by his terriers holding in his hand a length of orange billy band which trailed out over the choppy water. In the centre of the pond, sinking slowly, was the cheese kettle. The man who was supposed to be good with ropes and knots wound in the billy band sadly and as the last pan-head rivet disappeared he hissed one heartfelt obscenity. It was a word I would hesitate to use but as I picked up my chair, now my ninety pound chair, and plodded home, it summed up my feelings exactly.

The headless hare and Rabbit's reluctance to discuss the hunt fired up my curiosity. What had happened?

Mim had bullied Cockney Joe into taking her up the dale. 'Here for three weeks complete rest – on doctor's orders mind – an' all he does is play bleedin' cards an' drink,' she'd told Charlie. 'Well, I'm gettin' that bleedin' car out an' he's takin' me off for the day.' So the white Mercedes had pulled out of the car park that morning, taking with it the only other potential source of information that was close at hand.

There was nothing for it, I would have to go and see Long John.

I knew how to handle his geese by now, so when they came honking and hissing in a wing stretched phalanx towards the van I was no more than a little perturbed. The secret is the steg: the dominant gander. Turn his head and the other outstretched necks become less confident. They waver, turn back on each other and save their pride with a chattering neck swaying that says, 'All right, but next time we'll have you!'

I waited confidently by the van door as the flock raced towards me. At the moment I should have charged the steg, shouting and arms flaying, it stumbled, rolled over and lay on its side waving its neck and honking loudly. The hissing gang ignored their leader's plight and bore down on me. I turned and fled to a horsedrawn hayrake which stood in the centre of the farmyard locked in the dried mud, suffering two bites on the thigh and one in the lower buttocks before I could scramble on to the rake. Stood on the iron seat, well out of reach of the hostile beaks, I rubbed the bitten places and took stock. Geese are fickle things. Soon they would tire of their tormenting and so I mentally selected objects which could give me sanctuary and I made a dash for the farmhouse, whose door stood wide open. However, the strange downfall of the steg and the flock's unpredictable action had left me doubting my knowledge of goose behaviour.

The blue Bedford van Long John was using had not joined the row of MOT failures and stood against the piggery, and on the grassy mound behind the farmhouse grazed Polly, Long John's pony. With both modes of transport at hand the eccentric bachelor could not be far away.

My shout brought a barely audible response. A further shout brought a more audible reply, 'Up here.' I looked around the yard turning precariously on my small platform.

Sticking through the barn roof, where a sheet had been torn off in the January gale, were a pair of large dirty feet. I selected new points of refuge and bounded from hayrake to the piggery wall, piggery wall to the muckheap and from the muckheap I climbed the straw bales in the Dutch barn, leaving a flapping noisy wave of white pecking at my heels.

Long John was laid on the top layer of bales, a folded army

greatcoat under his head and a bottle of Swaledale Lightning in his hand. He wiggled his big toes slowly and stared at the thick yellow nails. 'Just givin' 'em an airing,' he explained. 'They did some miles last night.'

It was hot under the corrugated tin roof. I stretched my legs and massaged my thighs where the geese had bitten.

'Buggers get you?'

'Yes they're keen. Can't understand it, the old steg just keeled over.'

Long John blew down his nose. 'Ah, he'll be pissed again! Did he get up?'

'Didn't see, too busy.'

'If he gets on his back I have to turn him over, otherwise he'd be there all day.'

I peered under a rafter. The steg was walking slowly down the yard, his head swaying close to the ground on a cranked neck and his web feet slapping slowly on the dried mud.

Long John turned sideways and peered with me. 'Aye! He's pissed.' He rolled back and adjusted his greatcoat. 'Found out where I tip me mash after I've 'stilled off. Crafty old bugger keeps the others off an' scoffs the lot 'imself. He'll be as radgy as arseholes tomorrow.'

There followed a few hearty sniffs, a gathering in the throat, then he parted his feet and sent a ball of spittle flying between them.

'Heard about the hunt?' he asked.

'No, Rabbit was a bit reticent.'

'Not surprised – bloody disaster.' He pointed to his wagging feet. 'Them buggers must 'ave done thirty mile over them fells last night.' His arm flung out and tracked around. 'Devil's Leap to Bear Park, on to Ewesghyll, back again to Devil's Leap. I'm absolutely knackered.' The arm returned and tucked itself under the head of black hair.

'Planned like a military operation. Nothing could go wrong, nothing, that is, until you bring Rabbit on to the scene. I organises the hare, fixes some horns on, gets Harry the under-keeper to write out a chitty saying we can hunt it, stamped with the Estate stamp all official-looking like it was.' Long John pulled the chitty out of his pocket and dropped it on to the bale beside me. 'All Rabbit had to do was hide the hare, lay a trail to it, bring a couple of terriers and then let them find it. I took a couple of bottles of Lightning to fortify Joe and make it so he was not too inquisitive when we found the hare.' His brown eyes swivelled towards me. 'So as he wouldn't be asking too many questions like. About how come it's been dead two days an' is as stiff as a board.' Another gob of spittle described a flat inverted catenary between his feet.

'Then what happens? Rabbit, my accomplice, my thick-as-pig-shit accomplice, brings two terriers so old they couldn't smell a dead rat up a drainpipe and, piece de la bloody resistance, forgets where he's hidden the bloody hare. Meanwhile Joe's been at the bottle and is stoned. So we leave him sitting against a rock whilst we finds the hare.'

Long John folded his arms across his chest. 'Well! By the time we'd found the hare we'd lost Joe. Three o'clock this morning we found him. Fast asleep, sodden with dew, an' him supposed to be convalescing. I wonder if yon thick sod has remembered to take the head down to Totty's to be done right, 'cos I just shaved two patches an' stuck the horns on wi' glue.'

I told him of the headless hare hanging over Rabbit's draining board.

Long John grunted. 'Bound to get something right sometime

I suppose – law of averages.' He closed his eyes and shuffled his body.

'There's a Victorian fender in the stable, I pulled it down to polish and I can't seem to get it back right. Twenty quid if it's any good to you.' His chest began to rise and fall gently and his beard wagged as he chewed and sighed.

I picked up the hunt permit and folding it carefully put it in my shirt pocket and leapt down the bales to the farmyard, looking around warily for the geese. The steg staggered down the slope to the beck, his flock following him noisily.

As I pushed open the stable door Long John's head appeared where his feet had been. 'Oi! There's a fox hung in the pantry, take it across to Charlie for me – an' there's a bottle on the shelf for you.'

The fender was a good one. Its ends should have swept up to make rests for fire irons and in the centre should have been a swagged cartouche, but a hard night on the fells and recourse to an illicit still do not make for sound fender assembling. The curved end pieces were mounted back to back in the centre of the fender and the cartouche was bolted to one side where an urn-shaped finial was missing. I found the errant finial below John's polishing machine, checked that everything else was there and carried the fender out to the van.

Vicky scratched her head. 'Shouldn't they be . . . ?' She pointed to the central tangle of curved brass then her forefingers described a semi-circle.

'Yes and this bit?' I curved my hand elaborately through the air and brought it to rest on the cartouche.

'Ah,' she laughed, 'that goes in the middle.'

'Go to the top of the class in fender assembly.'

'Was it dear?' she asked.

'It cost me twenty pound and three goose bites,' I replied rubbing a bruised buttock.

Peter fetched a spanner and started taking the fender to pieces, working feverishly; he wanted to show us grown-ups that he too could work things out.

I had an attentive audience as I recounted a bowdlerised version of the hare hunt, then Vicky told me that Rabbit had been seen cycling off with a parcel of bloodstained newspaper under his arm, in the direction of Totty's cottage. The hare was off to be horned by a true professional.

By supper-time Peter had the fender reassembled as its Victorian designer had intended. There is good profit here I thought as I carried it through to the shop and set it around the feet of the lowboy.

The children were pyjamaed, washed and hair brushed, and ready for their goodnight kiss when I went back to the kitchen.

'Ah one moment, here's something for you to pin up in your curiosity corner. A licence for hunting a horned hare.'

Sally, with much ado, finally got the drawing pins pushed home. She spread her hands on the wall and read out Harry's legal sounding jargon. 'The said holder of this licence, is requested to take only one horned hare, observe the closed season and cause the grouse no disturbance nor harassment.' Sally nodded her head at every word. 'Signed: Harry Benson, under-keeper.'

She turned to me, a puzzled look on her face. 'I thought there was only one "r" in hare?'

Chapter 16

The taproom was packed. We were awaiting the arrival of the mounted head of the horned hare.

Mim perched on a stool beside her husband and pestered him for money to buy the opal brooch from Mucky Marion. 'Anything you want, you get. Me! I get bugger all.' She drained her glass and clacked her high heels across the concrete floor and up the steps to the lounge. The Colonel glanced sideways as she pushed up to the bar.

'Bloody men! 'Ere make it a double Charlie,' she growled.

Rabbit made a triumphant entry. Pausing in the doorway, he waited until all eyes were on him and the conversation had died down, then he drew the brown paper bag from the horned hair with a flourish and to loud cheers.

Joe was beside himself. He held the oak shield at arm's length and clenching his teeth shook his head and breathed in deeply. 'Wait 'til the lads in the smoke see this.'

Rabbit was happy too. He could see himself conducting rich and generous Londoners over the fells in a series of lucrative hunts. There were of course a few points that would have to be ironed out, and a less irascible partner would improve matters, but as far as he could see, this could, handled correctly, bring financial security at last.

The horns of Joe's hare were measured and compared with the ones on Charlie's. When Joe's proved to be a good half an inch longer, he flushed with pride, went and found Mim, put his arm around her, breathed a minor gust of stale beer over her tight *coiffure* and pushed a bundle of notes into the pocket of her bolero jacket. 'You get it dear, you deserve it.'

Mim pushed her glass to one side quickly. 'Here Colonel, keep yer eye on that for me. I've a bit of business to do.' The Colonel's only acknowledgement was to send a cloud of pipe smoke curling around the optics.

Cockney Joe was a generous man – generous and lucky. The latter quality Ted affirmed was due to his having a hand sized patch of blond hair amongst the light brown. It was slightly to the fore of his left ear and it fascinated Ted. 'Don't see many like that. Calf-licked that's what it is. They're always lucky buggers when they're calf-licked,' he told me from behind a wagging finger. 'Mucky Marion's father was calf-licked. Luckiest man ever, he was. If he'd have fallen off Lalbeck Town Hall he would have landed in a pair of carpet slippers.'

'The maharaja?'

'Maharaja? No, he was a stable lad. Went to India between the wars with a string of second rate racehorses. Came back under a bit of a cloud. We never did find out what happened but he never worked again, an' he was never short of the price of a pint.'

Mim was a long time at Mucky Marion's. The taproom was thinning out and only the Colonel was left in the lounge when

Mim retrieved her drink and turned her chest to him. 'What d'you think – nice innit?' The stem of the Colonel's pipe slipped on his teeth as he leaned forward and peered at the opal brooch. Mim's wide crimson mouth split to reveal her good teeth. 'My Joe's good to me, anything I want I gets.'

She did a little pirouette and then a saucy walk across to the taproom door. The Colonel screwed his eyes up, then looking sadly into the bowl of his pipe, vowed never to go south of Harrogate again.

The beer flowed freely but, as I had an auction sale on the following day, I paced myself carefully. Rabbit, Long John, Joe and Ted, having no such mundane events pencilled into their social calendars, drank without care. The stuffed head had been returned to Joe's keeping and he clutched it protectively to his chest. Rabbit received a well-aimed kick under the table when he blurted out to Joe, 'There's some wi' bigger horns than that.'

'Zip it,' advised Long John pleasantly, as Rabbit winced.

But Joe was happy with his hare and Mim, happy with her brooch, bent her thin chest to each of us in turn. 'What d'ye think? Nice innit?' We all agreed it was nice.

Charlie showed a mumbling Colonel to the front door and after throwing a towel over the pumps brought a crate of beer down into the taproom, where cards were produced then forgotten, feet were stretched out and Mim became a very efficient and solicitous waitress.

Ethel yawned and went to bed after laying the dishcloths over the towel rail and collecting the ashtrays.

We all admired Mim's brooch again, Joe's chin sank on to his chest as in his mind he relived, and this time took a more active part in, the hare hunt. I watched the clock nudge its minute hand to the half hour before midnight. Rabbit and Long John kept Mim busy. 'Gawd! I 'aven't time to breathe here. Charlie, they need buckets, not pint glasses,' she complained.

Charlie nodded his agreement and glanced at the rapidly emptying crate. 'Help yourself, Mim,' he said waving his glass towards the bar.

We heard the scrape and clunk of the gin optic twice, then Mim's voice through the serving hatch. 'Ice, Charlie, there's no bleedin' ice.' Charlie waved his glass again.

'Some in the fridge.'

Mim's shoes clacked on the concrete floor, and the fridge door opened with a suck, there was a piercing shriek then the sound of a glass shattering. Mim staggered back dropping down the two steps then reeled against the wall, a hand over her eyes and her thin chest heaving.

'Gawd, there's a bleedin' dead fox in there,' she gasped.

Charlie confirmed this laconically. 'Gettin' a bit niffy and couldn't get down to Totty's, so I shoved it in there – keep it cool like.' He leaned forward, a pleased smile on his face. 'Stop it going off, I thought.'

Mim fetched another glass and we heard the optic scrape and clunk three times then she lolled, iceless and dejected through the serving hatch. Her voice was quiet, a little sad and a little pleading. 'Joe, when are we going back to civilization?'

They left for civilization late Saturday morning. It was a bright sunny morning so Joe dropped the hood on the Mercedes and, carefully folding his expensive jacket, laid it on the back seat over the plastic bag that contained the mounted hare's head. Mim looked small and thin in the car. She pulled her handbag to her flat stomach with one hand whilst the other twisted her opal brooch.

Mucky Marion stopped her pram alongside the car and her mittened hands proudly passed a cake to Mim. 'There yer are dear. Look after that brooch now, gift of a maharaja that was.'

We waved from the top of the green. Mim's thin fingers sprinkled a goodbye and Joe blew the horn vigorously and grinned as the car scrunched out of the car park and swept down the dale.

Ted's eyes sparkled as he turned to me. 'By, he's a lucky bugger, a car like that and a fine-looking woman. Mind you, they're always lucky buggers when they're calf-licked.'

I was not in the best of moods as I parked the van at the top of the lane and looked down at the glinting roofs of two long lines of cars.

'Everybody's here,' Fatty called as he spun his car wheels up the grassy banking. A farm sale on a sunny Saturday afternoon must be the place to be I told myself as I trampled down the lane to the crowded farmyard.

The early eighteenth-century farmhouse showed its back to the baked mud of the yard and gazed with four bright curtained eyes down Blackaside ghyll. A low stone wall topped with wrought iron railings enclosed a front garden whose neglected lawn had been hacked to a pale stubbly neatness for the occasion. Delphiniums, lupins and gangly roses filled the borders except for one corner where rhubarb, its leaves as big as dustbin lids and veined and patterned like tortoise shells, overlapped each other in a huge green mound. A canny Dalesman I thought with a smile; the safest place on a farm for a bit of rhubarb.

The furniture was set out on the uneven lawn for it was only the surplus that was being sold off. Eddie Blenkinsop was retiring. 'Not leaving it too late like a lot of 'em do. Just going to enjoy life a bit an' they drop off the perch. Well, I'm not,' he told Drunken Sam, as he sat in the auctioneer's front room a week after his seventieth birthday. 'Get us sold up Sam, an' be done with it. Blackaside's been good to me, but it's not killin' me.'

Eddie had lost his wife some time ago and the last few years had been hard for him. There was a widow woman in Lalbeck who'd given Eddie his dinner every market day since his wife had died and Eddie had decided to sell up and 'do right by her'. Folk were beginning to talk.

Drunken Sam took the job with some reluctance; he was supposed to be retired himself and it would mean staying sober for a whole day. He phoned his old clerk up and went to see Long John. Would they turn out for Eddie? Of course they would, Eddie was well liked. A small hard-working man, he was reputed to have come into the dale wearing a boot on one foot and a clog on the other, and, knowing his careless attitude to his outward appearance, I don't think it at all improbable. I have quite often seen him cross Lalbeck marketplace on a winter's day wearing odd Wellingtons and his late wife's red macintosh.

Eddie screwed his face against the sun and peered up at me. 'What d'ye think?'

'Think of what, Eddie?'

'This stuff – furniture. Will it get away all right?'

Most of the furniture was junk: woodwormed plywood badly painted in pastel colours. Eddie's wife had been fond of what he called 'titivating'. Every chest of drawers, cabinet and cupboard had handle and knob painted in a garish gold, but amongst the rubbish were two really good pieces. Out on the lawn was an inlaid rosewood teapoy and in the dingy kitchen against a damp stained wall was a beautiful rent cupboard.

'You'll get more than you expect at the end of the day, Eddie,' I told him diplomatically.

'It's all good stuff, mind, t'owd lass did it all up, she wor' a good hand wi' a brush.' He shook his head. 'She wor' a good hand; you should have seen the state of some of this stuff when I brought it home. Out wi' the paint pots she'd come an' soon it wor' like new.'

Drunken Sam called to Eddie from the kitchen. There was some problem over a pedigree for the Shorthorn Bull.

The teapoy was beautiful. It had four foil-lined containers and two glass mixing bowls, one of which had a sizeable rim chip, otherwise it was perfect. The gadrooning around the lid was deep and crisp and the carving on its central column was restrained to the point of simplicity. Our early nineteenth-century cabinet maker had exercised his sensibility and not overshadowed his material with ornamentation. The wood was of the highest quality. Rich, hard, nut-brown with black veins that permeated it in long flowing curves, like wood smoke rising on a still summer's evening. The brass inlay around the lid and in long rectangles up to the knees of the elegant legs had aged to the colour of a less base metal.

Teapoys often look out of proportion: a small but stable box supported at a comfortable working height often results in heavy bases and thick legs. But here we had practicality and elegance happily married, beautifully made, and sitting confidently in the middle of a lawnful of sad colleagues.

Jack the Pat walked straight up to it and gave it a thorough going over. The tea containers were drawn out in turn, carefully examined, given a pat and slid back. The chipped bowl brought forth a wince but when he finally closed the lid, the teapoy got three pats.

204

'That's nice, that really is nice.'

Fatty watched him from the shade of the cow byre door. It was going to be an expensive piece of furniture.

Ted came stumbling across the lawn towards me. 'You're not interested in the Bamford Wuffler are you? I could do with that. Small field working, that's what they're good for.'

I assured him I had no interest in the little hayturner as we sat on the low wall, the gentlest of breezes rising from the ghyll and playing pleasantly around us. Cocks crowed in the distance and the river glistened below us like a thin silver rope. A skylark trilled unseen from a blue sky ragged with wisps of white like the trimmings from an old man's beard.

Sam had started on the cattle. Eddie was known for his shorthorns and a full set of the societies herd books had been brought out and laid on the stone bink, strips of newspaper set in each volume marking his entries. The knowledgeable ones ignored them, they knew that Blackaside Bouncer the fourth had fathered every beast that milled around the yard and that the six-year-old bull that poked its cocoa-coloured muzzle through the rails of its pen and bellowed its disgust at the crowd was one of the best 'getters' in the entire breed.

An American accent had been heard and rumours were abroad that Bouncer would soon be scrunching alfalfa and feeling the sunshine of California on his broad back, but Billy Potts scrubbing one Wellington behind the other and chewing thoughtfully on a hard rind of cheese knew otherwise. The bull would stay in the dale. He'd buy him, he'd told Ted, even if it meant opening one of the taped up biscuit tins he kept his savings in. 'There are some things in life you just have to 'av.'

Ted held his hand out and inclined his head. 'There, they're selling now, listen and see. I'll bet our Billy gets him.'

Sam has a strong voice. He'd strengthened it as a youth when he'd been sent up the dale on a 'measuring job' in his father's Austin 7, opening the sunroof and singing at the top of his voice. He had turned the head of many a grazing beast. Now the voice came to us strong and clear.

'I'm selling in guineas, make no mistake, it's guineas.' He gave the last word low growling emphasis.

The bidding opened at two thousand guineas and rose in one hundred guinea bids. There was no attempt to slow the bidding down and soon Sam was calling, 'six thousand guineas I have six thousand. You're out Mr Potts.'

Ted jumped up. 'Come on we shall have to see this.'

Sam stood on his box, his cane held high, ready to bring it down on his open palm. He stared steadily at Billy and Billy stared steadily back. The crowd was silent.

'I'll sell it,' threatened Sam.

Billy didn't move a muscle, he just stared at Sam as the cane wagged. 'It's going,' Sam warned. 'It's going.'

Billy waited until Sam pushed his lower lip out and drew his cane back slowly. At what he judged to be the apex of the arc the cane described against the blue sky. Billy raised one eyebrow.

'Six thousand, one hundred guineas,' Sam bellowed.

There was movement amongst the crowd, voices whispered and murmured, heads were shaken. Sam negotiated a right-angled turn and found his American. 'Now sir.'

A thin sunburnt man in a neat blue suit nodded his head. Sam executing a fast turn, swivelled back to Billy. 'I've got six-two Billy.'

Billy stared steadily into space as a fly crawled up his cheek making erratic turns and stops. Billy ignored it.

Sam smiled, 'Come on Billy, we've a lot to get through. Is it six-three?' He laid his cane on his shoulder. 'Come on Billy six-three. Let's be hearing you.'

Everybody was looking at Billy. Again he waited until Sam's cane hovered before he lifted an eyebrow. The American was agitated. He unbuttoned his jacket revealing a brass bullhead buckle which looked out of place on the sober suit. 'Does it take all damned day to buy a bull in this country?' he asked angrily. Billy allowed himself the thinnest of smiles.

The American walked up to Sam and thrust his brown hands behind the impressive buckle. 'Tell you what I'll do sir, I'll bid seven thousand pounds for that bull.'

Sam sniffed and laid his cane back on his shoulder. 'Guineas sir, we always sells pedigree stock in guineas.'

The man in the blue suit ground his expensive teeth. 'All right damn it, guineas!'

Sam looked from under his brows at a mummy-like Billy. 'What d'ye say Billy?' Billy left it as long as he dare. This time as the cane was poised he spoke softly and slowly. 'And a hundred.'

The American shouldered his way through the crowd to his car and roared off up the rutted lane raising a cloud of dust. Billy was shaken by the hand and congratulated and went on to buy two heifers and a cow with a calf at foot.

'In the Shorthorn trade with a vengence Billy,' Ted called to him, causing Billy to blow his cheeks out and roll his eyes.

The elegant woman took her high-heeled shoes off and walked on stockinged feet to the teapoy. She was tall and slim and although her ash blonde hair, some catty woman might have said, owed more to the bottle than to nature, she was

207

nonetheless a very attractive woman. She dropped her shoes on to the grass and with white-gloved hands raised the lid of the teapoy.

Sam having sold the cattle pushed his straw hat back and wiped his brow. He'd given Eddie a firm promise that he wouldn't drink – but this weather . . .

'It is as hot as a stoker's armpit and a man has to have a drink just to get through,' he told Long John who poured two measures of Swaledale Lightning into enamel mugs and passed one to Sam.

I left Ted when they started to sell the machinery and went back to the garden where the elegant woman, having completed her inspection of the teapoy, had seated herself on a low chest of drawers, crossing her long slim legs and lighting a cigarette.

Jack the Pat and Fatty Batty exchanged nods and prowled the garden like caged tigers and whilst Fatty only had eyes for the teapoy, Jack's attention was divided and soon he was in deep conversation with the woman. She was a woman who was accustomed to attention. She smiled, blew smoke from a pretty pursed mouth, and listened attentively to the suave Jack.

Fatty seeing the likelihood of this alliance of elegance and wealth being to his disadvantage scowled and came and sat next to me on the wall. 'Jack and a woman and fine furniture: a formidable combination.'

'He'll buy it,' I said, absent-mindedly watching a sheep cur hustle a flock of ewes into hurdled pens. The dead stock took a long time to sell largely because Eddie felt compelled to give the history of every piece of equipment. He told them where he'd bought it, how much he'd paid for it and how long he'd had it. Sometimes it helped, sometimes it didn't, but Sam was very patient. He had a healthy slice of commission coming for this sale and his wife was off to her sister's for a week. There were several days of serious drinking in front of him.

Eddie denied us the provenances of the furniture. 'Stuff I don't want – it all has to go,' he said hoisting himself up on to a five-barred gate alongside Billy. 'I'm glad you got Bouncer, nice to know he's staying in the dale.'

Billy sighed. 'It'd been a bit cheaper if it hadn't been for bloody colonials pushin' their noses in.'

'Well you've got a fine animal there Billy. You've seen the stuff he's got – best in the dale, aye, an' a bit beyond.'

Ted bought his Bamford Wuffler. 'Not cheap,' he sniffed, 'but it's a good 'un.'

Sam, red in the face and perspiring freely, mounted his box in the centre of the garden. The titivated furniture was dispensed with quickly; a gaudy chest of drawers, its eau-de-Nil carcase splattered with gold stars was had for two pounds, and the hall wardrobe, perhaps a little too much for most people with its panels of pink ragged in silver and lined about with Tuscan red, went for a miserable pound.

'Lot of furniture for a pound,' observed Sam sadly as he steadied himself on Long John's shoulder.

The elegant woman and Jack the Pat had gone to stand in the shade of a rowan tree which hung its windswept head over the yard wall.

Fatty retreated to the cow byre door, whilst I moved along the wall until my arm was brushed by cool rhubarb leaves. It was a good position. Sam and Fatty were clearly visible and I was half hidden by a group of farmers who had gathered at the top of the lawn.

The rent cupboard, after much whispering and nodding between Sam and Long John, was carried out into the garden. I caught John's arm. 'Tell Sam that as long as I'm sat on the wall, I'm bidding.'

John grinned and went to whisper into Sam's ear.

The bidding opened at fifty pounds and Fatty joined in when a flat-capped farmer shook his head at a hundred pounds.

Sam didn't give me away. He took Fatty's bids then looked vaguely at the house for an opposing one making Fatty growl, 'He's taking 'em off the wall,' and leave his doorway and advance into the crowd.

I could feel his eyes on me. I pulled a knee up to my chin and stared intently into the rhubarb. At a hundred and fifty pounds I felt that's enough and rose and stretched my arms.

Sam waved his cane around the throng asked if anybody would go anymore, then he gave me the slightest of smiles as the cane thwacked into a plump palm. 'Mr Batty.'

The teapoy was carried from the ranks of the lowly and set before Sam. Long John opened the lid and held the good mixing bowl aloft. Jack moved slightly away from the elegant woman and cupped a hand under his chin as Fatty retreated to his doorway. Sam began a paean of praise that stopped the farmers' gossip and made the dealers edgy. As soon as he had finished his loving tribute to the star of the sale Jack called from the shadows, 'One hundred pounds.'

The elegant woman raised a gloved hand. Sam, sensing a battle was at hand and with an auctioneer's eye on the commission, beamed. 'And twenty-five,' he said confident that the healthy increment was fully justified.

The bidding was brisk. Neither hesitated, making Sam's cane wag like the tail of a tired dog. At two hundred and fifty pounds the woman shook her head and giving Jack a glassy smile picked her way through a crowd of admiring farmers.

I had experienced an interesting but barren afternoon. Fatty stood looking at his rent cupboard. 'I don't know who it was but somebody made me pay for it.'

'It's nice, though. Be a good seller,' I told him happily.

'Never got in at the teapoy. Who is that woman?'

I couldn't enlighten him. She had walked with some difficulty up the lane followed by Jack and as she got into her car and folded her elegant legs up and tucked her skirt in, I could see him bend low and produce one of his flamboyant business cards.

I helped Billy and Ted load the cattle. The bull was the easiest. Billy slapped its massive rump across the yard and up the ramp, whilst Ted stood back, arms folded across his chest. 'He's made a bit of a hole in thi' biscuit tin.'

Billy was happy; he bolted one of the internal gates behind the massive beast and gave it a final slap. 'Aye, but there's some things you just have to 'av.'

I keep Widgeon's chair in the bedroom, angled to the window. I can lean back and see across the green over the washfold and down the fold of the dale to the carefully planted coverts on the estate. It is a good place to sit for a few minutes at the end of the day.

Vicky, scented and pink from her bath, pulled her towelling robe around her and sat on the broad window-ledge. She leaned forward and played with her toes, her blonde hair spilling around her knees. I told her of the elegant woman and Jack the Pat buying the teapoy. She looked down at her toes and wriggled them. 'The woman who made the curtains for us tells me Jack has some lovely inlaid work-boxes. I've always fancied a good work-box.' She gave me a sideways glance and her mouth parted in a roguish smile. 'I'll have to go see him some-day.'

I reached forward, grabbed a small toe and twisted it until she winced. 'You keep away from that terrible man. If you want a work-box, I'll get you one.'

Chapter 17

Mrs Smythe-Robinson's hat bobbed and ducked around the lowboy, its feathers dancing and catching the light. Well-gloved hands tried the drawers, then splayed across the top and shook it. 'Seems quite stable. No woodworm?'

'No woodworm Madam, it's as sound as a bell.'

She worked a searching finger over the nicely patinated top. The finger stopped abruptly. 'That mark, will it come out?'

I bent over the lowboy and looked at the faint black ring; ink, undoubtedly ink. 'No, to take that out would ruin the patina, it's just part of the character of the piece, every knock and dent, every stain acquired over the years is like a pedigree, and if they're not too obtrusive they're best left. Part of the character.'

'Well it's too dear.'

'For you Madam, I'll reduce it, by twenty pounds.'

The searching finger was pressed into her cheek. 'Make it thirty.' Without any confirmation or otherwise she pulled a cheque book out of her bag and set me rummaging over the counter top with one sharp word. 'Pen!'

Jack the Pat's ploy had worked and I was still ten pounds up so I raised no objection when the good lady gave me a brief smile. 'Bring it round this afternoon. Smythe-Robinson will be in. I'll tell him where I want it.' She paused, hand on door-knob and, staring at some elevated point in the Colonel's ivy, asked me how the children were. I told her they were fine, thanked her for asking, and began to warm a little towards her.

Arrogant, rich and prickly to deal with, she had bought, over the year, quite a few decent pieces from us and her cheques were always good. She turned slowly and gave me a head to toe appraisal, clicked her tongue and slammed the door behind her.

Mr Smythe-Robinson was fast asleep on a sun-lounger. I shook him into a yawning wakefulness. 'Ah! Lowboy, in the library, follow me old chap.' When the gods smile on me I shall have a library like the Smythe-Robinsons'.

A partner's desk scattered with silver-framed photographs occupied the centre of the room which was lined with book-shelves. A club fender embraced an Adam fireplace on which stood a French novelty-clock in the form of an elephant, the sunburst pendulum swinging from its curled trunk. Two high-backed leather chairs were set in front of the French windows, a small modern coffee-table between them.

Mr Smythe-Robinson pointed at the incongruous little table. 'She wants that out. The lowboy in its place and one chair by the fireplace. Put the coffee-table in the garage would you? There's a good chap,' he said, walking out of the French win-dows and across the lawn to his sun-lounger.

We always have to run around the carriage trade a bit.

That's another thing that's going to change when the gods smile. I took the drawer out of the lowboy to make it easier to carry and propped the French windows open.

As I lifted up the drawer I noticed a splatter of woodworm holes I hadn't seen before. Mr Smythe-Robinson was once more fast asleep so with heart pounding I crept like a thief into the kitchen. Where do the well-heeled keep the shoe polish I wondered? Under the sink seems to be a classless place; disinfectants, fly sprays and shoe polish. With a skill born of fear and an ear cocked for the sound of a car I mixed light tan and medium, and then to my delight I found a tin of pure beeswax. Soon I had an acceptable colour and a good stiff consistency. I knifed the filler into the holes and then turned the lowboy in the sunlight. Were there more? Thankfully there weren't, so I slid the drawer back into place and had just returned the tins when the honk of a car horn made me jump.

Through the kitchen window I saw not a car but an ancient sit-up-and-beg bicycle ridden by an old man. Bolted to the handlebars was a wooden platform on which sat a Jack Russell terrier and attached by an elegant swanneck towbar was a trailer loaded with what looked like a giant, black, canvas ball. Rough hewn poles were strapped alongside the trailer and lashed to the crossbar of the bicycle was an enormous shotgun. The terrier raised itself on all four legs to balance as the bicycle and trailer jolted across the flowerbed and out over the lawn to the sun-lounger. A further blast from the horn brought a bleary eyed Mr Smythe-Robinson up on one elbow. The cyclist saluted and got an angry wave in return. A further salute and then the man dismounted and pushed his ensemble the way he had come. Remounting at the top of the drive I saw his grey head speed over the top of the beech hedge down the Old

Drove Road. The two loud honks he sounded as he passed the area of the sun-lounger went unacknowledged. I closed the French windows and drove off quietly.

When I've milked the goat and fed the poultry I like to spend some time with Topic and her foal. Sometimes I yoke the mare up and with Starlight trotting alongside I lead them down the green lane letting the mare stop to graze the bankings when she feels like it. If the sun is still warm I lie in the cart, my legs dangling over the tailgate, and watch the sky through a filigree of green. The swaying of the cart and its many stops and starts have a soporific effect and sometimes I awake to find the sun low in the sky and a chill breeze playing about my arms as I scramble stiffly out of the cart and lead the mare home.

The green canopy stopped its slow sliding by. Topic whinnied and the foal halted its leggy cavorting and ran to her side. I knelt up in the cart to see what had startled the ponies. In the centre of the lane thirty yards away stood the bicycle and trailer I had seen that morning. A rough tent had been pitched between two may bushes and the old man and his dog were walking up towards me. A toothless mouth broke into a wide grin.

'I thought she'd got loose. I didn't see anybody with her.' He spoke softly to Topic stroking her neck and breathing into her nostrils. 'They're a grand pair. They look as fit as lops, pair of 'em. I've just got a brew on, fancy a pot?'

I climbed out of the cart and followed him and his dog to the tent. A billycan, hung on a gallows of willow, danced gently and bubbled over a small fire.

'Sit yer darn.'

He brought three enamel mugs out of the trailer and poured water from a bottle over them. 'It isn't often we have company is it Monty?'

The dog cocked his ear and inclined his head. 'By the way I'm Pigeon Pie and this is Monty. Was that your van I saw up at Smythy's this afternoon?'

I told him it was. He put a spoonful of tea into each mug and with spurts of steam rising from the fire, tilted the billycan over each mug in turn with a forked stick. 'He's all right is Smythy. Don't say a lot but he's all right.'

The mugs were set in front of me and a column of condensed milk run across them. 'Me and Monty, we lets 'em cool a bit, don't we lad?'

He sat on the banking beside me, a small man, thin and tanned. He wore baggy corduroys and a navy blue waistcoat on which were two rows of medal ribbons. The top row had a small figure eight attached to one ribbon. 'You're the antique man then,' he said.

'That's right. Might have something for you.'

A bright eye swivelled on to me. 'Oh aye, what's that?'

'I've a seven pound tin of black powder going cheap.'

'Black powder eh? Well there's powder an' there's powder.'

'This is Walkers Parker and Company.'

A pink tongue flicked over his lips. 'Good stuff Walkers Parker. All their stuff was good.'

'Interested?'

'Oh aye. If it's not too dear.'

'Couple of quid if it's any good to you.'

He reached forward for the tea, his laughing mouth showing his gums again. 'Couple o' quid, that's my kind o' money.'

Monty wagged his tail as Pigeon cooled his tea with water

and stirred it with a brown finger. 'Just right Monty, couldn't get better at the Ritz.'

Through the open flap of the tent I could see the big shot-gun. 'Ten bore?' I asked him.

He pressed his lips together in a wide smile and half closed his eyes. 'Eight bore,' he said with pride. 'The owd cow, I calls her. Not with any disrespect like, but 'cos she feeds me an' now an' again brings me a bit o' cream.' The gun was laid on a piece of sacking, an oily rag trailing from its muzzle. It was a percussion gun, the heavy hammer was worn and smooth and shaped like a dolphin and the long barrel browned and polished to a rich cinnamon. It was slightly swamped at the muzzle and here and there along its length were old delves, not too serious but showing dark on the glowing metal. The stock was in proportion to the barrel, heavy and inelegant, but it too, was highly polished.

'Beeswax,' said Pigeon handing me a mug of tea. 'A lot soak the stocks wi' oil. Weakens 'em eventually.'

'Must have a hell of a recoil.'

Pigeon laughed and rubbed his right collar bone. 'Aye she gets yer there if you don't watch her.' The tea wasn't bad.

Topic, no longer alarmed, grazed high on the banking and Starlight once more ventured from her side to press a velvet muzzle here and there into the hedge, her ears pricked and alert.

Monty's pink tongue chased his empty mug across the grass as Pigeon brought a shiny tin box from his waistcoat and started to roll a cigarette. He nipped off the straggling tobacco and reached into the fire for a glowing twig. 'He's all right is Smythy. I was in North Africa with him. Kept me out of the glasshouse many a time. He was the scruffiest officer in the Desert Rats and that,' he added with a little guffaw, 'took some doing. I shoots over some of his old quarries in the back end.

'Fancy a brace of wild duck?' I told him I did. The cigarette hovered between two trembling fingers. 'Well now, we may be able to do a bit o' trade with this powder.'

It was quite dark when I backed the coup cart under the barn and pulled the jingling harness from Topic.

Vicky was a little annoyed. 'The children are in bed. Where've you been?'

'Get out your recipes for wood pigeon and wild duck,' I told her. 'I've been doing a bit of a deal.'

The gun could be heard quite distinctly. It didn't have the crack of a game gun, it had a long rumbling report. We heard it four times in the morning and three in the afternoon.

Pigeon was shooting from hides he'd set up around the wheat and barley fields to the south of the village.

Ted's Fergie screeched its brakes down the track and rocked to a halt alongside the washfold. In the link box was a wheel-barrow full of cement, several buckets and Baz. He had been engaged by the Parish Council to effect some repairs to the old sheepwash.

'It doesn't want to look freshly built,' the Colonel had cautioned him. 'Just put it back in some order and prevent any further deterioration.'

When Baz had pulled down one bulging wall and sorted the stones out on the green, I took a mug of coffee out to him. 'You heard him did you?' he asked, pressing a hand into the small of his back.

'Pigeon Pie?'

'Aye he's here again. Missed last year 'cos he shot himself in the foot, although how the hell he managed with that length of barrel I don't know.'

Perhaps, I thought, that's the real reason he calls it 'the owd cow'.

Baz sipped the coffee noisily. 'Hell of a character – him an' that little dog. You want to get talking to him. Nobody knows more about wildlife than Pigeon.'

'I met him last night. Seems a nice enough chap.'

'Don't get him on about the war though; once he's back in the desert you won't get the sand out of your boots for a month.'

He threw the dregs of the coffee on to the grass and handed me the mug. 'Well, I'll have to get on, important job this, and I've no doubt the clerk of works will be across in a minute.'

The Colonel's gate creaked and we heard him call his Labrador. 'Here dog. Bloody dog, come here!'

Baz picked up his level, unravelled his line band and winked. 'Make it look technical, eh. Blind him wi' science.'

The Colonel hrmphed a good morning and shouldering his stick stood, legs slightly apart, and ran his eye over the huge stone toppings. 'You will have noticed the lichen on one side of the stones.' Baz bent over the wheelbarrow of cement and ignored him. 'Stones want to go on the way they came off.'

Baz sliced his trowel through the cement then turned slowly and smiled at the Colonel. 'I'm not bloody stupid. I just look stupid.'

We got another hrmph, the stick was tucked under the arm and then, hands clasped behind his back, the Colonel strode off. 'Good man, good man,' he muttered.

After smiling and shaking his head at the Colonel's retreating back, Baz laid a scaffolding plank across the beck. 'Now with a bit of luck we get some peace till dinner-time.'

Baz was proved to be wrong. Everybody in the village had something to say about the washfold.

Ted spat into the beck. 'Ought to be completely pulled down. It's been a nuisance since I wor a kid. Pull it down and build some stocks.'

'Stocks?' Old Mr Hall cried, leaning heavily on his stick. 'What the hell would we want stocks for?'

Councillor Ted pushed his belly out. 'You builds some stocks. Very photographic, stocks. Then you puts a collecting box near 'em inviting contributions for their upkeep and the upkeep of the green.'

Rabbit, immediately seeing possibilities, agreed enthusiastically. 'Get the parish to do it Ted. That's a damn good idea.'

Mrs Lewis called her father from the shop door. 'Paraffin!'

Old Mr Hall scratched at his balaclava then jerked his slippered feet up the track. 'Stocks! Might not be a bad idea, stocks. We could shove these bloody paraffin wallahs in 'em for an hour or two.'

Ted, encouraged by Rabbit and Baz, was determined to pursue his plan of having some stocks on the village green. Charlie was for it, the Colonel against, the rest of the village about equally divided. Secretly Ted got Baz to earmark some stone and then went to see Richard Radford. Good thick elm-boards he wanted, and two sets of holes, one for adults and one for children. This was one battle the Colonel would lose.

'Progress, that's what it is,' Ted told us in the taproom. 'How many villages can you think of that has a new set of stocks?'

Vicky brought the gossip from the shop. Ted was going to have the stocks made and get Baz to concrete them in late at night. The opposition to the stocks centred, naturally, around the Colonel. When he called on Ted at milking time, Ted listened politely to his objections. Then, wielding his yardbrush with vigour, he splattered the Colonel's immaculate brogues with cow dung. He apologised profusely, then as the Colonel picked his way out of the yard, Ted, a disdainful curl flaring his well-cut nostrils, advanced behind him, his upturned brush a foot from the cavalry twill-covered buttocks.

'*Fait accompli* and sod the planners,' he grinned as the Colonel stalked off across the green. He was just about at the spot where Ted planned to put the stocks when the jubilant farmer cast his parting shot. 'And sod the stick in the muds!' he yelled.

Vicky scrubbed vigorously at the fish slice. A *batterie de cuisine* is all very well on the pages of a glossy magazine but in reality it is a nuisance. Hung with bunches of herbs and drying onions they do give a certain ambience to the kitchen but when all your utensils are on show, they have not just to be clean; they have to look clean.

The scrubbing stopped and she leaned forward over the sink. 'There's a tramp with a dog in the yard.'

Pigeon Pie and Monty were sat on the steps of the apple house.

'That's Pigeon Pie, he's come for the black powder,' I told Vicky as I pulled on my Wellingtons.

I put the tin at Pigeon's feet. 'Couple of quid, all right?'

He prised the lid off, sniffed at the powder and rubbed some between his fingers. 'A bit crystally, slow burning stuff but it'll be all right in my long barrel.'

I told him how I tested it with the Colonel's eprouvette but he didn't seem impressed. 'Vary a lot them things,' he announced loftily.

The dogs sniffed up at Monty and the most beautiful cat in the world peeped at him from the apple house window, yawned, decided he didn't warrant closer inspection and went in search of mice.

Pigeon rose to his feet and gave a little bow when Vicky brought mugs of tea out to us.

'Most kind, madam, most kind,' he smiled as he put his tea on the step to cool and brought out his tobacco tin. 'How long have you been here? This place was empty last time I came.' I told him we had been here eighteen months. The match flared, Pigeon wrinkled his eyes against the smoke, then advancing his lower lip blew a column of it into the air. 'You've made it nice. It's good to see it lived in and a bit of livestock about the place.' Monty took two or three laps at the tea. 'I missed coming last year, had a bit of bad luck.'

Feeling it might be a touchy subject, his shooting himself in the foot, I diplomatically asked him, 'You just go after pigeons?' knowing full well he didn't.

'No, no, anything in its season, but I'm known for pigeon shooting. I've studied their ways you see. They can be crafty can woodies, but I knows their ways. I knocks 'em down, don't I Monty?' He gently pushed the dog away from the mug and raised it to his mouth, the loose turkey skin at his throat pulsing as he swallowed. 'I'm not an educated man but I've studied nature's ways, and we don't do bad, do we Monty?' The dog stared expectantly at the mug. 'Most of the time we lives off blue milk but now and again we gets some cream,' he laughed. Pigeon took another gulp then gave the tea back to Monty. 'But whatever it is the good Lord sends us, blue milk or cream, we shares, don't we Monty?' The dog's tongue searched noisily into the mug.

Pigeon nipped the glowing tip from his cigarette, blew on it and pushed it behind his ear. 'No. I'm not an educated man. I've read three books, I read the *Bible, War and Peace*, and *Wuthering Heights*. I started on one called *Finnegan's Wake*, but I couldn't make ash nor coke out of it, so I said to meself, Pigeon you must be a three book man, so I've left it at that. Read nowt since.'

He took his empty mug and washed it in the stream. 'Now this powder, two quid you say?'

'Must be worth two quid, Pigeon.'

'Not arguing about the price, it's just that, well, start of the pigeon shooting me and Monty is always a bit strapped.'

'Take it, pay me later.'

He held out his brown hand. 'Very decent of you. We'll not forget, will we Monty?' He wheeled his bicycle and trailer out of the Dutch barn and after stowing the black powder away carefully, patted Monty's platform. 'Come on boy, early start tomorrow.' Monty leapt on to his platform. Pigeon paused, foot on raised pedal, 'Thank yer Missus for the tea. We'll not forget will we Monty?'

Baz didn't have a happy time rebuilding the washfold. 'Wish I'd never taken the damned job, clerk of works never off me back,' he complained.

If it wasn't the Colonel pestering him it was Ted, for he had an old photograph of the washfold and he scrutinised almost every stone Baz laid then hurried home to find his spectacles. 'Not as it was, not as it was,' he jubilantly told a disinterested Dolly.

Ted knew he had a real battle on his hands over his plan for putting stocks on the green and the washfold was putting shot in his locker.

Those lazy, warm, barley-water afternoons of high summer, Baz scraped his trowel on the rough hewn stones and the distant report of Pigeon's old cow could just be heard over the tinkle of a thin beck. We dug up the second early potatoes and squeezed squeaky pea pods. 'Nearly ready,' we said eyeing the fat Muscovy ducklings.

I was away at an auction when Pigeon went around the village selling his 'woodies'. He went from door to door, the faithful Monty at his heels and his belt hung with pigeons.

'Pigeon pie, missus?' he asked at every cottage.

Vicky bought six. The old man turned the birds over for her. 'Look, missus, good young ones, pink legs and downy under the wings. That's what to look for in woodies.'

The big brown casserole-dish was brought out and Vicky tripped off to the shop for bacon and mushrooms whilst I took the plump birds into the barn to pluck. Young pigeons are easy to pluck, a wet thumb rubs them bare in no time. We fried them in butter over an open fire until they were a golden brown then wrapped them in bacon and set them carefully into the casserole. I left Vicky peeling mushrooms and raided the onion bed, picking from a crowded row and quelling my peasant misgivings at taking immature vegetables by telling myself they were thinnings.

Dolly's recipe called for sherry, and as we had none, Vicky poured half a bottle of Rioja into the casserole. I groaned and went to milk the goat. Elspeth looked around and stopped chewing as I pulled at her udder. 'Sorry old girl, but it was a Gran Reserva.'

We sent Peter scurrying off to Nellie May's, a fat pigeon clamped between two plates, then we sat, and dispensing with cutlery, ate like our forefathers must have done, pulling off legs and tearing the meat from the breastbone, gravy running down our chins; wine rings on a planked table. It was gorgeous; a little lapse into primitive and satisfying gluttony.

Baz had nearly finished the washfold. He had raked back the joints and brushed the macaroons of dried cement from the grass. All it needed now was the toppings.

He tapped on the kitchen window and pointed down the yard. 'Give us a hand wi' these old lad?'

The toppings were heavy. We dropped each one on to its cement bed and as I breathed heavily and stretched my arms Baz tapped and wedged until they were level. As we lowered the last one into place, Pigeon honked his horn and pulled up with a screech of brakes that nearly sent Monty toppling over the front wheel. He took two pound notes out of his waistcoat pocket and straightened them between finger and thumb. 'There you are friend, two quid and we're much obliged, aren't we Monty?'

Baz raked the back of his trowel under the topping and flicking the excess cement expertly into his wheelbarrow smiled up at Pigeon's blackened face. Three days of black powder shooting and primitive washing facilities had given it a decidedly dusky look.

Baz, still smiling, stared at his wheelbarrow where the cement had made a ringed impact then looked up at Pigeon. 'By thar' mucky Pigeon, thar does look mucky.'

Pigeon's toe raised a pedal and his toothless mouth broke into a laugh as he released the brake and joggled down the track.

'Aye, but we're right bonny when we're washed,' he called over his shoulder. 'Aren't we Monty?'

Chapter 18

The wall on our eastern boundary is substantial. Over six feet high and dry-stoned it has, over the years, been pointed here and there with cement to strengthen it and several of the rough-hewn copings are cemented in place.

It stood ten feet from the Dutch barn and parallel to it, so all we needed were some tin sheets and a few purlins and we had the makings of a good cart shed. Patches of old whitewash stuck to it in places and set in one big stone was a tethering ring. I remembered Edward Raphael Bunney's watercolour and the pantiled cart shed. Pantiles were beyond our means, red bitumen on corrugated iron would have to do.

Peter and Sally protested angrily as I swung my bill hook into the scrubby trees. 'That's our wilderness, you can't chop that down.'

Wilderness or not it had to go. Our plans for walling the Dutch barn in to give us much needed storage space would mean that the coup cart would have to be housed elsewhere.

'There used to be a cart shed here,' I said defensively, 'I've seen an old picture of it.'

Sally stuck her lower lip out and glared at me. 'Heidi and her babies live there.'

'Heidi?'

'Heidi the hedgehog.'

Hedgehogs aren't my favourite animals, they are far more vicious than people imagine. Early spring one had scrunched its way through an entire brood of my Muscovy ducklings.

I stuck the bill hook into the corky bark of an elder. 'Well they've got notice to quit.' I rolled the tangle of briar, nettle and goosegrass away from the barn and was allowed to set fire to it only after the children had poked their way through it making sure Heidi and her young were not curled up in it. Thick grey smoke filled the garth and swept over the wall, thinning out across the fell.

My pick had just levered out the second of the rotted stumps of what must have been the original cart shed poles when Ted appeared through the smoke, coughing and spluttering.

'What are you on with? I thought you were burning the place down.'

'Bit of restitution, Ted. I'm putting a cart shed up.'

'Restitution?'

'Yes, there used to be one here so I'm putting it back. Restitution.'

Ted leaned against the wall and lifted his cap and scratched his head. 'By, yer going back a long ways.'

'It was on one of Edward Bunney's paintings, and they're always truthful.'

'Aye, aye, now then. Yer right, old Edgar pulled it down,

them pantiles edging that garden.' He pointed to the onion plot. 'They're off the roof. Aye, I'd forgotten that cart shed. Edgar used to keep t'snowplough in there 'cos he had the contract for keeping the road open from the bottom of Sparrow Bank to Yarker Lane end. Used to like to see it snow did old Edgar. "White gold", he called it.'

I smiled at Ted and held up a finger. 'Have a look at these.' I turned a rusty pile of shackles over with my foot.

'Them's off the snowplough right enough,' Ted confirmed holding his hands out. 'A fall like this, six or eight inches, they'd put a couple of shires in, but I've seen it this deep.' One hand went back to scratch whilst the other was held out two feet from the cleared earth. 'Then they'd have six pulling it. I've ridden on the leaders many a time when I was a lad. The plough had a big tiller bar on it an' after a good fall there'd be four or five blokes steering it through the village.'

I gathered the rusty ironwork together, put it in the apple house, and was throwing the rotten stumps in the fire when Ted stopped me. 'Here give me a couple, I might just have a job for them.'

'They're rotten, Ted.'

'Just right,' he winked and went off happily hugging the rotten stumps to his raggy sweater.

That night as I had my few moments in Widgeon's chair I saw Ted creep out on to the green, a draining spit in one hand and the two stumps under his arm.

Ten paces from the washfold he looked around furtively, dropped his load and began to dig out two squares of turf. He buried the stumps and replaced the grass carefully and then, by the light of the full moon, he knelt and brushed away all the remaining soil.

229

Like a good poacher he didn't walk straight home. He shouldered the spit and walked along the bottom of the green, past the Colonel's, up the snicket behind the old wheelwright's and on to the common.

I crept along the landing and into Peter's room and saw Ted climbing the back wall into his farmyard. 'Goodnight Ted,' I called, as loud as I dare.

The draining spit clattered into the yard and the big hands, white in the moonlight, slipped from the wall top. I couldn't see his face but I knew he'd be making one of his best mumpy mouths.

We had come to call Friday rent day, for that was the day of the week I took Nellie May her ten bob and half a dozen eggs in payment for the bottom land.

She was getting to look really old. Her face had been nutbrown with dark eye sockets and lined like the craquelure of an old vase as long as we had known her; but now she was bent almost double and moved about the cottage holding on to the furniture.

'I'm as fit as a flea on a butcher's dog,' she told me defiantly when I asked after her health, 'it's just me bowels. Bowels is everythin' to owd folk, keep yer bowels right an' you're right.'

The villagers worried about her, but the old lady was fiercely independent and resented any intrusion into her life. Mrs Lewis was allowed in once a week when she took her groceries and our children were always welcome along with Ted, but anyone else who went uninvited up to the cottage got short shrift.

'Off with ye, I'm all right,' she would shriek at them.

I put the eggs and the fifty pence piece on the sideboard. She nodded and sank back in her chair. 'Send your bairns up to see me, I've a little job for 'em. Want 'em to get me some greens.'

Sally and Peter stood bright eyed by the kitchen table. 'We've a 'portant mission for Nellie May,' Sally blurted out.

'And I've written a letter for her – a secret letter,' Peter added excitedly.

Sally, not to be outdone, unfolded a piece of lined paper. 'And these are the drawings of the greens she wants. Nellie May said you can show your Mum and Dad but nobody else.'

Vicky looked at the spidery drawings. 'Yellow Melilot and Gentian,' she said as Sally climbed up on her knee.

'Nellie May's told us where to find them. What are they for?' the children asked. Vicky shrugged.

They took a basket from the pantry shelf and Sally painstakingly folded the paper and put it in the purse which hung around her neck. They were just pulling the heavy kitchen door behind them when I called out to Peter. 'What was in the letter then?'

His eager face reappeared. 'It just said, "Tell Apple to come."'

'You'll be no good in MI5,' I grinned as his face clouded over and he bit his lip. 'It's OK, Mum and me won't say a word,' I reassured him.

Nellie May rewarded the children for their herb gathering. She gave Peter a sword stick, which caused us a little consternation, and she gave Sally a camphor wood box covered in Victorian scraps and full of old photographs and bits of cheap jewellery and dried flowers. 'It was her diddy box when she was a little girl, travelling in a caravan,' Sally explained. 'And her father used to carry this stick when they went to race meetings 'cos there were some roughs about then,' Peter added excitedly.

We extracted a solemn promise from Peter that he wouldn't fool about with the sword stick and emptied Sally's diddy box on to the table. Amongst the photographs were several of the village, mostly sepia and white. They showed unmade roads, horsedrawn vehicles and, surprisingly, a lot of vegetation around the cottages. The Ship was clothed in ivy and a plum tree grew against the wall of Ted's house. On one photograph a group of tough-looking men, waistcoated and cloth-capped, stood in an aggressive way outside the Miner's Arms.

'That's Mrs Lewis's shop now,' I told the children.

Vicky picked up a photograph and stared at it long and hard then turned to me. 'I bet that chap there,' her finger curled under the photo, 'is Ted's dad.'

The man stood square to the camera, his head back and his thumbs tucked into his belt. His mouth, under a walrus moustache, was pushed forward – Ted's mumpy mouth. He was holding a horse which was highly decorated with what looked to be real flowers. Several children in buttoned boots, the boys in tweed suits and the girls in long dresses with overhung blouses, stood to one side of the horse and behind them, just visible, was a ragged stump. A board with two semi-circular cutouts hanging from it was partially buried in the grass. The village stocks. But was the picture taken of Ramsthwaite? I fetched a magnifying glass from the shop and we jostled our heads together looking for something to fix the photograph geographically. In the top right-hand corner we could just make out the eaves of a house. The guttering was supported on stone kneelers and fed into the downpipe through a waterbucket on which was the date – 1887. It was Jubilee house. The stocks had been a good fifty yards from where Ted had buried the stumps.

The following morning Heidi and her brood were found safe in the orchard and I, with a smug smile on my face, took the photograph round to Ted. 'Recognise him?'

Ted fetched his glasses and held the photograph two feet from his face. 'That's my father. Where did you get this?'

'Nellie May gave it to Sally.'

'And that,' a thick fingernail almost hid one of the beribboned girls, 'is Mrs Thompson – Baz's aunt.' He looked over the photograph carefully. 'Aye, that's my dad. Hell of a horseman he was! That's a good type, that 'oss is. Look at the feather on them legs.'

'Nothing else of interest Ted?'

'What d'ye mean?'

'Well this here.' I pointed to the stocks. A grin broke across his face. 'Hey! Can I borrow this?'

That night I kept a vigil until well after The Ship had closed and only the odd cat was abroad in the village, for I fully expected Ted to exhume his stumps and resite them to correspond with those in the photograph.

Vicky yawned and pulled the quilt up to her chin. 'Come to bed, you can see in the morning if he's shifted them.'

The stumps hadn't been moved but Ted was quartering the green probing the grass with a thistle dagger, his draining spit on his shoulder.

'Lost something?' I called cheerfully.

He held a finger up in recognition and went on with his silent probing.

Ted's presence in the taproom was, for once, eagerly awaited. He hadn't time to pull his stool up to the domino table before he was bombarded with questions. 'What was he doing?'

233

'Bit of restitution,' was the only answer we got.

To nobody's surprise he uncovered the two stumps and then he did the rounds with the photograph. 'See, there used to be stocks alongside the washfold.'

Vicky was puzzled. 'How can he say they were near the washfold when the photograph clearly shows them outside Jubilee house?'

God, auctioneers and parish councillors move in mysterious ways I told her.

Parish council meetings are usually boring. There are axes to be ground and backs to be scratched and the long rambling monologue is in the armoury of both grinder and scratcher.

The parish council owns the lordship of the manor and along with the Drainage Society controls a fair amount of land. There are nineteenth-century charities to administer, rents to collect and grazing rights to be put out to tender. Rabbit scoops up a handful of small but well-paid jobs and one or two he regards as sinecures and his by rights.

We waited, arms folded, wriggling our buttocks on the hard folding chairs for 'any other business'. Ted opened an impressive folder. 'Mr Chairman . . .'

The Colonel blew down his pipe sending an eruption of ash over the table. Rabbit was in the front row. He hitched his chair forward and leaned on the baize-covered table until the Colonel waved him away. 'Members of the public can't lean on the table.'

Ted began again. 'Mr Chairman, the question of the stocks.'

He spoke for half an hour on the advantages they would bring to the village and ended by producing the photograph. 'This photo shows without a doubt there used to be stocks and

234

I, with a bit of clever detective work, have actually found the rotted remains.'

The Colonel was badgered by Ted and Rabbit into holding a site meeting. 'On the green, 8 pm Wednesday,' he snapped curtly, slamming the minute book shut. 'Meeting closed.'

Miss Wells gathered up the books and papers and went off home to type up the minutes whilst the rest of us wandered along to The Ship.

The children were sent on a further herb hunt. Wood Betony and St Johns Wort the old Gypsy wanted this time.

'She ought to see a doctor,' Mrs Lewis told us sadly. But the old woman was as fiery as ever. 'I'm all right, damn you,' was her answer to every query about her health. So Ted and Mrs Lewis got their heads together.

Something had to be done about Nellie May. I broke a confidence and told them that I thought she had sent for Apple Tom. How she knew how to get in touch with him was a mystery, but Ted thought they had places they could write to: settled down Romanies who could pass on messages. They decided that as she didn't seem to be deteriorating they would wait for a week and see if her nephew turned up. If he didn't they would go and see Dr Nichols.

Apple Tom appeared within the week. He backed the Yorkshire bow top hard up to the cottage and carried the old lady into it. 'She hasn't been sleeping,' he explained, 'but she'll sleep in there all right.'

His wife unfurled a tarpaulin and supported it from the side of the van with rough poles then rolled stones to make a fireplace and soon the black iron cauldron was bubbling away.

Roddy, their son, was nowhere to be seen and neither was the coloured Galloway, so Sally and Peter went and asked

Apple Tom where he was. 'Blaeberrying on the tops,' he told them. 'Good money in blaeberries. Get yourselves a can and get up there, plenty for everybody.'

Ted knew where we could find bilberries and took a delight in telling us. 'After making funeral pie are you?' he laughed as he set off up the moor to see to his sheep.

Sunday afternoon I put the pack saddle on Topic, Vicky made sandwiches and filled flasks, and Peter and Sally splashed happily away in the sink washing two aluminium milk cans. We were off bilberrying.

It was a warm sunny afternoon with a soft easterly breeze. Sheep bleated to errant lambs and just occasionally the pipe of a curlew scythed through the air. I like the smell of the moors, I like the warm muskiness that rises from the dry matrix of heather stalks and the dank peaty places.

Our little troop was soon strung out up the track. The dogs rushed ahead plunging through the heather, the children danced and skipped waving their cans in the air whilst Vicky and I padded on behind leading Topic and Starlight on long lines. Ted had drawn a simple map in the dust of the yard. 'Up past where you dug peat last year and keep on.' A big hand cautioned us. 'Keep on! D'ye hear?'

Yes, we heard, and we promised to keep on.

'You'll see down below you the chimneys of the old smelt mill, keep them to your right and keep on, right away on. There's a bit of a tarn, it'll probably be dried up this time o' year, but keep on.'

'Is there anything we can look for that'll tell us here's bilberries?'

Ted sniffed, and looked up to the sky, and thought deeply. 'No, you just have to keep on till you come to 'em.'

The children dashed into the old peat diggings; they kicked their heels into the dark brown springy mounds and jumped down into the shallow pits with screams and shouts and flailing cans.

The dogs poured themselves over the diggings, tails wagging madly and noses working furiously. The scars we had left so raw-looking last year had started to heal. They were still clearly visible but bracken fronds curled over the edge of them and moss had begun to dapple the dark brown with bright green.

The children and dogs lay out on the soft peat mounds; it was time for a halt. Pop and chocolate were distributed and the canvas water bucket brought out and filled for the ponies. They weren't at all hot but I had some misgivings about them drinking, so much so I sacrificed a handkerchief, washed out their mouths with it, and poured the water back into the plastic container.

We lay on our backs and listened to the panting of the dogs and the ponies blowing through their nostrils as they nosed through the ling. Above us was a beautiful blue sky, paling at the horizon and lightly ragged with white, way out over the plain of York. I eased my hips into the peat and folded my sweater for a pillow. The bilberries could wait.

Vicky knelt on the diggings getting brown patches on her knees as she searched through the flora. Her tiny notebook came out as she squealed with delight: two new finds, Bog Violet and Bog Stitchwort. The children pushed their blonde heads against hers, and the dogs, expecting food, pushed between the kneeling bodies. Topic stood over me blocking out the sun and breathing a marshy breath over me; I waved her away and closed my eyes. Someday I would bring a tent up here, light a fire, cook a simple meal and lay for hours on the dank earth, just listening.

'Uncle Ted said we had to keep on.' Four sunburnt arms pulled me to my feet and we tramped on, keeping the smelt mill chimney to our right.

Ruins from the Dales lead-mining past always fill me with a degree of sadness; it was such a hard and dangerous life for the miners. The heaps of spoil they cast over the fells still only support scant growth, and the narrow paths they trudged morning and night, knitting sheaths tucked under their arms, can still be seen. Early man dug the useful but toxic metal from simple bell pits and progress was slow until the Industrial Revolution put fearsome tools into the miners' hands. The Dales were raped until cheap Spanish lead quenched the fires and stopped the wheels for ever. The stone buildings they left were robbed of everything useful: doors and beams, slates and lintels were carted away and nature began her healing process.

The little tarn, as Ted had predicted, was dry; sheep lay on the warm cracked mud. They arose stiff-legged, stamped their feet and shogged off in protest at our arrival. They had been recently shorn and bright red daub on shoulder and rump marked them as Cousin Leopold's.

We kept on, a path no wider than my sandal led up a gentle slope to mark a stone that Ted had failed to mention, leaning its lichened side to the heather. We touched it in turn and the dogs lifted their legs to acknowledge its presence.

The children found them first. Yells of 'They're here! They're here!' made Vicky and I pull on the lead ropes and quicken our steps. Small hands with purple stained fingers held out the tiny black berries, the purple blue bloom rubbed almost away by eagerness.

'Can you eat them?' Sally asked naively.

I took them from her palm and squashed them between my lips, the warm juice had a slight bite to it. 'No, only grown-ups can eat them,' I teased her.

I took the panniers off Topic and tethered the two ponies. The cans were slow to fill for although there was an abundance of fruits, stained lips and tongues showed the route most berries were taking.

'Baskets is no good. Take cans,' Dolly had said. We soon saw why. The tiny black orbs are so fragile they burst, spilling their full black dye with alarming ease, and our hands were soon as purple as our mouths.

'Come on!' I shouted to the children. 'We need two full cans for funeral pie.'

Peter dropped on his haunches and looked at me with a sad face. 'It isn't for Nellie May's funeral is it?'

'Bless you, no,' I laughed. 'You'll see why it's called funeral pie when Mummy bakes it.'

Vicky and I finished the picnic, then pressed lids on to two full cans of berries and stretched rubber bands over them. The hard-won fruit we treated with care, for bilberry pickers need old clothes and patience, a lot of patience. We picked up scattered sweaters and sandwich wrappers and loaded Topic's panniers.

In retreat our little army reversed its order. Vicky and I led with the ponies, and the dogs, tongues lolling, brought up the rear. At the peat diggings I lifted a tired child into each pannier, where they sat, knees drawn up to their chins, milk cans cradled to their chests.

They were half-dirty children we chased up the stairs to bed. A cursory wash of hands and mouths with a face cloth and solemn promises to brush their teeth well having been given with a nodding of tired heads.

The first Muscovy ducklings were ready. I sorted the new potatoes until I had a panful that were no bigger than pigeon eggs and shelled a piggin full of peas. The children gathered watercress, then sneaked crisps from the bowl. Vicky rolled out pastry for the bilberry pie and I, with slight misgivings, swopped Ted a young Barnevelder cock for a quart of fresh cream.

Mrs Lewis rapped the linen-clad cheese. 'Aye, that's ready.' A healthy wedge banged the scale down. A bottle of Rioja was decanted, sniffed at, raised to the light, sipped and approved of. The children chopped mint and dipped forefingers in the cream; we were ready for our first duck dinner of the season.

It was a warm evening so I propped the back door wide open and put up our square of netting which keeps inquisitive hens out. Elspeth put two feet on to the orchard fence and bent her head to peep into the kitchen. I carved the duck, a shade too fat perhaps but the pricked and salted skin was crisp and the fresh sage and onion stuffing made the mouth water.

We don't like our duck rare, and the grainy brown slices were awaited eagerly. The potatoes were rolled in butter, then the peas, wrinkled-skinned peas, that had just the right skin popping resistance to our teeth. We had set aside two cupfuls of bilberries and made a sauce, a smidgin of brandy giving it a delightful piquancy. There is a lot of debris with duck. When everyone had finished I combed the bones from the plates and into the dish of a happy cat and threw some of the softer bits of skin to two very attentive dogs.

Vicky brought the funeral pie from the oven. 'See why it's called that. It's as black as a crow's hat,' she laughed, dropping big dollops of cream over the lattice of pastry she had laid across the pie.

'Is it worth the labour?' I asked the children. 'Stained fingers and tired arms?'

'Mmm!' was all the answer I got from the two pairs of purple lips.

'Wensleydale all right was it?' Mrs Lewis asked Vicky when she went along to the shop.

'Well, there's none left! That should tell you something,' Vicky smiled.

Mrs Lewis leaned over the counter and beckoned Vicky closer. 'A social worker came to see Nellie May this morning,' she whispered. 'Apparently the old lady listened to her politely for half an hour or so then shooed her out of the van and off the common. "You might have a lot of fine cerstifticates young woman but they don't give you the right to talk to me as if I was a five-year-old bairn," she shouted after her.'

'I think she must be getting better,' Vicky said quietly.

Chapter 19

Apple Tom was taken with the foal. 'She'll make fourteen two,' he predicted, as I waited for the dreaded question.

'How much?' he said quietly.

'Tom, join the queue. If I decide to sell her there's one or two asked for her already.'

Vicky, hanging out her washing in the orchard, overheard, and at lunch-time I got a good dig in the ribs. 'Get the Snows rung up, we can't afford to keep another pony and it'll be weaned soon.'

I was reluctant to ring the Snows and had been putting it off as long as I could. Long John wanted the foal and now so did Apple Tom. With either of them it would have a hard life. They would look after it but it would have to work for its keep.

Vicky brought the address book from the shop and shuffled the plates to make room for it. 'There you are,' she said after rumpling a few pages, 'get them rung up.'

Mrs Snow was very interested in Topic's foal. She and the good Doctor would ring us back and arrange a visit.

*

The parish council had assembled on the green when the Snows' car pulled up at the shop. Ted carried a folder under his arm and continually looked at his watch; the Colonel was untypically late. Dr Snow watched the group as he held open the door for his wife. 'Looks like the start of a revolution.'

'Democracy at work,' I told him. 'We are on the verge of acquiring a new set of stocks.'

The Snows liked the foal. Topic was petted and congratulated as her offspring was trotted around the garth.

'Good bone. Good bone,' the Doctor muttered as, with arms folded, he watched her intently. Vicky brought coffee out and all four of us leaned over the garth wall and watched the grazing ponies in silence.

It looked as if the Snows would be happy to buy Starlight but how much should I ask them? If they didn't buy her she would have to go to Long John and my little white lie of some months standing would have been to no avail. The Doctor after exchanging looks with his wife and receiving a little nod, asked in the same manner as Apple Tom. 'How much?'

Cap in hand I walked to the centre of the garth, my eyes were fixed on the foal and I was thinking furiously, we'd paid top price for Topic and put her to a good stallion and she had produced a superb filly. They had both had the best attention and they looked a picture, coats shining like wet coal in the evening sun, bright eyed and alert; Topic well-muscled with just the hint of a grass belly.

Starlight was good on the lead rein and having been constantly handled since birth was amiable and easily managed, but she was not the mature pony broken to saddle and gears like Topic had been. And yet she was so well put together, so pleasingly marked, we could, I felt, be looking at a future best

243

of breed. There was a lot of work to go into the animal and although breeding Dales' ponies was the Snows' hobby and they were very well off I didn't think they would be disposed to pay much more than the going rate. Half the price we had paid for Topic seemed cheap, and three quarters too dear so I did a mental calculation based on two thirds Topic's price and put fifty pounds on for talking money.

Dr Snow winced. 'You think a lot about her. I'll give you a ring.'

Vicky bit her top lip after we'd seen them off. 'I think you overdid it a bit there.'

'Well it's given us a breather,' I said philosophically.

The parish council were still on the green. The Colonel was jabbing his stick angrily into the turf and Ted, looking over the heads of the little crowd, pushed out his lips and flapped his folder against his thigh.

He's winning, I thought.

'How did you get on with yer big buyer then?' Apple Tom stuck his head over the wall and laid his tobacco pouch on a flat topping.

'All right, we're near enough. Wants to see her when she's weaned,' I lied.

Tom smiled. 'It'll make a big 'un, she'd pull a wagon all right. A bow top, not one o' them Reading wagons, 'cos they takes a big 'oss.'

At the price we were talking I didn't think that Starlight would end up between the shafts of a bow top, for the Snows, as I told Vicky, hadn't seemed frightened to death. I leaned over the wall upwind of the cloud of blue smoke that hung around Apple Tom's head then drifted gently over the garth.

'There's a good few years in the skewbald surely?' I asked him.

'Oh aye, she's sound, but I like to have one coming on. Owt happens to your main shaft horse and you're stuck. I like to have one coming on.'

Roddy was sitting on the caravan steps, a chocolate cake on his knees. He broke off a large piece and munched steadily away.

'Did all right with the blaeberries?' I asked, remembering Apple Tom's word for them.

'Aye, done well has t'lad.'

When I told him of our little expedition, he turned, lifted a foot to rest on the wall and laughed. 'Aye yer earns yer keep when yer pickin' 'em. Lad's fingers is still blue.'

Tom's wife pushed past Roddy and went to collect the washing she had laid out to dry on the gorse bushes. Apple Tom's eyes followed her. 'Good at fettlin' and washin' t'wife is – nowt at cookin'.' He stubbed his cigarette out on the wall and after blowing on it put it behind his ear. 'Well if them posh folk don't come through, I'll give you a price on her.'

He walked slowly across to the bow top and mounting the steps leaned down and broke a sizeable piece of Roddy's chocolate cake, the child's protests, muffled by a full mouth, going unheeded.

Ted spread his arms on the gate and his foot, after two or three attempts, found the right place on the rails.

'Good sense has prevailed,' he said with a smile. 'We're going to have a new set of stocks. Owd stick-in-the-mud over there were fairly trounced. Showed council the photo and me stumps, pointed out the undeniable advantages and good sense prevailed.'

The discrepancy between the position of the stumps and the stocks in the photograph puzzled me. 'What I can't understand Ted, is this.' I waved my stick towards the stumps, now dug around and exposed. 'Stumps there, stocks on photo, there.'

Ted eased himself off the gate and looked up at the sky. 'Bit of rain in the offing,' he said absent-mindedly, then without another word disappeared into the feed house.

Richard Radford knocked on the open door. 'Can I come in? I'm on the cadge.'

Vicky sat him by the table and poured out a glass of barley water for it was a boiling hot day. Topic and her foal pushed their heads into the elder bush to escape the flies and the hens dustbathed languorously in the dry earth under the Dutch barn.

Richard took a long drink. 'Councillor Ted has commissioned me to make some stocks. He first approached me a couple of weeks ago when he just wanted a rudimentary set-up, but he came down last night and all that has changed. It's being funded by the parish now so we are to have a very sophisticated affair.'

He took a piece of paper from the breast pocket of his shirt and unfolded it. 'See, a set of stocks in best elm, one bench and one box for contributions.'

Vicky pressed forward to look at the sketch.

'Problem is,' Richard went on, 'old ironwork. I can distress timber OK but I need some old blacksmithed ironwork.' He inclined his head forward and gave me a wide grin. 'Councillor Ted told me you have some shackles – came off the old snowplough.'

I leaned my arms on the table. 'And is Councillor Ted going to pay for them?'

Richard laughed. 'Don't think so, but I'm authorised by the parish council to give you a few quid for them.'

The apple house was cool. The iron shackles, delved with rust, clanked like jailer's keys as I lifted them down for Richard to look at.

'They'll do, a good old look about them,' he said as he sorted them out, laying them in some sort of order on the flagged floor. 'These six – how much?'

It would, I felt, be nice to get something out of the parish council. 'Will they stand a fiver, Richard?'

The cabinet maker drummed his fingers on the flags. 'Three quid! I'll go to three quid on their behalf.'

'All right, it's in a good cause, I suppose.'

Richard was taken with the idea of making the stocks, so much so that he had pushed more lucrative cabinet work aside and drawn some thick elm boards from his wood-shed soon after Ted had left. Now he had the ironwork, he worked, according to Gwen, half-way through the night to finish them.

'You know how it is,' he said apologetically as I put the duet stool on his bench. We were waiting for a prie-dieu to have a waggy back braced and a new pediment for a longcase clock and his workshop was overflowing with furniture awaiting his attention.

'I'll look at the clock tomorrow, I promise.' He crossed his heart and looked waggishly at Vicky.

'If I'd have known I wouldn't have sold you the damned ironwork,' I growled.

Richard ignored me and taking Vicky by the arm led her out to the back yard to look at the stocks. 'Just need a bit more distressing, then a bit of oil. What do you think of the ironwork?' he said turning to me. He'd wire brushed the shackles, painted them matt black and then wire wooled most of the paint off. They had been cut and bent to clamp the boards and to form two rudimentary hinges.

'Very good Richard, you could with a bit of practice, take over from Arthur the famed table faker.'

Richard shook his head. 'I've got a long way to go to equal Arthur.' He reached up and took a chain flail from the crook of an apple tree and gave it to Vicky. 'Go on, give 'em some pasty, they could do with a bit more distressing.' Vicky swung the flail lightly.

'Go on!' Richard urged. 'There's a hundred years to go on 'em yet.'

He had made a small box with a sloping lid and screwed it to a post and above the generous slot he had routed a neat inscription – 'Contributions towards upkeep of the green'.

'Very concerned about the wording of that Councillor Ted was.' Richard flipped open the lid. 'And of the dimensions too. Generosity will flow into this box, according to Councillor Ted.'

Vicky, tiring of distressing, handed me the flail. 'Go on, you put a few years on them.'

I flailed vigorously, trying to imagine where the stocks would receive most wear. Richard had heated an iron on his stove and scattered several burn marks over the bench. He'd eroded the tops of the posts with an axe and then a sander and when I stopped, breathless, to stand back and survey the results of my flailing, I could easily picture some poor miscreant locked in there on a hot summer's day, pestered by flies and small children, continuously easing his aching buttocks on the knot-swelled bench.

'They look super Richard, you've done a good job there.'

'Make sure you don't end up in them, that's all,' he joked as we went back to the cool workshop.

'Duet stool, usual problem, Richard. Too many bums, wants setting up and blocking, that's about it.'

I pushed my head close to his and smiled. 'Favours, good customers, good payers, people who don't whine when their stuff gets pushed back for restitution work.'

He held up his hand and closed his eyes. 'All right, all right, clock tomorrow, prie-dieu day after, then I'll have a look at this.' Cabinet makers' days are like country miles; they have a great degree of elasticity.

Baz dug out the old stumps and concreted the stocks and bench in place. They had been stained and creosoted, the bench top had been sanded to a silky finish and they looked good. Ted took himself off to the shop and selected a lock for the contribution box and with a smugness born of achievement handed one carefully labelled key to the Colonel.

'I suppose, as Chairman, you ought to have one,' he smirked. The Colonel accepted the key with grace and calling his dog to heel clicked his tongue all the way across to The Ship.

'How has he done it?' Vicky asked as I slumped into Widgeon's chair. She was sat up on the bed and indulging in her usual bedtime toe wiggling.

'Done what?'

'You know – got the stocks near the washfold.'

'Ted has two weapons in his armoury, rustic charm and pig ignorance and I suppose he applied, as usual, a little of both.'

The cabinet maker's day stretched threefold before Richard backed his van up to the shop and flung the doors open.

'*Voilà!*'

There, wrapped in blankets was the prie-dieu, the clock-case and the duet stool. We heaped praise and vegetables upon him for the shop had been getting to look a little empty.

Fiery Frank and Little Petal called in the afternoon. The little man couldn't get over the stocks. He photographed Little Petal, baby on knee and feet secured between elm planks. 'Every woman ought to spend an hour a week in them,' he declared. 'Discipline 'em a bit and give 'em time to cogitate on how fortunate they are in their menfolk.' Vicky hit him on the side of the head with a wet dishcloth.

Little Gunnar was coming on grand. He was shown ducks and hens, goat and foal and laughingly held on Topic's back, his tiny hands grasping at the wiry black mane.

After a period of waning, Fiery's attire had waxed full again. The hunting-pink waistcoat was slapped with gold as he picked his way through the shipping furniture, his sovereign rings clattered on bureau and mirrorback and his tooled leather cowboy boots shone with care.

Vicky, an intent look on her face, stabbed a finger at his ear. 'What's this?'

Fiery grinned sheepishly. He had acquired a gold earring. In deference to the heat he drew the paisley neckerchief from his neck and knotted it around the wing mirror of his van. 'It's hot guv. What about a small libation?'

Vicky brought cool barley water from the pantry and filled tall glasses. Little Petal dipped her finger in the glass and wiped it along the baby's lips, the little face crumpled in distaste.

'Takes after his father,' she muttered happily. 'Drop of beer and he grins like a pot dog.'

'You don't look after stuff guv,' Fiery complained as he

pulled the tarpaulin off a marble-top washstand and looked with distaste at the ridge of poultry droppings which had built up below the tiled back.

'They must have roosted there for a month before you sheeted it up,' he complained.

'It's a preservative Fiery.'

'Preserve be buggered, it'll take me an hour to get that off.'

I knocked a further pound off the price to pacify him and watched him pull the drawers carefully from a hideous 1930s sideboard.

'Coming into its own, this stuff.' He looked at me warily. 'Mind you it's got to have been looked after.'

'It has,' I assured him. I'd bought it from Mucky Marion and as he opened the cupboard doors I prayed that the inquisitive monkey hadn't found its way in there.

Fiery pronounced it 'OK at a price'.

I leaned against my new cart shed and watched Fiery whistle and probe his way through the furniture. 'Give us a price for the lot,' he said after a long deliberation.

'Fiery, every price I've given you is rock-bottom trade – the death.'

The little man kicked his heel into a post. 'Aye, but if I took the lot.'

There were ten pieces of furniture and as I added them up in my head I increased each price by a pound then told Fiery the total. 'Comes to £245, but tell you what, take the lot and I'll knock ten quid off.'

Fiery sniffed and giving the post one last vicious kick spat on his hand and held it out. 'You're allus good to deal wi' guv.'

We roped Marion's sideboard on to the van roof and Fiery, after helping Little Petal to her seat, looked up at the sky. 'Hope it doesn't come on to rain. The weather this side of the Pennines is about as predictable as a baby's bottom.'

Ignoring the slur on the broad acres I banged the van side. 'Off with you man before I have you flung in the stocks.'

Every time we asked Ted about the siting of the stocks he employed the politicians' technique of asking us a question instead of giving the answer to ours. He would prattle on for a minute or so then it would be milking time or there would be some other urgent farm business he suddenly remembered.

But the stocks were a success. Children romped over them, visitors stood and smiled at them, photographed each other in them, and coins clattered into the collection box.

Dolly, brushing dead flies from her pantry window-ledge, called to her husband, 'See what you're bringing into the village.'

Ted, his spectacles on the end of his nose, pulled down the net curtain. A foreign car, expensive-looking and gleaming black, had driven across the green and up to the stocks.

Ted, like the rest of the parish council, has a thing about motor vehicles on the green so he pocketed his spectacles, folded his paper and changing his slippers for boots, marched out to do battle.

The car belonged to a professional photographer and he along with his female model were unloading a mass of equipment on to the green. The photographer had spent years on the staff of a national newspaper and had, of necessity, developed ways of dealing with irate officials. The village was praised, the stocks were praised, and Ted's house was singled out as a candidate for a calendar. The photographer made a square with his fingers and squinted at the farmhouse through it.

'Yeah! Yeah! July or August – it would be ideal. Know who lives there?' he asked innocently.

Ted bristled with pride. 'As a matter of fact I do.'

'A discerning man, obviously.' The model smiled and the photographer held out his hand. 'Benson of London.'

Ted shook the hand and smiled back at the model.

'This village is superb, surprised it's not been found before,' Benson grunted as he lifted a huge tripod out of the car boot.

'Terrif,' the model said as she slid into the back seat and started to change.

Ted glanced towards his pantry window, there was no Dolly in sight so he hedged nearer the car. 'Kind of photos you taking?'

Benson flicked the legs of the tripod apart. 'Quality stuff; for the glossies.' Benson's model backed a shapely rump out of the car. She was wearing tiny skin-tight shorts and a Nell Gwyn blouse that caused Ted to swallow hard and take another glance at the pantry window. 'Come on Gloria, let's have you in the stocks.' Benson gave Ted a lewd wink.

'Terrif,' Gloria beamed and poked tiny feet into the stocks.

Gloria smiled and smiled, she twisted this way and that, lifted one shapely leg and then the other and raised a brown shoulder to nuzzle against her long blonde hair and make Ted swallow again.

'Come on squire, your turn, sit here with Gloria. Go on put your arm around her.'

'Terrif,' whispered Gloria brushing her head against Ted's big chest.

'Give us a smile squire.'

Ted's grin was ear to ear and he was far too occupied to see Dolly shake her duster from the bedroom window and glare down at him. Benson wasn't ungenerous, a handful of coins clattered into the box, then he asked Ted, 'Where can you get a decent lunch squire?'

Ted stood up and offered his hand to Gloria. 'Allow me my dear, I'll escort you across to The Ship, an excellent hostelry kept by a good friend of mine.'

Ted paid for his little bit of naughtiness; his meals were late and cold and Dolly didn't speak to him for three days, and when the promised photograph of him and Gloria in the stocks arrived, he wisely pinned it to a beam in the haysel, well out of Dolly's way.

Children are observant. It is probably their height that gives them a different perspective of the world. The time they have to wait around, seen but unheard, isn't always, as we adults think, wasted.

Peter sat patiently on a sack of potatoes in the village shop awaiting his turn while Mrs Lewis and Miss Wells discussed the gypsies. He noticed that the card of locks hung on the brown press door had an unusual feature: every sixth lock had the same key. The lock, bought by Ted for the coin box would have in the second lock on the third row, an identical twin. This lock for some reason had been purchased out of turn. Peter's innocent enquiry brought a surprised look to Mrs Lewis's face. 'Funny you should ask that,' she mused. 'Rabbit insisted on that very one.'

Ted enjoyed having his leg pulled about Gloria. 'Some day,' he told us in the taproom, 'I'll show you a photo. Fine-looking woman she is.' He stood with his back to the mantelpiece and raised his glass, 'Here's to fine-looking women. What do you say Rabbit?'

Rabbit was a little drunk. He'd been in the taproom since opening time and had, as Charlie put it, downed a few.

He raised his glass and threw back his head and laughed. 'Aye, here's to fine-looking women, and,' he said slipping side-ways and spilling a little beer, 'here's to restitution.'

Chapter 20

I hate doing the accounts. Receipts go missing, bank statements don't tally with our book and always there is some major item I manage to forget. I'll finish off a month's accounts and throw my pen with a satisfied air into the desk ledge only to have Vicky stick her head around the door. 'Don't forget we paid the carriage on that longcase clock.'

I groan and with crossings out and insertions make the sheet of paper before me even more of a mess. It is, my family tell me, the only time I become bad tempered.

My pen doodled on the blotter, there was something sadly wrong. Fiery had been twice that month and paid cash. Jack the Pat had bought an inlaid whatnot and paid cash. According to the books we should have had a substantial amount of cash in hand – but where was it? The neat tin box with little trays, lined about with gold, held only a moderate amount. I leaned back in my chair and thought hard. All the auction accounts had been paid by cheque, the household bills were paid by cheque and Vicky's housekeeping money, alarming as I found it, didn't come anywhere near the sum that should have been in the cash box.

I could hear Vicky's iron dunking on the kitchen table but I hesitated to call for her assistance; it was always something so obvious I had overlooked. I'd give it ten minutes then go in, brew some tea, and bring the subject up gently.

We try to keep the business transactions well apart from the smallholding affairs. Vicky nodded at the spike which stood, frilled with bills, on the mantelpiece. 'Anything among that lot?'

I found a feed bill I'd settled with cash and also an account from Richard for the longcase clock and the prie-dieu. An improvement I thought, as I pencilled in the amount I'd paid Richard.

I was relieved when Billy Potts' cattle truck juddered to a halt outside the shop, darkening the windows and wafting a scent of diesel exhaust through the open door. Billy, never a man to come straight to the point, wandered around the shop, hands clasped behind his back and humming to himself. The diesel exhaust was superseded by the pungent smell of cow and Billy's Wellingtons left ribs of dried fibrous dung on the carpet. He opened boxes, peered inside, closed them; tilted vases, rubbed a thumb over the base, hummed to a longcase clock until it struck the hour then came and sat, to my dismay, on the duet stool.

'They tell me you're a chair-buying man.'

'Bought a few in my time Billy.'

'Now then, I have a chair I might be persuaded to part with. Damn good chair, sound as a bell.'

'What's it like Billy? Describe it.'

'Well – it's got legs, and a back, covered in this stuff.' He plucked at the Berlin work-cover of the stool.

'Arms, has it got arms?'

'Oh aye. Big strong arms.'

'Have you got it with you?'

'No, tha'll have to come up. I'm not putting a chair of that quality into a mucky wagon.'

Altonshotts is a bleak place. The stone-roofed steading squats down below the narrow road, hugs a few gorse bushes at its flanks, and hunches its back to the fell like a flagellant awaiting the lash. The storms that howl over the tops, swoop over the ling, and shriek their fury at man's temerity of raising stone on stone in this wild and lonely place, are storms of the highest order.

The stone gateposts, slabs of Yorkshire gritstone encrusted with lichen, dangle a thin iron gate over the dried mud of the yard. Several hens, aged and scaly-legged, search dried lumps of nettle, and from a low byre, its roof a patchwork of tin, stone, and asbestos, roared the mighty Blackaside Bouncer, Billy's pride and the toast of the dale.

Billy slapped its wet, primply muzzle. 'Thought they'd take thee to Americy, did they? Well, they thought wrong. Thar staying here wi' thi' uncle Billy and getting him some good stuff.'

The bull clattered its copper nosering on the top of the ragged door and bellowed.

'They can hear him in Lalbeck on a still day,' Billy laughed. 'Hell of an animal. I'm having his picture painted.'

We left the bull and walked through the unkempt orchard, surprising a goat which leapt from a bed of chervil and minced away to watch us with baleful eyes from a safe distance.

'He's a damn nuisance.' Billy waved a deprecating hand at

the goat. 'Show thee where I'm having Blackaside's picture done.'

He led me out into a pasture where the thistles had been recently dagged and lay dying in the afternoon sun.

'Here,' said Billy, stopping and holding out both arms. 'With that bit o' good walling as a background an' Penhill in the distant. What d'ye think?'

I half-closed my eyes and pictured the magnificent bull against the bit of good walling. 'Just right Billy. Get him to subdue the walling and just ghost in Penhill.'

Billy put his hands in his pockets and grinned. 'It's a her, not a him, but I'll get her to do just that – subdue the walling and ghost in Penhill.'

Why I had suddenly donned the mantle of art expert I didn't know, but my little observations had obviously pleased Billy and a happy chair-seller is always easier to deal with.

'This chair Billy,' I prompted him.

'Aye, up in the house.'

We are a nosey lot we dealers. As Billy and I walked through the kitchen, I stopped to fuss an old cringing farm cur and give myself more time to take things in. A long dresser base, bare of polish, was cluttered with Billy's cups and trophies and on one corner of it stood a small galvanised bucket.

'The hen bucket,' Billy explained.

It had been thumped, clattered, scraped on to the dresser top until it had worn a ring almost through the boarding. Under the small paned window stood a white pot sink. Three brass taps, on lead stalks and encrusted with dried soap, leaned over it at drunken angles. The table was covered with an oil cloth and scattered over its top were dirty plates and mugs. A hen strutted between the plates and spotting a crust of cheese seized it with a throaty clucking and dropped to the floor. Billy batted it with his cap and retrieving the cheese washed it under the middle tap.

'Bugger wor off wi' me supper,' he explained with a grin.

The hen, feathers ruffled and complaining noisily, sought refuge under a long oak settle that was piled high with old copies of *Farming Weekly*. The tab rugs which covered the floor and overlapped each other with a dangerous thickness were dull and flattened. The arch of the fireplace had a small Yorkshire range fitted into it and ashes spilled from the rufous fire bars out over the enamelled hearth tin and lapped a wave of brittle-looking cinders against the brass fender. Billy dabbed the cheese dry with a khaki handkerchief and put it on the mantelshelf between the American gingerbread clock and a lonely little Georgian chamberstick. I remembered Ted telling me with pride that Billy was the tightest man in the dale.

'Chair's through here,' he waved towards the best room.

Parker Knoll make very good chairs and no doubt with the passage of time the simple but effective lines of their furniture will make it collectable.

Billy grinned, 'I reckon if you gave Rabbit forty-five quid for that old wreck of a chair, this must be worth a hundred.'

He reached down, shook each arm then lowered his bulk into the chair and folded his arms, no doubt to emphasise the chair's comfort, then beamed up at me. 'Damned good chair.'

'It's a bit young for me Billy,' I told him gently.

'Young! What's tha' mean, young? I've had it twenty-five year.'

'Relatively young.'

Billy's smile faded. 'Tha' doesn't want it?'

'Afraid not – too young.'

Billy sucked his teeth. 'Too young. Never had ought refused 'cos it was too young.'

The best room was like a funeral parlour. Heavy drapes half-obscured the small windows and all the furnishings were heavy and covered in a moss-green material. Family portraits stared down sternly from the damp walls and the neat mahogany dining-table was almost hidden under a moss-green chenille cover, its tassels waving a handspan from the dark Axminster as a gentle breeze blew from the kitchen door and stirred up a mustiness that tickled the nostrils.

Billy leaned forward on the table. 'No good. Well that's capped me. I thought we could have a bit of trade there.'

'Is there anything else while I'm here?'

Billy turned and sat on the table, one leg swinging, its Wellington setting the tassels dancing again. 'Come wi' me,' he said at last. 'There's some owd stuff in the barn you can look at.'

It took my eyes some time to become accustomed to the gloom in the barn. There were no windows, just owl holes in the end furthest from the house, and the beige and grey of the roof was pinpricked with points of light where slates had slipped and been frost chipped.

The cow stalls stood empty and hung with cobwebs, their floors thick with old straw and dung and dimpled by cloven feet. Stacked against one wall was a pile of old furniture covered in straw and dust. There were three chests of drawers, a dresser base and a complete bedroom suite, all in painted pine. I took the drawers out into the light of the yard to make sure they were pine and looked carefully for plywood panels, but there were none. It was all good mid-Victorian Baltic pine. The bedroom suite had a simulated ash finish and was beautifully lined in faded red and the washstand, topped with rose marble, carried eight large tiles each depicting a scene from Shakespeare's plays.

'There's some more up here,' Billy called, raising a ladder and banging it against the haysel.

I followed his Wellingtons up the creaking rungs. A box-bed made from wide pit-sawn planks was rat-gnawed past redemption and a neat mahogany commode only swung one door from splayed hinges as a result of years of neglect. In the corner was a pile of chairs, simple country Chippendale style with solid square legs and lyre splats. All the drop-in seats were missing but apart from sprung joints and a crusting of bird lime they were quite sound.

'Is it all for sale Billy?'

'Could be.'

I wrestled the chairs free from each other and sneezing from the dust set them out in a row. There was a set of eight.

'These are good chairs, Billy.'

'Me mother brought them wi' her when she came to Altonshotts . . . ' Billy sat on the box-bed chewing a straw and swinging one leg. 'T'owd man niwer liked 'em.'

'You wouldn't have the bottoms would you?'

Billy spat the straw out. 'If I remember rightly they were burnt. We burnt a lot of stuff when the old girl died.' He selected a new straw and after wiping it through his fingers clamped it between his teeth and folded his arms. 'Looks like we can do a bit of trade after all.'

'The bedroom suite and the chairs are OK. The rest is commercial but not −' I wagged head and hand.

'Not worth much?'

'No, it's pine. It'll strip, but the chests are a bit big and the box-bed,' I gave its dry and ribbed boards a kick, 'is past it. Only worth a couple of quid for interest value.'

'Well now, what's to be done?' murmured the master of Altonshotts.

I was worried that Billy, now seeing his disregarded furniture in a new light and applying new values to it, would have it moved en bloc to a saleroom. The dealer's ploy of belittling everything wouldn't work with Billy, he is a seasoned dealer himself; I would have to tread very carefully.

I straightened the line of chairs. 'You see what I have to do, Billy, is work backwards. I have to imagine these chairs renovated: new bottoms, set-up, blocked and polished, and then set a price. Then I have to deduct the cost of the cabinet work, allow for having them on my hands for months, possibly a year, and work out the best price I can give you.'

The new straw followed its predecessor in a flat arc to disappear over the edge of the haysel. 'Best possible price! That sounds all right. That's my kind of talk.'

Knowing what his answer would be I still asked the question. 'Do you want me to give you a blanket price for the lot or individual ones and let you have a think?'

The Wellington stopped its pendulum swing and the folded arms dropped loose. 'Give us prices on stuff an' I'll have a think.'

I fetched my notebook from the van and began by listing the pine. There was nothing unusual about these pieces so pricing them was easy, but the bedroom suite and the chairs were difficult. I watched Billy's face intently when I gave him the list but it betrayed nothing.

'Come on, we'll have a cup of tea. Then, I'll have a think.'

The hen was pecking around the table legs. Billy shooed it out then guided the old dog to its bed by the fire. 'She's nearly blind, but she war a good 'un in her day.'

The dog turned its oily blue eyes to me and settled its chin on its paws. Billy fussed about the dresser. 'Now then, where did I put that teabag?'

He filled a black iron kettle from the centre tap and lit a gas ring, throwing the spent match on to the lava-like flow of ash. 'This bottle gas costs a bloody fortune but when I comes in late I don't feel like lighting a fire.'

Billy took a pince-nez off the mantelshelf and leaned against the dresser, his lips moved and occasionally he lifted his eyes from the list, obviously trying to place an item in his mind's eye. 'Why is this chest of drawers worth more than the other two?'

'Because it's small and has canted corners.'

'Smaller! And it's worth more?'

'Yes.'

'Funny; smaller and worth more.'

Hung over the fireplace on a reckon was a lipped griddle-pan. The congealed fat that covered its bottom was patterned around the edge, like ice on a winter's pond patterned by the feet of mice. Two hams, dark with soot, peeped through skirts of dried sage and mint that swung from the centre of the main beam. Billy saw me looking at them. He glanced at me and then at the griddle-pan. 'Tha' can have a slice if tha wants,' he said in an unconvincing way. I declined his offer, thanking him profusely. I realised that for a man who makes his own envelopes, to offer a slice of ham, was, to say the least, unusual, and a compliment. Perhaps I had overdone the prices a little?

'It's air-dried the Cumberland way, then done wi' black treacle, best you can get.'

I thanked him again. The hams sleeping up there like giant bats looked delicious – but the pan, I shuddered and turned to the taps. Why three I mused – hot, cold and tepid?

Billy took his pince-nez off and rubbed his eyes, then nipped the bridge of his nose. 'Aye, I'll have to have a think, just leave it wi' me for a day or two.'

He poured boiling water into two mugs and slopped the tea-bag from one to the other with a bone-handled fork. Being unable to contain my curiosity any longer I asked him why there were three taps.

He folded my list and filed it along with his cheese between the clock and the chamberstick. 'Ah now, this one,' his big hand slapped the first tap, 'is from Shotts Beck, and this one,' the hand moved on, 'is from a runnel that comes off t'moor top.' He handed me a mug of tea which was the colour of those expensive ciders one can buy; very very pale golden. The last tap was slapped. 'And this,' Billy said in a low voice, 'is corporation water.' He turned a red and solemn face to me. 'I have to pay for that.'

He sat on the dresser, his baggy corduroys bowing a line of trophies and stared at the least-favoured tap. 'I only use that when I have to. Shott's Beck tap goes off when it's drought an' that off t'moor tap gets tiny pink worms in it sometimes, so I'm forced on to corporation water.' I peered with some concern into my tea made from t'moor tap.

To my relief I could see nothing, not even the fleck of a way-ward tea-leaf. Billy watched me, a twinkle in his eye. 'Nay yer all right, they won't be here for a month yet. Don't do yer any harm but,' he shrugged his shoulders, 'better without 'em. Ted's father put the water in, made a damn good job he did. Apart from corporation stuff it's gravity fed.'

The water that was paid for and not gravity fed received another long hard stare via its encrusted tap. The trophies clinked back into line as Billy rose and drained his tea. 'Well, I have to feed round.' He nodded at the mantelpiece. 'I'll have a think and let you know in a day or two.'

Blackaside Bouncer bellowed on seeing Billy at the farmhouse door. 'He knows it's tea-time, t'owd lad. Wait till I get his picture done, that'll set folks talking.' Billy waved a backhand wave. 'I'll let you know in a day or two.'

He disappeared into the feed house and I could hear a rattling of buckets then Billy's deep throaty voice. 'I'm Billy Potts of Altonshotts, I've yows as big as cows an' cows as big as elephunts.'

Billy took two days to think over the prices I'd given him. 'It's the chairs that worry me,' he confessed, settling himself on the creaking duet stool. 'They are a hell of an age. They were mi' mother's folk's and I've been thinking about them a lot. Other stuff you can have, but I think I'll keep them chairs.'

'A lot of work on them Billy.'

It was a hot day and the combined odour of feet and dung that rose from his Wellingtons caused me to lean back in my chair. We sat in silence for a while, then Billy muttered a few don't knows, slowly and in a muted voice.

'Go to Richard and see what he says Billy. He'll give you a price for doing 'em up.'

Billy smiled sheepishly. 'I know, I've been. He's not a cheap man, is he?'

'He's good; slow, but good.'

'Well they're no good stuck up in t'haysel, I might have three done up and sell five.'

The English tradition favours two and its multiples – a set of four, a set of six and so on. So I told him. 'Spoil the set Billy, keep two or four not an odd number, that's continental.'

'Continental? Having three is continental? Well, I better make it two, how much then for the six?'

I now had another problem to explain. The value of sets of chairs increases disproportionately to the number. A set of eight is valued, not as one might think, at twice the value of a set of four, but at three times.

I looked at Billy for a long time, wondering how I could best explain that I couldn't give him, as I was sure he would expect, three quarters of my original price.

'Sets, Billy, are important: four, six, eight, and so on. You've got to have a set to get the best value.'

I drew sets of chairs on a piece of paper and starting with a plain balloon back at fifteen pounds showed Billy how the values escalated disproportionately as they were doubled up.

'It's a graph like this Billy,' I said, my pencil describing a parabolic curve.

The cattle dealer leaned forward propping his elbows on his knee and pushing his lips out not unlike his cousin Ted's mumpy mouth. 'Aw, take the soddin' lot,' he sighed, raising his heels and dropping them to the floor and sending up a stench which made me abandon sketches and graphs and lean back against the till.

'Cash!' he called over his shoulder. 'Not that I don't trust you, but cash is a lot easier.'

I stood the wardrobe on end on the roof rack and propped it with the box-bed. The chairs, two chests and the washstand almost filled the van. I pushed until the creaking of chair joints stopped me pushing; I just couldn't get the last pine chest in.

Billy stood and watched me with some amusement. 'Leave it an' I'll chop it up.'

'Not likely Billy. It's the best bit of pine here.'

'I'll bring it down for you. Time I had a ride out.'

Billy reversed the Rolls-Royce from its tin shed and with much grunting hitched a decrepit pig-trailer to it. He wiped his hands on his trousers, then together we lifted the pine chest and laid it on its back on the stained straw.

'You wouldn't believe the trouble I had getting a tow bar for this Rolls. I went all over. Ended up ringing 'em up at Crewe.' Billy put his head back and pursed his mouth. 'We don't advocate the fitting of tow bars to our cars,' he said in a mocking voice. His big hand shook the tailgate and his voice resumed its natural cadence. 'I ask you, what good is a bloody car wi'out a trailer?'

I paid Billy out, counting the notes carefully on to the counter.

'Any luck money, Billy?' I asked hopefully.

'No,' he grinned, 'but tha' can have this.' He gave me a large slice of ham wrapped in the shiny cover of a *Farmer's Weekly*.

'Best ham in Yorkshire. Just show it the pan. Just show it the pan.' He folded the money lovingly and pushed it deep into his inside pocket then he gave a theatrical wink which employed all of the right side of his face and two thirds of his mouth.

'An' don't thee tell anybody I've given thee that ham. I've a reputation to maintain.'

Chapter 21

I reversed the van behind Otto's garage, brushing the rhodo-dendron along one side and leaving tracks in the damp pine needles. The garage doors had been pushed open and Otto was putting on a linen jacket over his cream suit and fussing with beige driving gloves.

'Today is Sammy day off, so we go in Duesenberg.'

The car smelt as cars used to smell – of leather and oil. I stretched my legs down an enormous tunnel and pressed my back into the deep upholstered seat. Otto drove in a very flamboyant way; gravel rattled under the mudguards as we set off down the drive at a spanking pace.

'Sale start at ten thirty, we be there at eleven, plenty time.' Otto grinned exposing his gold teeth to glint in the morning sun. 'Jade on sale this afternoon. Plenty time.'

He swung the car on to the tarmac and with a throaty roar we accelerated under arches of trees. It was a big car on a long wheelbase and the suspension, soft for a car of the mid-1930s, made it seem as if we were gliding on a cushion of air, out of contact with the road. There was no vibration and as we swept down the sun-dappled road the engine noise was drowned by the rush of the wind and the hiss of the tyres.

Otto was a dial tapper. One gloved hand clutched the huge steering wheel whilst the other floated and fluttered like a beige dove between the gear lever and the dashboard. The ammeter was his *bête noire*. The smallest of the dials, it was easily accessible and received more than its share of Otto's heritages knuckles.

'She's charging OK,' he kept saying. 'She's charging OK.'

Otto cornered with panache. He did as he had been told and accelerated the big car around corners, but the fluttering hand was often late to the wheel. We mounted the verge in an alarming way, our bodies were flung sideways and clouds of dust exploded from the nearside wheels. It was like riding with Toad of Toad Hall.

The car was a real head turner and was accorded more courtesy than one normally meets on the road. These courtesies Otto acknowledged with a wave of the dial-punishing hand. Lorries slowed down, tractors pulled on to the grass verge and the general *hoi polloi* of the road stepped aside as we sped gleaming and crisp towards the sale.

The large country house had been in the same family for generations and the last of the line, elderly and failing in health, was taking up residence in the South of France and had instructed his solicitor to dispose of the estate.

Otto, high on the mailing list of many leading auction houses, had received a complimentary catalogue which now lay, shiny and expensive-looking on the rear seat, three of its entries ringed in ink.

The house, ivy-covered and castellated, was fronted by an impressive set of steps watched over by a life-size pair of stone lions. A smooth undulating lawn, recently mown, slipped down to a rush-bordered lake where coots and mallard sent arrow-head wakes rippling across its surface to gently sway the waterlilies and flag irises. At the side of the house, on what had once been grass tennis courts, was a marquee. Large and white, its guy ropes taut and businesslike, a frilled canopied walkway connected it to the house like an umbilical cord.

Otto took great care parking the Duesenberg. He did not want it under any trees and he wanted it well away from other cars. 'If it get sticky, Sammy complain. If it get scratched he go barmy,' he explained.

When the car was parked Otto pulled off his gloves and driving coat and, throwing them on to the rear seat, plucked out the catalogue and a gold-topped cane. 'We look, then come back,' he said, taking my arm and steering me towards the marquee.

The soft opalescent light of the inside of a marquee is probably a part of its magic. Auctioneers of county standing know its value; they are never loath to erect a marquee.

I have studied marquees. I've wondered at their size, then paced out their dimensions, patted canvas panels galore and tested a thousand guy ropes. I've run fingers on their massive central poles, approved of their neatly coiled ropes and just stood, hands clasped behind my back, and smiled at their acres of canvas. There is something very English about them. They are at the same time, robust and flimsy. They appear with the ease and quickness of a mushroom. They smell good and they protect us from the elements without isolating us from them. The faintest patter of a laconic shower is conveyed to us and

271

the most footsore of breezes pause and gently paw a canvas panel.

Otto opened the catalogue and passed it to me.

The auctioneer, a third generation one, was pin-stripe suited, flanked by clerks, and elevated high above the general crowd. He sat at a table covered with Irish linen which was standing on two green baize-covered tables. The marquee was crowded: every chair was taken and a crust of people, three deep at the side and twice that depth at the rear, pressed against the ordered rectangle of the seated ones. They were selling the glass and ceramics, really good stuff; *façon de Venise* goblets, Bohemian cameo vases and squat German rummers, old and heavy with seed.

Hung on frames down one side of the marquee were some superb paintings waiting to come under the hammer. Mostly Victorian genre; cattle knee deep in Highland lakes, girls on swings in blossom-heavy orchards, village scenes and a cottage interior by Carlton Alfred Smith that was so beautiful it took my breath away. It was quite small and in a badly damaged frame and showed a young girl with a kitten on her knee reading to an old man. The light from a small latticed window fell on to the book and reflected into her face; a face so lovely and gentle, so innocent and sweet. She had obviously read a passage which had caused the old man to laugh and now she looked at him, her eyes full of love, the beginnings of an impish smile just opening her pretty mouth.

I pushed my way through the crowd until I was right in front of it. A steward eyed me warily as I took it from the stand and held it to the light looking for repair marks and overpainting. It was clearly signed and the catalogue stated unequivocally 'by Carlton Alfred Smith'. There was none of the jargon employed when there are doubts about a painting's authenticity. It was undoubtedly genuine; in need of cleaning and reframing, but genuine.

Otto shouted across the marquee. 'My friend, we eat.'

The auctioneer smiled wanly and, with a thousand eyes on me, I replaced the painting and worked my way, with many apologies, through the crowd.

'That painting Otto,' I said as he spread a tartan rug on the grass. 'It's superb. Do they give an estimate? I never thought to look.'

Otto was on his knees peering into the open boot of the Duesenberg. 'It nice picture. They think two to three hundred.' Otto has a near photographic memory. He reads a catalogue from end to end and can reel off, weeks afterwards, prices and descriptions. I crossed my legs, closed my eyes and thought about the Carlton Smith.

Otto pulled a wicker basket out of the boot and with a rattle of cutlery dropped it on to the rug.

'Mrs Sammy pack our lunch. See what she give us, eh?' He knelt over the basket like a happy child, his rings catching the sun as he brought pots and jars, bottles and plates and laid them around himself at arm's reach.

We had duck pâté on slivers of crispbread and smoked salmon on triangles of brown bread. Otto, surprised at my rejection of it, sat cross-legged and spooned an entire jar of caviare between his gold teeth. He opened a bottle of good claret and after much sniffing and viewing poured it into two goblets he hung between the fingers of a cupped hand. The wine was delightful; it was a chateau bottled wine and a very expensive one. Otto refilled the goblets and grinned happily. 'Now, *mon ami*.' He lifted the lid from a silver entrée dish with a melodramatic flourish. In it were two pork pies, neatly quartered and garnished with sprigs of parsley.

'They from eminent porky pie maker Monsieur Thievy Jack,' he laughed. His left hand brought a silver model of a donkey from the basket and placing it in the centre of the rug he gently depressed its tail. The lids of the panniers slung each side of the animal opened; one was full of mustard, the other apple sauce. He rocked to and fro with laughter, slopping a little wine on to the cuff of his cream jacket.

'Otto know how to live. Good claret, good porky pie and good company.'

Perhaps it was the wine, perhaps it was the marquee. It was probably an amalgamation of the two, peppered with Otto's *joie de vivre* and salted with an unaccustomed association with wealth. But at two thirty I found myself with sweating palms and thumping heart at the back of the marquee having paid four hundred pounds for the Carlton Smith.

Fatty Batty and Elly were staring at me. In fact the whole of the Ring was staring at me as Otto patted my shoulder. 'Nice picture, nice picture.'

Still numb and feeling a little sick I positioned myself for the jade. We had worked out a little ploy. I would do the bidding and bid as long as Otto held his cane to his chest; when he dropped it to the ground I would stop.

The first lot was a mutton-fat jade bowl, rare and of good quality, but it did not appeal to me and Otto soon dropped his cane leaving the auctioneer to bring down his gavel in favour of a smiling Martin de Trafford. The second lot, a very rare Pi disc, went the same way. The table screen, spinach jade, beautifully carved and lodged on a cinnamon red base was what

Otto had set his heart on. With one eye on the wealthy widower and one eye on the auctioneer I bid on until the price was sufficient to bring a hush over the blasé crowd. I knew it was Martin who was bidding against me. He was sitting in the front row, legs crossed and his catalogue held to his chest which he flicked forward to bid, and this he did with an automatic regularity.

I looked across at Otto. The gold knob of his cane was pressed firmly against his tie as he stared expressionless at the translucent roof. I dived behind Fatty Batty and billowing out canvas walls worked my way to the other side of the crowd thinking that perhaps Martin, seeing the bids come from a different direction would think he was up against a fresh bidder and lose heart. I reappeared beside Canary Mary and Piccalilli.

'Bid when I tap you on the shoulder,' I whispered. The auctioneer raised his gavel. Otto was glaring at me.

'Here!' shouted Mary, somewhat hesitantly.

The auctioneer smiled. 'Fresh blood.'

I winked at Otto who managed the smallest of smiles, but Martin was not to be put off, his catalogue flicked, perhaps a little petulantly now, but still with the same regularity. I watched Otto like a hawk; the screen was getting really expensive. The steward, now aware of the value of his charge, gripped it harder and raised his eyebrows. Otto's cane was still pressed to his tie. Mary gulped, as I tapped her again and again: here she was, Queen of the Fleamarkets, out for the day to glean amongst the linen and household goods bidding five thousand pounds for a jade screen. She dropped one hand to Piccalilli's head and nervously massaged the dog's ear until he winced.

Five thousand pounds. The auctioneer leaned forward and looked over his glasses at Martin. 'The bid is against you, sir.'

Martin shook his head. The auctioneer looked around then brought his gavel down. 'The lady in the yellow hat,' he announced, then leaning towards his clerk he permitted himself a rare joke. 'The lady in the yellow everything,' he giggled behind his hand.

Otto threw his arms wide open and gave me a continental hug. 'Well done my friend.' He turned to Canary Mary and took her hand. 'And who is the lovely lady who help Otto?'

'This,' I told him, 'is Mary. Canary Mary.'

Otto bent and kissed the hand. 'You my dear, like all beautiful women, have the ability to be a little bit naughty – yes?'

Mary smiled, a shy schoolgirl smile, and Piccalilli pushed between us and, looking up at Otto, wagged a happy tail.

Canary Mary had a problem: her car wouldn't start. I tried, Otto tried, a steward tried, and a passing man who looked as if he should have known all there was to know about cars tried, but to no avail. Mary looked worried.

'Don't worry,' Otto told her. 'You come home with Otto.' He arranged for the car to be towed to a garage and signing a blank cheque gave it to me. I collected the jade and my painting and a bag full of assorted junk Mary had bought.

They walked in front of me to the Duesenberg deep in conversation, he in his pale cream suit and she in various hues of yellow, the ginger dog at their heels. A tone poem no sane artist would dare to tackle.

I staggered behind them; five thousand, four hundred pounds under one arm and ten quid under the other.

Mary gasped when she saw the car and Piccalilli raised a leg and washed a handspan of dust from a rear spat to show his approval.

I packed the purchases into the boot and as I opened the door and encouraged Piccalilli to jump on the back seat a Rolls-Royce drew up and an old man wound down the rear window and beckoned to me.

He was wearing an Inverness cape and a pearl grey fedora. His face was thin and white and he breathed with obvious difficulty, expelling the air with a mechanical force.

'You bought the Carlton Smith?' Watery blue eyes looked steadily into mine.

'Yes, I like it.'

He smiled a thin smile. 'It was my daughter's favourite. She had it in the nursery when she was very young, that's why the frame is damaged. I never had it repaired.' He stopped and resumed the mechanical breathing then smiled again. 'She died in the war. I was going to keep it but sometimes it is best to sever links.' He stared fixedly at the back of the chauffeur's head then smiled again. 'I bought it from the artist – for rather less than you paid for it.' A little guffaw brought on a spasm of coughing and he tapped on the glass partition. The window closed and the car glided away.

Vicky held the painting at arm's length, a stunned look on her face – I had just told her how much I had paid for it.

'Ye gods,' was all she said.

I promised to sell my shotgun, my silver mounted driving whip and a pair of martingales to help pay for it. These enormous sacrifices did not, I felt, receive the recognition they should have, for all my wife said, over and over again, was 'ye gods'.

In a churlish mood and feeling guilty at using up so much of our working capital on an impulse buy I set off to mooch around the village. I kicked the stones down Mill Lane and threw one at a rabbit on the common, I leaned over the wall and watched the fish rise in the mill pond and cursed the spot where my cheese kettle had sunk. I ignored Rabbit's dejected wave and stood with my back to the pinfold and watched a helm cloud, heavy and black, brush the flat top of Penhill. We were in for a storm.

John Barleycorn has many enemies. He's railed and ranted at, decried, has blame heaped upon his cheery head but sometimes he is the only friend a sensitive man needs.

Billy Potts sat in the taproom, a half pint of bitter, barely sipped, in front of him. He sat on a stool, his legs wide apart and his hands grasping his knees like enormous red crabs. 'Where's Rabbit? Should be in by now.'

I shook my head and went to sit in the corner under the dartboard; it's just the place for a miserable man to sit and reflect.

Rabbit, I knew, was sat out in his overgrown garden, an upturned peggy-tub, the one he uses for forcing rhubarb, providing him with a fairly comfortable seat and a drop-head sewing machine, its iron frame red with rust, serving him equally well as a table. He was playing with a young ferret, but he was not a happy man.

Late bees hung on the lips of the foxglove bells, moths jittered in a billow of activity over the giant privet hedge he thought best left uncut. His terriers licked tired paws and lay back in the still warm grass with satisfied sighs, and from over the mill dam, across Mill Lane, came the occasional plop as a lazy fish rose to a careless fly.

Rabbit had paid the last instalment on his rates and bought a new pair of boots. His dogs were working well, his ferrets fierce but pliable, he was healthy and Mucky Marion had brought him, that very morning, one of his favourite cream cakes, yet he was not a happy man.

The access to his Golconda had been blocked, the silk thread that connected the spider with his fat fly had been severed: Ted and the Colonel had changed the lock on the contributions box.

The two agents of Rabbit's financial downfall stood shoulder to shoulder in the lounge, looked at each other, and for once, exchanged smiles.

Ted stayed in the lounge as long as he could. He farmed his own land and had money put by, so much in fact he had been forced to remark more than once, 'Folk'll be capped when I go.' But for all his social and financial standing in the community he still felt a little uneasy in the lounge. The dingy taproom, spartan in the extreme, was his natural habitat and the unusual presence of his cousin Billy in the taproom and the knowledge that he would have to fork out for a substantial amount of beer if he joined him, kept him hovering at the Colonel's elbow.

The Reverend Sidney, always breezy, and in Ted's eyes a bit of a parasite, pulled off his bicycle clips, ordered half a pint and called Ted 'my good man'. This brought a frown to the farmer's face and sent him hurrying down the two worn steps, to give me a friendly nod and sit alongside Billy.

'Where's Rabbit?' Billy asked him.

'How should I know? I'll tell you one thing though. Idle sod won't be working, wherever he is.'

Billy nodded in agreement. 'Aye, if poaching began with a "w" and had four letters in it, there'd be a lot more pheasants about.'

The cousins laughed and raised their glasses. Ted on thumping his glass back on the table after a healthy and throat-pulsing swallow saw to his dismay that Billy's glass was now completely empty and that his cousin was smiling at him with childlike affection. He clicked his teeth and taking Billy's glass rattled it noisily in the service hatch. 'Same again!'

Billy coughed. 'Make it a pint this time cuz. I'm a bit clagged.'

The revenue from the box after the lock had been changed had surprised everybody. It had bought petrol for the parish mower and provided money for a sack of bulbs to be planted on the green by the schoolchildren. It had paid Baz for cleaning out the pinfold and Richard for repairing the seat on the common.

The washfold, sympathetically renovated by Baz, had grown back its pink lace of creeping cranesbill and the broad elm board that sat easily in its stone slots had swelled and gathered around its water-pushed side a debris of plants and twigs, small stones and caddis fly larvae. It formed a pool as big as a table top and two handspans in depth. The parish council, ever concerned with the safety and the well-being of the children of the village, had decreed that one board would suffice: it showed the intent of the washfold without creating a hazard.

The village was looking good. The pub had benefited, and so had we; Mrs Lewis was selling more ice cream than she had ever done and on a fine day cameras clicked the length and breadth of the green.

The ruttle boxes, lucrative as they were, had become a chore to the children. I wheeled them out every morning and replenished them as needed. Roddy was fascinated by them. 'Damned good stuff here,' he'd told Sally and Peter. 'A real winner mateys.'

But the delights of summer days in the dale exercised a stronger pull and Vicky and I were pleased that it did. We had let them gorge on their profits and they had hoarded crisps and pop, sweets and chocolate bars in their bedrooms like two squirrels. We insisted on vigorous tooth cleaning and Nellie May wagged a warning finger at them. 'You'll ruin your stomachs.'

Charlie at The Ship beamed as only a satisfied landlord will. The tables were full every lunch-time. Ethel and Mucky Marion sweated in the kitchen and Susan had been taken on as waitress. There were only two black patches in Charlie's life. Yorkshire weren't doing well and a host of beetles had invaded his cellar.

Rabbit could only offer his condolences on the cricket but the beetle problem he had cured. 'There yer are Charlie, damned good hedgepig that, she'll soon shift 'em.' He'd smiled, and after handing the cardboard box over the bar had scrubbed his stubbly chin and inclined his head slightly. 'Must be a two pint hedgepig, that.' Charlie had given him three pints for it and the children had looked in vain for Heidi.

'She's gone off to be queen of a wonderful underground world,' I told them. 'She lives on beer, beetles and meat and potato pie.' They looked at me in a puzzled way and put a saucer of milk and bread out for Heidi's brood now, thankfully, weaned and independent.

Ted had returned the old photograph. Vicky had run her finger across the top of it. 'That's how the clever old devil did it, he's cut the top off the photo.'

The photo-cropper sat opposite me, responding in a reserved way now to his cousin's *bonhomie*, for *bonhomie* costs money. 'We're reviving the village fête and show. Used to be a grand day,' he told me, as the first big drops splatted on to the window.

*

Vicky was already in bed. I sat in Widgeon's chair, the oil painting in front of me, and told her of the parish council's decision to hold the fête again.

She listened in a petulant way giving me no more than a cool 'really', or a disinterested 'oh'. The storm broke, rain lashed on the window and thunder rumbled overhead. She leaned up and hugged her knees. 'You're a neddy,' she said slowly. A flicker of lightning lit the room. I saw that her eyes were soft and that the beginnings of an impish smile was just opening her pretty mouth.

Chapter 22

Good shopkeepers that we are, we keep our daybook meticulously. Sales and deposits, purchases and breakages: little happinesses, little sadnesses, all recorded in Vicky's neat hand. Tucked in amongst the mundane entries of materials bought and rates paid are details of our house calls. The addresses are carefully underlined and some have magic names. There is Crackpot Ings, Halfpenny House, Donkey Fields and Three Mare Close. Lovely names that owe nothing to artificiality, they are honest names that have grown as the buildings themselves grew – out of the dale.

Vicky squared the sandwiches and wrapped them neatly in greaseproof paper; she laid two apples and a flask of coffee alongside them and looked me up and down. 'You want a thick sweater on, it'll be cold on the tops today.'

Thick-sweatered and well-provisioned I ushered the dogs into the back of the van and set off up the dale. I had two delicious names to add to our collection that day: Tête Beche Cottage and Mouse Castle.

Tête Beche has the kind of garden many strive for but few achieve. The wide borders are curving cushions of colour: marigold and lavender giving way to massed dahlias which hold the eye with a sheer intensity of colour until it is stolen away by majestic ranks of delphiniums, hollyhocks and sunflowers interplanted with golden rod.

Aaron Simpson is well known for keeping his purse strings tied. He only grows a plant or a bush if he can beg or filch the seed or a cutting from a neighbour. He sees no distinction between the cultivated and the wild, incorporating feverfew or ragwort into his beds if the shape and colour of the plants suit his needs.

Wherever the raw materials come from, Aaron instinctively knows how to use them to their greatest effect.

'Nurserymen are thieves to a man,' he'd pronounce on one of his rare visits to the Fighting Cocks. 'Nature's bounty and they want to empty your purse for it.'

A weak sun had dried the dew from all but the deepest hollows in the Yorkstone path as I rang the bell and stepped back to admire the neat eighteenth-century cottage.

Aaron led me down a stone-flagged passageway, which was lined breast-high with firewood, to the kitchen. A lathe stood under the window, a milling machine sat comfortably between the cooker and the sink, and, bolted to a good period dresser, was an archaic bench drill. Aaron's kitchen is his workshop for he is a fanatical model engineer and that was the reason for my visit to Tête Beche. He wanted his models valuing.

Properly scaled and engineered models are difficult to value. Hundreds of hours of painstaking and skilled work can go into a model which is perfect in every way but has little appeal to the layman. A cross-sectioned model of a diaphragm pump, no matter how exquisite, fails to excite, whereas the locomotive and the Merryweather fire engine incite an immediate response and bring out the schoolboy in every man.

Aaron waved me to the solitary chair. 'Tea?' he asked.

I thanked him as he sprinkled what looked like a handful of dried horse manure into a tin jug, then he curled his ragged sweater around his hand and lifted a black kettle from the fire. After swilling the jug around for a while he plonked it on to the milling machine table.

To the left of the fireplace stood a huge livery cupboard. Aaron took a key from his pocket, unlocked the doors and swung them open to reveal three shelves lined with superb models. 'These are what I want you to look at.' He glanced across at the tin jug. 'I'll just get some pots.' Clumping over to the sink he began to rummage through a pile of dirty crockery.

A breathtaking model of an 0–4–0 tank engine in NER livery sat on a length of track on the middle shelf. It was a live steam model and I could see from the discoloration around the smoke box and fire pan that it had been fired up.

Sometimes, as every child knows, the eye is not enough; we have to touch. I touched. I touched the wheels, the valve gear, the steam dome, even the crashed coal in the hopper.

Aaron pushed an enamel mug into my hand. I must have looked a little guilty about the touching for he smiled up at me and nodded at the engine. 'Go on thee touch it. I have to touch it missen sometimes.'

'It's beautiful Aaron.'

He grinned and ran a thin hand through his white hair. 'Aye it is grand. Over 2,000 hours in her, reckon she'd be cheap at a pound an hour.'

Aaron spent all his waking hours gardening, model engineering or scouring the countryside for firewood. This one engine must have represented three or four years' work. I looked along the shelves. There were two beam engines, a double-acting mill engine, a horsedrawn tram, two waterline models of tugs and several stationary and pumping engines and on the top shelf was a delightful four-wheeled carrier's wagon and a threshing machine with tiny bags of wheat resting against a back wheel.

Meticulously scaled, beautifully crafted and superbly finished they were the lifetime's work of a skilled and dedicated modeller. How could I possibly value them accurately?

I had some catalogues of specialised model sales and with a phone call or two I could get near enough for insurance purposes. 'Is it a valuation for insurance you want, Aaron?'

He scratched his head, closed his eyes, then gave me a slow sideways look. 'I just want to know what they're worth.'

I couldn't possibly just give a figure off the top of my head, the collection warranted a thorough evaluation and it would entail a lot of work. 'For a proper written valuation we charge two and a half per cent,' I told him.

Aaron jerked his body around to face me. His pale blue eyes stared into mine, his jaw dropped open and wagged two or three times before the words came. 'Two and a half per cent, you'd want two and a half per cent?'

'That's it Aaron. It entails a lot of work.'

'Entails a lot of work.' He stabbed a finger at the shelves. 'Them's entailed a lot of work. Tha' wants two and a half per cent of all them hours I've stood at that lathe, two and a half per cent of all them hours I've sat at that bench – just to tell me what they're worth?'

He took the mug out of my hand and hurried me down the passageway. 'Per cents! Per cents! It's per cents that ruin a man.'

The heavy door clumped behind me and two heavy bolts were shot home.

I let the dogs out into a steady drizzle and poured myself a coffee. Wiping the condensation from the inside of the windscreen I could see Aaron climbing the fell behind his cottage, his body rocking as he stabbed his legs into the scree, his tightly rolled firewood sack under his arm. I suppose a man needs some fresh air when he's been damned near frightened to death with talk of per cents.

I pulled the van off the road and on to the sheep-cropped turf. It was lunch-time. Behind me lay a dale veiled in a white translucent mist; before me, one dappled in sunshine.

The dogs raced after the crusts I threw into the heather, their strong stumpy tails wagging like mad metronomes.

The visit to Aaron's had wasted the best part of the morning: petrol and time, two of our most precious commodities, wasted. 'Well!' I thought. 'I'll waste a bit of time on myself.'

I called the dogs and ran pell-mell along the Old Drove Road. It was a delicious day and waiting for me was Henry Lee-Carew, D. Litt., and Mouse Castle.

Henry's directions were full and accurate. I turned left at the cattle grid and proceeded for four-tenths of a mile before turning left after the rowan tree. A note ringed in red had instructed me to 'reverse van to here', so obediently I reversed until the briars and blackthorn scraped the sides of the van, then I leapt out of the back doors to a yapping welcome from Henry's Jack Russell.

Mouse Castle is a Victorian folly. Built by a rich landowner as an estate boundary-marker it had seen life as a shooting box and shepherd's hut and had then lain derelict for years until Henry had found it. Barely eight paces square with its crenellated walls, leaded lancet windows and mock portcullis, it is an aristocratic little place. The Virginia creeper which covers all four walls was shaded from a blush pink to a deep red and showed here and there a waxy yellow leaf.

Henry's garden is a jungle. Cotoneasters, briar and quickthorn, berberis and Russian vine are massed around the house. It's a garden for bird and hedgehog, a haven of food and shelter, marred only by a yapping but harmless dog.

Henry came up the path to meet me. He is a very tall man. Hunched in the back and a little springy in the knees he does tend to resemble an untidy question mark, but he is still an impressive figure of a man and when questioned about his great height he straightens himself slowly, grimaces a little, then with a smile announces, 'Half an inch of leather under my heels and I'm two and a quarter yards.'

The tiny lounge was comfortable and warm. Colourful Ghiordes prayer rugs were scattered about a pearwood floor and a good fire crackled in the dog grate. A cottage suite and coffee table were the only furnishings, with the exception of a chiffonier occupying the only gap in the bookshelves which lined the walls from floor to ceiling. Books are Henry's passion. He lifted a pile of them from the settee and waving me to a seat stationed himself in front of the fire.

His wife Dora waddled in from the kitchen with a tray of coffee and biscuits. 'Enwee told me you were here.' She smiled and setting the tray down dropped into a chair. 'Sit down Enwee, sit down.' Henry sat and rubbed his knees. Dora leaned towards me. 'We haven't a good leg between us,' she confessed.

Henry smiled across at his beloved Dora. 'We've magnificent bodies but cheap legs.' Dora rocked back in her chair and laughed. They are a lovely couple.

When Henry resigned his teaching post and buried himself in the dale with his books he had no intention of marrying. However, within a month of his arrival he was walking out with the rotund little Dora. She had kept house for her two bachelor brothers since leaving school and they had treated her like a slave. When she and Henry married and moved into Mouse Castle it was as if the gates of paradise had opened for her. She was somebody. She was cared for and loved, for the first time in her life, and she in return responded with a complete and all-enveloping love for her 'Enwee'.

Every morning when Henry takes his walk with the dog she struggles upstairs and watches him from the landing window.

'I love you Enwee Lee-Carew,' she says, and sometimes her soft brown eyes fill with tears. 'If folk knew what I did they'd think I was crackers,' she'd confided to Elsie in the Post Office.

Elsie's a blabbermouth so folk do know, but nobody thinks Dora is crackers.

Henry is a good talker and both Dora and I are good listeners. Time flew by. Through the lancet window I watched the sky streak with pink and then darken as rain clouds crowded over the fell top. Henry's bantam cock crowed in a half-hearted way and then clucked a stiff-legged walk up the ramp to the hen house followed by his little harem. Dora must have heard the tales of Henry's National Service a half a dozen times before but she still laughed until her cheeks glowed. There was no clock in the room and I never wear a watch but it must have been late afternoon when I prodded Henry gently towards the reason for my visit.

Dora struggled to her feet and waddled off to the kitchen. 'I'll leave you two to it.'

Henry nodded. 'It's the chiffonier we're after selling. We're just desperate for bookshelves.'

It was a fine rosewood chiffonier, more Regency than Victorian, with good colour and crisp ormolu mounts: it would be an easy seller so I offered a good price. He shrugged his shoulders. 'Yes, that seems all right. Are you interested in the things on it?'

There was a Staffordshire figure with plenty of colour and a lobster-tail helmet of the Commonwealth period. I was a little out of my depth with the helmet. It was such good quality and so well preserved it aroused my suspicions. Was it a Victorian copy? I felt the thickness of the metal, tested its weight in my hands and screwing in my eye glass worked the segments, looking for an evenness of pitting which would suggest acids had been used to accelerate ageing. I looked around at Henry because sometimes a vendor's face can tell us what we want to know. 'A Victorian copy?'

Henry nodded and smiled. 'A good one, eh?'

It was a good one and in the right quarter would fetch its money. I had no wish to jeopardise the deal over the chiffonier so I offered what I considered to be top price. Henry winced. 'I paid more than that for it, years ago.'

'Well, it is a copy Henry, and it's finding the right outlet. I could have it years.' Mentally I upped the price on the Staffordshire and Henry brightened a little when I made him my offer.

'OK, swings and roundabouts I suppose,' he shrugged.

I gathered the Staffordshire represented a good profit for him and he was willing to offset the helmet against it.

'Dora! Dora!' he called down the passage. 'A little of your beetroot wine wouldn't go amiss.'

Dora poured two generous glasses and stood back smiling, bottle in hand. The wine was a good colour and it had bite without being fiery. It tingled in the mouth, then left it warm and suffused with a blackcurrantiness which was very pleasant.

'It's very good – beetroot you say?'

Dora smiled and refilled my glass then she waddled off to the kitchen. 'I'll write out the recipe for you,' she called over her shoulder.

Henry waited until she'd gone, did a sideways twist of his body to make sure she was out of earshot then put a finger to his lips. 'The wine she makes is all right but a bit bland so I fortify it a little with brandy.'

We loaded the chiffonier with some difficulty. Henry, like a lot of tall men, is a poor lifter. Once safely inside the van I cocooned it in old blankets; to mark it would have been a crime.

The dogs bounded up and down the track, goading Henry's terrier into a frenzy of barking, as Dora pushed the helmet and Staffordshire into my arms and tucked the recipe into my pocket. 'Now make sure them beetroots is good and juicy – no woody 'uns.'

Henry gave me a broad wink. 'Yes, take care over the main ingredient.'

Vicky was delighted with the chiffonier. Rosewood is our favourite, especially if it is not too high Victorian. She ran her hands over it lovingly and gave me one of her endearing smiles. 'Shall we keep it?'

I shrugged my shoulders. It would be a prestige piece in the shop and it represented a lot of money, but it was beautiful, and, coming as it did from Mouse Castle, I too was tempted to keep it for ourselves. However, it was far too good to go in the kitchen and our lounge was fully furnished. 'It would go in the dining room,' Vicky suggested hopefully.

'It would look ridiculous in an empty room on bare floor-boards,' I replied half-heartedly.

Vicky pushed her lower lip out and looked up at me. 'It wouldn't look ridiculous anywhere, it's beautiful. Anyway, it's time I had something – you've got the Carlton Smith.'

I gave a deep sigh and turned away. Vicky knows when she's won, she grabbed me around the waist and waltzed me around the shop.

I sat the Staffordshire and the helmet on the counter and went in search of the children. One of the advantages of keeping an antique shop is that history pours through your door, objects which have lived through years of tumult and social change make it almost tangible, and here were two good lessons for the children, for the Staffordshire figure represented Queen Caroline, the sad wife of George IV, and the helmet, although a copy, recalled the stirring years of the civil war.

Sally and Peter stood quiet and attentive until I'd finished, then Sally with just the hint of a smile pointed with a charmingly crooked finger to Queen Caroline's neck. 'Did the naughty King have her beheaded, 'cos her head's been off?'

I took a magnifying glass and inspected the figure closely. A thin line around the neck confirmed Sally's words, the figure had been repaired. I waved them out of the shop and dropped my head into my hands.

Peter paused in the doorway. 'These Cavaliers and Roundheads, Dad, which side were you on?'

The duster missed him but caught a small fairing and sent it crashing to the floor to explode into a thousand pieces.

I bent my head against the rain as I hurried across the green to The Ship. An acquisitive wife and hawk-eyed and cheeky kids can send a man to the pub when it isn't fit to turn a dog out.

'This man looks as if he's had a good day,' Ted greeted me.

I told him I had been to see Enwee and Aaron.

'Did tha' manage to do owt?' Rabbit asked.

'Well I did a bit with Enwee but nothing with Aaron.'

Ted smiled. 'Tatey Beech, that's where Aaron lives. It's French for arse-about-face.' He looked around authoritatively and paused for effect as I pulled a buffet up to the table and waited for him to go on. 'And I'll tell you how it became to be known as Tatey Beech.' He stretched his legs out and joined his hands together across his waistcoat.

The wind was rattling the door latch and slapping fingers of rain on the windows; it wasn't a bad night for a tale.

'Well, Aaron went down to Lalbeck for some stamps. This was years ago. They had a little machine set in the wall then – for stamps. Well he'd got three or four stamps out when he noticed they were all arse-about-face. Well! He'd run out of change but he knew he were on to summat, so he got a kid to stand by the machine and see nobody else used it and ran down the market place like a clipped cock. I wor doing t'milk and it wor payday so I had me old cash bag on.' Ted stopped and took a long drink. 'Well! Aaron shoves his hand in me bag and ruttles round until he had a fistful of pennies, then back up t'market place like a clipped cock again.'

Rabbit leaned forward and held his hand to Ted's chest whilst he explained to me. 'This wor before Aaron did his leg in.'

Ted glowered at him until he removed the offending hand then continued. 'Well! Aaron got another couple of bum stamps, then they all came good 'uns. Still he kept putting money in till all t'stamps were done. Yer see, he wan't going to leave any stamps in that there machine in case there was some more bum 'uns.' He leaned forward to me and whispered quietly. 'Did I tell thee they wor penny stamps?'

'No you didn't Ted.'

He leaned back. 'Well! They wor, and Aaron thought ah, might be t'same in halfpennies. Down he came again, split-arsed across the cobbles, his boots striking sparks, rattled in me bag again an' off wi' a fistful of halfpennies. Well! He got nowt out of t'halfpennies but good 'uns. But them arse-about-face penny 'uns, they was auctioned and fetched a lot of money: enough to buy Rose Cottage and change its name to Tatey Beech in honour of what had brought him the money.'

Rabbit scratched his nose. 'Myrtle!'

Ted blew his cheeks out and looked at him hard. 'What d'you mean Myrtle?'

'That's what it wor called, Myrtle Cottage, not Rose.'

'Well, does it matter?'

Before Rabbit could answer, Ted half turned his back on him and grinned at me. 'An' another thing: I never did get that brass back off Aaron.'

Rabbit lifted his legs up on to a buffet and stared at his mud-caked boots. 'An' tha' widn't get it back either – tightest man in the dale, Aaron.'

Ted banged his pint on to the table and stared at it until the froth-covered waves subsided and then turned to face the old poacher. 'No! Ar' Billy's tightest man in t'dale.'

Rabbit, in a slight huff at Ted's earlier treatment of him, couldn't wait to contradict him. 'No! Aaron's the tightest.'

Ted, seeing family honour at stake prepared for battle, spreading his knees and leaning forward in a belligerent way.

'Ar' Billy meks his own envelopes out of brown paper.'

'Aaron sieves his ashes and weighs t'nails in for scrap.'

'Ar' Billy can mek a teabag last a week.'

'Aaron drinks camomile tea and grows it hisself. Anyway your Billy has a Rolls-Royce.'

Ted looked uneasy, and swilled his beer around in his glass. 'Aye but he had it given. Lady Brown gave him t'car and a courtin' suit, an' them cars weren't valued like they are today.' He turned to me and explained quietly. 'You see her Ladyship wor very fond of ar' Billy when he wor young man.'

Rabbit leaned back and laughed. 'Her Ladyship wor fond of a lot of young men but she didn't giv 'em all a Rolls-Royce.'

Ted blew his nose and emptied his glass. Rabbit's was already empty and the two men stared at the offending pint glasses in silence until I took the hint and passed them through the hatch to Charlie. Being as we were on the brink of having one of the outstanding questions of the day settled once and for all by these two experts, it would have been churlish, indeed silly, to do otherwise.

The two men smiled their approval at the full pints but remained silent. With money invested I had to have a result so I prodded them into action. 'Could anybody else be considered the . . .'

They broke me off, crying in unison. 'No! No! It's between Aaron and Billy.'

They took long pulls at their beer, smacked their lips, sniffed, and bent themselves once more to the task.

'Ar' Billy cuts his own hair.'

'Aaron has never bought a piece of coal in his life.' The two protagonists leaned back deep in thought.

A log settled on the fire, Rabbit's dogs scratched themselves and yawned, eclipsing the steady tick of the wallclock until their two tired heads flopped back to the floor.

It looked like a draw. I thrust my hands deep into my coat pockets and tapped my feet on the concrete floor, this was most unsatisfactory, money invested and no conclusive result. I could have told them that Billy had, quite unprompted, given me a slice of ham, but this I felt was a temporary aberration brought about by his receiving a substantial amount of money for something he looked upon as junk. It would have clouded the issue. Anyhow, I'd promised to say nothing.

Suddenly Rabbit brightened. 'Your Billy once gave me a goose egg.'

Ted eyed him suspiciously. 'A goose egg? Wor' it addled?'

'No! It was a good 'un. Ad it for me breakfast.'

A sly smile came to Rabbit's face as he watched Ted make his mumpy mouth and squirm in his seat for a full five seconds. Then he put the knife in with slow meticulous words. 'Aaron would never give you a good egg.'

Ted shook his head sadly, conceding defeat. Then he rose with the measured dignity that befits a parish councillor, buttoned his overcoat and walked slowly to the door and opened it. He paused, letting a cold blast of air brighten the fire and chase the cigarette ash from the tables, then turned and smiled at us.

'Aye, but Aaron's a lot older. Wait till ar' Billy gets a bit of age on his back.'

Chapter 23

I was in trouble over the bee-saving kit. I didn't know that the Victorian pressed glass tumbler and the creased postcard that had stood in the window bottom for days had any special use.

'Any bee trying to get out of the window we save –' Sally started to explain.

'Yes,' Peter interrupted. 'We put the glass over the bee, slide the postcard up to trap it, then fling it outside.' It seemed an admirable idea, so I went, rather sheepishly, and retrieved the tumbler from the thirty pence ruttle box.

We have loads of bees around the house. The Colonel keeps a hive and so does Miss Wells. Our tangle of nasturtiums and our herb garden literally vibrate with bees on summer afternoons. Sally and the cat watch them intently, the dogs occasionally snap at a lazy one that drones too near their tired heads, and sometimes one buzzes into the house to butt against the window panes and make Vicky a little nervous. The bee-saving kit, now properly acknowledged and housed on the comb box, came more and more into use as the summer days lengthened and the wealth of pollen dusted the bees and filled the little pots that Sally insists they have strapped to their back legs.

They drone off across the green in a low swaying flight like heavily laden bombers. Our garden, plundered of its wealth by these gentle raiders, looks no worse for it and the fruit on our trees sets well and in autumn bends boughs down to within range of our nibbling goat.

Next year, we tell ourselves, when we've got a bit of wool on our backs, we'll buy a colony. Fresh honey on home baked bread we do have, but it is Miss Wells' honey.

She buys pretty labels for her jars. They are in ivory, bordered by pale flowers and have a dark brown line which runs fiercely along its straight paths, but when it comes to the corners it flings itself into several gay little arabesques then descends to coil in a somewhat laboured way, into a message. 'This honey is from –' And here Miss Wells writes, in a delicate hand, 'Miss Wells'.

Her back porch is not a typical country back porch. It is too ordered. The geraniums grow evenly, the hanging fuchsia arches its stems and droops its lovely flowers in a perfect hemisphere and the dog lead hangs on its hook.

She handed me the jar of honey and then she folded a schedule for the village fête and with one of her nice but restrained smiles tucked it between jar and hand. 'We expect some good things from your two,' she said taking the money from my open hand; her smile became less restrained; in fact, quite abandoned.

'It's time you gave us a little talk you know. We have a cancellation, the pot-pourri lady is ill. What about Thursday?'

The children pinned the schedule to their picture wall and leaned against it and considered what to enter. Sally changed her mind constantly. From an edible necklace to handwriting, from handwriting to a garden on a dinner plate then back to the edible necklace.

Peter had no such problem. 'A homemade desk-tidy,' he cried and immediately seeing the possibilities of several items in the rattle boxes, he dashed out to retrieve them.

Vicky shook her head. Sewing, cooking and flower arranging seemed to be the only things open to her and she was loath to take on the village matrons in any one of these fields.

Odd free moments I got in the shop I made notes on the antique trade, because before Miss Wells had gently closed the porch door behind me she had extracted a promise from me to talk to the Women's Institute.

The village fête and show began to intrude into my life. Embryo edible necklaces and several patterns of desk-tidy lay on the dresser and in the wide window bottoms.

Sally lolled on my knee and kicked her new sandals on to the rug. 'You could do a plate of four eggs,' she said in a wheedling voice. 'You're always on about your Barnevelder's brown eggs.'

I promised to enter a plate of eggs and sent the happy child to pester her mother. 'Surely there is something you could do, Mummy?'

I was just expanding a good idea I'd had about we dealers being custodians of antiques when Ted, the doorbell still jangling behind him, dropped heavily on to the duet stool.

'This is the bit I don't like,' he said leaning forward. 'Cadging.' He almost whispered the word.

'Cadging! Ted, you're always bloody cadging.'

He pretended to look offended, made a cursory mumpy

mouth, then stabbed a finger on to my knee. 'No, for the fête, the white elephant stall, you must have something?' He looked around the shop then back at me and grinned.

'I'll seek something out. When do you want it?' I asked him.

'Soon as poss.'

'This afternoon, Ted, I will deliver unto you.'

He paused, his hand on the doorknob. 'I'll have to take more brass than old General Disorder over there. I allus did in the past.'

'The Colonel? What's he doing?'

'Same as usual, clay pigeons.'

I searched the caravan, the loft of the apple house and the smallholding in general for stock for Ted's stall.

Vicky is not a hoarder like me, her definition of junk has a low threshold.

She added a food mixer, antiquated but sound; a violin with no strings and a hideous vase in the shape of a gaping-mouthed fish to my wheelbarrow load. Then she returned to the kitchen for more. The vase I agreed with, but the mixer and violin? I pushed the wheelbarrow round to Ted's before we were ruined.

'Smashin', that's smashin'.' Ted delved into the barrow picking out items which caught his eye and set them out on his bink. He held the fish vase at arm's length and smiled at it. 'By, that's grand! That'll fetch a bob or two.'

My little talk to the Women's Institute went very well; the dear ladies were a grand audience. They listened attentively, laughed at my little jokes, and then drowned me in tea.

Unbeknown to me, Dolly had confidently told everyone that I would be doing valuations, and consequently nearly every lady huddled a bag of some description to her legs.

I looked at Staffordshire figures, carriage clocks, snuff boxes and a variety of buttermarkers. Some ladies with knowing smiles produced fleams and mazling irons, buckers and rowelling stones, but I had spent enough time with Long John's collection to enable me to identify them all.

Mrs Henry Lee-Carew brought a calf-bound book of botanical prints which made me sigh. It was very beautiful, easily the most beautiful thing there, and Dora glowed with pride when I told her so.

From the far side of the dale had come Mrs Kolakowski. A woman to whom work is a religion. She farms, with her husband and son, some of the hardest land in the dale. The grass is scant and windbent and soon browned: the soil is thin on the rock. But they prosper. They prosper because they work like dogs. The light in their cheese room is burning past many a midnight. She had brought nothing, but her leathery brown hand closed on mine. 'You have in your shop a painting. One man two sheeps?' I confirmed that I had. 'This painting you ask a hundred pounds for?' I nodded again.

'I have painting, one man three sheeps. How much mine worth?' She released my hand and folded her arms, a satisfied look on her face.

I asked her the usual questions. 'Is it on canvas? Is it signed? How big?'

She mumbled her replies, each one prefaced with 'I tink.' The solid hard-working woman was not to be moved. Her simple philosophy was unshakable, more sheep – more money.

'Bring it to the shop Mrs Kolakowski and I'll put it under the glass: it sounds very interesting.'

The satisfied look gave way to a wide smile. 'I bring it, and other tings, too, OK?'

Canary Mary had been very quiet all evening. There had been some problem the previous month over the jar of lemon curd she'd entered in the Preserves section of their competition. It was rumoured that she had bought a well-known and expensive lemon curd and transferred it to her own jar.

Stephanie, the vicar's wife, who was judging the competition, had got around the problem quite nicely, disqualifying Mary's entry because she'd used a metal lid. Face had been saved without a major ruction but Mary was still sulking; she likes to win. I took my umpteenth cup of tea and went to sit with her.

'You didn't bring anything for me to look at.'

'Haven't got anything,' she replied petulantly.

'Mary, I was hoping a colleague in the trade would have helped me a bit.'

She obviously enjoyed being classed as a colleague and she smiled a little as she dipped into her bag. 'I was going to show you this, but you didn't seem to have time for old friends.'

I apologised. 'I was a bit nervous, Mary. It's the first time I've done this.'

She brought out a tiny but superb boudoir clock set with brilliants. Two cherubs held a gold banner high and the clock, in the form of a ball, nestled in its folds.

I took the clock and walked back to the table. 'Ladies! Ladies! If I could have your attention please. I would like you to see what Mary's brought. It is a superb boudoir clock.'

There was several oohs and ahs and soon I had a circle of jostling ladies around me as Mary smiled from her third row seat.

'Could you tell me how much it's worth?' she called.

I could have walked up to her and jammed her custard

yellow cartwheel hat over her ears, for she knew it was valuable, and in this condition, quite rare.

Dora looked at me balefully. Her book of prints, calf-bound and beautifully produced had, up till now, given her a clear lead. Upset Dora or upset Mary? I dithered and dallied.

'Well, it's French. Late nineteenth-century. Superb craftsmanship. Very desirable.'

Mary's eye never left me. Her smile had become more of a smirk. I sat down in the front row and the ladies formed a semicircle in front of me, Dora hugging the book to her bosom, a set look on her face. Her Enwee had chosen the book carefully, and, I suspected, not without a touch of devilment. I looked up at Dora then back at the clock.

'I'm glad you brought this Mary,' I lied. 'It illustrates a point. I've seen some superb things here tonight, things I never thought I'd see up the dale, and two of those things are rather special, Dora's book and your clock.'

I heard Mary's chair creak as she leaned forward. Dora edged to the front, her legs ached but she chose not to sit: Enwee's book was important, it was going to get its rightful recognition.

It went very quiet. The clock ticked away in my hand, a hurried mocking tick. I was thinking furiously. The prints were more valuable than the clock, but the clock was, on the face of it more desirable, more tactile; women touched it and smiled.

I cleared my throat. 'We have here an example of the best craftsmanship from two centuries. The book is of the eighteenth, the clock, the nineteenth. You could take the valuations of a hundred dealers, some would come down in favour of the clock and some in favour of the prints. Personally I think the clock is slightly more valuable than the prints, but if I was offered a choice I would take the prints, because sheer value is not the criterion of a knowledgeable collector.'

I risked a glance at Dora, she was smiling. Her Enwee was a knowledgeable collector, that she knew, and I, a knowledgeable dealer, had told everyone so and that I preferred the prints.

Dora was happy and Mary was satisfied. The yellow cartwheel swayed from side to side as she graciously accepted compliments about the clock.

Mrs Smythe-Robinson, who with uncustomary sensitivity had elected to bring only a simple knitting stick, now eyed Mary with envy and wished she'd brought the Clichy paperweight which stood on the oak lowboy.

Miss Wells thanked me profusely and presented me with a cake. The ladies clapped and all of them insisted on shaking hands with me.

Dora pulled on her navy mac and winked an unpractised wink before she waddled off, clutching her book tightly, to get her lift home.

I took Mary's clock back to her. She was as happy as a sandboy as she wrapped it first in blue tissue, then in newspaper and nestled it safe into the middle of her bag. The hall emptied fast, leaving three of the more forceful volunteers washing up noisily.

I put my hand on Mary's. 'How much for the clock?'

She pursed her lips and shook her head. 'It's not for sale.'

'I'll give you a good price.'

'It's not for sale!'

'It's a nice piece Mary. Where did you dig that up?'

'From a friend. Got it from a friend.' She began to hum and pull her clothes about, a sure sign she was not pleased with my questioning.

I stood up and looked down at her for a moment. 'If you ever do want to sell it.' She hummed a little louder and clattering her chair back gave me a glassy smile and gathered up her bags.

Dolly had been washing up. 'We should have a roster,' she complained without conviction. 'I always seem to get stuck with it.' I knew she was happy getting stuck with it and I pulled her leg gently about it as we drove home. 'Some as never gets their jewelled hands wet,' she said primly, nursing her basket and crossing her feet.

We stopped at the fish and chip shop in Lalbeck for I had hatched a little plot with Vicky. We would change into our pyjamas and sneak upstairs and catch the children sitting in the landing window. After a few mock tellings-off, I'd produce the fish and chips and we'd all sit cross-legged on the landing carpet and have a little feast, and now there was Miss Wells' chocolate cake too, an unforeseen delight.

Dolly had come prepared; she had extra newspaper to wrap around her steaming parcel and a thick tea towel to tuck over her basket. The tucking finished she leaned back. 'What are you putting in the show?'

'Eggs! A plate of four brown eggs.' I grinned at her confidently. 'Bound to win, my Barnevelders.'

She sniffed and mm'd. 'You'll have all on because –' She stopped suddenly and turned to look out of the side window.

'Because, Dolly. Because what?'

'Well, I shouldn't tell you this but . . . '

There was a long silence, before I said, 'Go on.'

'He fiddles!' she blurted out.

'Fiddles! Who fiddles?'

'The Colonel,' she whispered. 'He boils his eggs in coffee

grounds, makes 'em real brown, a deep brown. He's started saving all the coffee grounds already.'

Vicky had hidden our things in the pantry. We changed quietly into our cold night things, shivered, and tiptoed up the steps.

'What's this,' I cried as a creaking stair gave the game away too soon. We chased the fleeing children and caught them, carrying them back to the landing, all wriggling arms and legs.

'Punishment time,' Vicky laughed, 'no vinegar on your chips.'

We sat on the narrow runner in bright moonlight and ate our chips and chocolate cake as I told them of my little talk.

'You've no chance,' I told the happy children. 'You're the product of two fruit cakes, you've no chance at all.'

Vicky supervised a tooth cleaning operation whilst I went downstairs and made tea.

'You enjoyed your talk then,' she said pulling her dressing gown around her shoulders. I confessed that after worrying about it for days I had enjoyed it. They had made it easy for me with their good manners and enthusiasm.

'The mystery of the clock,' she said. 'Tell me about the clock again.'

'Don't mention clocks, and books and eggs.'

'Why eggs?'

'Come on it's bedtime. I'll tell you in the morning.'

I spent all afternoon experimenting with different stains. Rosewood was too intense, American walnut a little wan and cedar far too reddish, but mahogany with just a dash of yew proved ideal. It took the natural bloom off the eggs but this was soon replaced with a rag and some glycerine. The eggs, their natural golden brown advanced to a deep chocolate, stood in the window-sill for two days and showed no sign of fading or patchiness. I filled in my entry form with confidence; all I need do now was to search through the egg basket every day and choose perfectly formed eggs, to apply my new found technique, and the coveted red card was mine to pin behind the apple house door.

Vicky disapproved. If the Colonel won by fiddling that was his business, we didn't have to stoop to his level.

'Put four honest eggs in and take second prize. It'll mean more than a fiddled first,' she advised.

Egg men, real egg men that is, are not satisfied with second place no matter how honestly it's been achieved. They have culled the producers of malformed and crissled eggs ruthlessly from their flocks and they've fed for colour, which is not a cheap or easily understood exercise. No, it had to be first by fair means or foul.

'Just this year,' I promised, 'then no more fiddling, I'll win honestly next year.'

I put my much loved shotgun into the local auction to help pay for the Carlton Smith and to my vexation it didn't do very well. Perhaps I expected too much for it because like many dealers I find it difficult to value my own possessions, but if I was disappointed Canary Mary wasn't. Her medals after being subjected to the corrosive and ageing influence of rabbit droppings looked very authentic. One collector eyed the particularly nasty looking stain on the ribbon of the Waterloo medal. 'Could be blood,' he said in an awed voice. I was itching to disillusion him.

'Rabbit shit,' I was on the point of saying when Mary gave me a very hard look.

The medals, held at arm's length, by an unusually fastidious steward fetched a high price, making Mary's smile as wide as a hayrake.

'Come and sit here.' She patted a vacant chair. She's a good provider is Mary, her huge bag starts a sale day half-filled with food and ends it fully filled with junk. The boiled egg sandwiches with just a smidgin of mayonnaise and black pepper were delicious. 'Not too hard, people always overboil eggs, don't you think?' Mary playfully smacked Fatty Batty's hand as he nodded his agreement and reached for a second sandwich.

'Hard boiled. Hard boiled,' I said more or less to myself, thinking of the devious Colonel and his coffee dregs. 'Mary, you've put a weapon in my hands. A weapon I shall use to smite the mighty. Hip and thigh.'

She gave me a puzzled look and then another sandwich.

'Hip and thigh,' I said again lifting a corner of the sandwich and smiling at the yellow discs snug in their annuli of glassy white.

Ted chuckled when I told him of my plan. The more he thought about it the more he chuckled, and when I said I couldn't wait to see the Colonel's face he burst out laughing, a deep laugh that shook his body and made him roll sideways in his chair.

'I can swing it – you leave that to me.' His red spotted handkerchief: the one that people refer to as a rick cover because it is so large, covered his face, was then pressed to his eyes, then under his nose and then thrust into his pocket. 'Aye, we'll spike the bugger, leave it to me.'

I left as a fresh spasm of laughter shook his body.

Vicky was surprised when I did two consecutive days in the shop without complaining once and when various members of the fête committees came on their cadging expeditions I showed a generosity which brought smiles to their faces.

Yes, they could borrow the cannonballs for putting the shot. We'd be delighted to lend Topic for pony rides. And the Tombola? 'Why of course, here's a pair of good brass candlesticks Mrs Smythe-Robinson.'

Chapter 24

Long John looked down at his bleached and rumpled jeans. 'I'll either have to stop suppin' or stop pine strippin'.'

He had fallen into his stripping tank again. The mild caustic had cracked his boots and left a white rime about them, had bleached his clothes and taken a little hair from his legs; otherwise these submersions seemed to do the tough bachelor little harm.

His tank is massive and he falls into it three or four times a year. You could drop two family saloon cars into that tank and still tuck in a wardrobe, and it is this sheer size which presents the problem. A chest of drawers floats half submerged and can be re-orientated and piloted by a little skilled work with a pitchfork, but a press top or a bedside cabinet bobs about high in the tank steered here and there and clunked against the side by any capricious breeze that deigns to curve around the barn wall. These, then, have to be weighted, and it is this weighting, which involves a precarious hand and knees crawl-out over a scaffolding plank, a coping stone or a clock weight, under one arm, that brings about the stripper's downfall. It requires a cool head, good judgement and an impeccable sense of balance – skills that Swaledale Lightning, even in moderate quantities, tends to blunt.

Long John's raven black hair fell over his face and his beard, a silver hair glistening here and there, was crushed into his chest. He thrust his hands deep into his trouser pockets and shuffled the white rimed boots. 'I think it'll have to be strippin',' he sighed.

It was, I felt, a wise decision; he is not good at stripping. He forgets things. A Georgian serving table on finely turned legs had been hauled out of the tank after it had sailed merrily about for three weeks, its top planks skellowed and warped beyond redemption, and a superb corner cupboard jostled the tank side and suffered a continual battering from a leviathan wardrobe until it completely disintegrated. Long John had combed the surface of the tank with a cowling rake. The panelled door and two shelves were retrieved along with some puzzling bits of moulding and a dead hen, but the rest he never found.

The Colonel had sent me to borrow Long John's quoits, but good manners decreed that we discussed the weather, the price of hay, and that I enquire about his health, his pony and his geese before coming to the point. It was enquiring after his health that had brought up the story of his latest submersion. The preliminaries over I got down to business.

'The Colonel's sent me up to ask if we can borrow your quoits for the fête.'

The rimed boots ploughed the gravel into the ridges then flattened them. 'Can't lend yer me own, nobody's ever cast them except me and me dad.'

I sighed a dejected sigh and turned to look down the ghyll. Long John's feet stopped the gravel scrunching. 'But I've a set of ladies quoits in the barn you can borrow.'

Quoits is a simple game: a simple test of coordination between hand and eye, but amongst some Dalesmen it has donned the mantle of a religion. Cheating and heated tempers are not unheard of, so when the Colonel had asked me to run the quoits match I had flatly refused. The Colonel had taken upon himself an enormous workload and I had promised to organise a fifty–fifty auction for him and act as his ADC, but running the quoits match I felt required someone with a little deviousness in him and the strength of will of Attila the Hun. There was a dearth of such men in the village. The Colonel himself possessed the requisite qualities and Rabbit could, if money was involved, be prevailed upon to exercise some strength of will, but by three o'clock he would be drunk. The Colonel snorted, hrrmphed and postponed the clay pigeon shoot until after tea; he would run the quoits.

I had cut a forty gallon drum in half to make a barbecue, scrounged an armful of electric fencing stakes to carry the white tapes for the children's sports, prevailed upon Fiery Frank to bring his amplifiers and speakers, and now, with four sets of quoits borrowed, I had all but fulfilled my duties.

In the pantry my eggs lay serenely on a delicate wedgewood plate and an edible necklace and a desk-tidy had pride of place on the dresser.

Vicky couldn't find anything to enter. The children sat on my knee as I read through the produce section.

'A fatless sponge' brought a negative shake of the head from their mother, 'four melting moments' a look of horror and a 'Victorian sponge' a curl of the lip.

'You've got to do something,' Sally cried as I turned to the flower arranging section. Soon Vicky was bullied into entering an arrangement in an egg cup.

Peter cried with delight, 'I've got just the egg cup.' He ran and retrieved from a ruttle box a blue-banded and stemmed cup that had just the tiniest of chips on the rim, but it was, we all agreed, a superb egg cup.

The fête was to be opened by Mrs Smythe-Robinson at one o'clock but all entries had to be in place by nine forty-five, so as the church clock in Lalbeck gave one solemn dong, and with fifteen minutes to spare, I crossed the village green to Ted's five acre, carefully balancing the family's skills and efforts on a tin tray.

The Colonel's eggs were already in place, along with the Martins' and four that Rabbit must have purloined on one of his mooches. They looked like four of the Colonel's which had not been helped on the road to perfection by boiling in coffee grounds: they were well-formed but of a very inferior colour. As for the Martins' eggs: well, how can common Rhode Island Reds be expected to match Marans and Barnevelders? The Colonel had, I had to admit, achieved a good colour, but mine were definitely superior.

Miss Wells ticked our entries on her list and gave a rather anxious look at the eggs. She was to judge the produce class and the Colonel had won the egg section for as long as anyone could remember. She did not know that Ted, as the chief steward, was going to guide her through this difficulty and neither did she know that Rabbit had sat in her porch in the early hours of the morning and laboriously counted the dried peas she had borrowed from the shop and housed in a spaghetti jar.

I wandered around the marquee; the grass was getting

crashed and mingling its smell with that of dried cow pats. Miss Wells had taken my tray and having printed the relevant numbers on the little cards with a round hand pen she placed our contributions here and there. Sally's necklace outshone the others and Peter's desk-tidy had enough compartments, little drawers and pigeon holes to impress any judge. Vicky's egg cup full of mignonette and lobelia foaming around a group of harebells was pretty, but overshadowed by the rumbustious entry of Mrs Lewis and the flamboyant, gravity defying sprays that Susan had teased into her egg cup. I went home to a late breakfast. I was to keep shop in the morning then take Topic down for rides in the afternoon.

Fiery Frank tooted his horn as he sped past the washfold and into the field raising a cloud of dust and soon his amplifiers were blasting out the Beatles and Elvis Presley interspersed by country and western songs from the little man himself.

The fête brought us no trade. People peered in the open door, dawdled outside the window, then hurried on to the field. I sold a butcher's steel to a myopic man who fingered the knurling round and round for what seemed an age and a tin of wax to a woman who enjoyed its smell so much she stood stock still with it glued under her nose whilst I drank my coffee.

The children came begging for more money and I had no sooner sent them off happy and put my slippered feet up on the duet stool than Billy Potts shogged in and waved them off. 'There's 'ell on over the eggs.'

I tried not to look too interested.

'Aye, it wor a draw between thee and t'Colonel's, so ar' Ted said they had to break one off each plate open and judge 'em

314

on yolk colour as well.' Billy made the stool creak as he leaned forward and laughed. 'T'bloody Colonel's wor 'ardboiled – tha's won.' He clapped a big hand on my knee and shook it. 'Tha's won. Tha's won.'

Vicky was late but happy, Peter and Sally had got firsts and she was quite thrilled with a third. 'And you, you devious, underhand fiddler, you got a first.'

'I know,' I said happily, 'but you have to fight fire with fire.'

'Was it yours or Ted's idea?'

'Bit of both,' I confessed sheepishly.

After a spartan lunch I harnessed the pony and put the foal in the apple house and chained the dogs in the yard. Vicky put sprigs of lavender in Topic's blinkers and with the coup cart swept out and fitted with our garden seat I set off for the fête.

Mrs Smythe-Robinson shortened my cart route appreciably. 'Once around the field, ten pence,' she said authoritatively, and I with a shrug, complied. It seemed expensive to me for 500 yards in a bumpy cart with no springs, but people seemed to enjoy it and every time I returned with a happy load there was a little queue waiting. It was tiring leading Topic in the hot sun but the pony made light work of it. She was fit and threw her head into the collar willingly, for to her a couple of adults and a bench full of children was no load at all.

The quoits match was in progress and whenever a quoit hit a pin as we passed she raised her head and sometimes gave a little nicker but she behaved like a lady and I had no qualms about letting Peter take over.

I patted Topic's neck. 'Another couple of turns then give her a rest, take her up in the shade and wash her mouth out.'

Peter nodded and dropped the pins in the tailgate, took the

slack out of the reins and clicked his tongue. 'Come on girl,' he said gently. Then 'walk on' in a good strong voice Mr Hall would have approved of.

The Ship's tug-of-war team took on ballast in the taproom and Ted settled himself on a straw bale to watch the mothers' race. 'There's some fine-looking women in this village,' he told a bemused Reverend Sidney. Sally claimed her prize money and joined the queue at the ice-cream van, and my cannonballs thudded on the dry earth, an alarming distance away from the sawdust circle, for the arms of Dales farmers can have a terrible strength in them.

It was time for me to help Sam with the fifty–fifty auction. There was nothing of particular interest, it was predominantly unwanted household goods that had found their way into the small marquee, but leaning against a pole was the Reverend Sidney's hated bicycle. Sam gave me a knowing look. 'We've to keep that out of Stephanie's way till it's sold.'

I spun the rear wheel and tested the brakes. The wheel ticked crisp and even and the brakes snatched the movement out of them; the bearings were firm and the tyres were good. 'Be interested in this,' I told Sam. 'Damn good bike.' I lotted up and wrote owners' names and reserves into Sam's book and laid the goods out in order on the trestle tables.

Viewing was an hour before the sale and Long John, brown-smocked and efficient, firmly turned away a constant stream of inquisitive folk.

We had put several items into the sale. Nothing special, just sound stuff that finds itself amongst a table top lot in a conventional auction.

It was hot in the tent and a drop of Swaledale Lightning with a dash of lemonade was welcome. Sam and Long John forwent the lemonade and with the odd belch and some lip vibrating blows made a serious attack on the bottle.

'I've donated two bottles to the Tombola,' Long John told us with a sacrificial look. 'Good stuff, three months old.'

Sam was round-eyed at the generosity his friend had displayed. 'Two bottles?'

Long John's beard dipped on to the lapels of his smock twice. 'Two bottles.'

'Which are them John? 'Cos there's a few bottles on that stall.'

'It's in a port bottle and a tonic wine bottle.' Sam nodded gently as he stored away the information. 'Port and tonic wine.'

I tied electric leads into neat bows, taped lids on to casseroles and marshalled wine glasses into sets. 'All done Sam. Ready for the master's touch.'

He waved me a sleepy goodbye and dropped his body somewhat recklessly into a canvas chair. Long John, sprawling on the grass, raised a lazy arm. 'Stick a note on the door, pal. No viewing till four o'clock.'

I blinked at the bright sunlight and rubbed the sellotape on to the canvas. I had done my bit.

Ted's white elephant stall had drawn a good crowd. The violin had gone and so had the food mixer but the fish vase still rose gaping-mouthed on its thick tail.

'Sixteen quid Ted. It's not worth sixteen quid,' I told him.

The old farmer pushed his mumpy mouth out at me. 'Can't be far off, I've had a lot of interest in it.' The vase soon lost my attention for laid behind it was a bee smoker I'd lent Rabbit and alongside that a garden spray Ted himself had borrowed.

'That's mine Ted, and that's mine,' I cried, pointing at the smoker and the spray.

He sucked his teeth and looked, not at me, but at Mrs Lewis who was hovering over the fish vase. 'Give us a quid apiece for 'em,' he whispered out of the side of his mouth.

I reluctantly bought my spray and smoker back and went on to the Tombola. Mr Martin, smart-suited and very much the bank manager, spun the drum. 'Anything ending in a five wins,' he said cheerily.

There were several bottles of wine, included amongst them the tonic wine and two bottles of port. Which one was Long John's? It didn't matter because I won nothing and from the look of the tables neither had anyone else. I had two further turns and screwed all fifteen tickets up and then threw them into the waste basket without getting a five. 'It's a fiddle,' I joked.

Mr Martin, unflurried as ever, denied it and even looked a little hurt. 'Perhaps the fives for some inexplicable reason have grouped together. I'll give the drum an extra turn,' he offered, but I'd had enough of Tombola – apart from the wine, packets of sago and tins of peas failed to excite.

Peter was resting Topic again. A group of children gathered around the pony, some patting and offering grass, some just looking. I put the smoker and spray in the cart and straightened up to find a suave-looking Jack the Pat.

'When are you starting the rides again?' he smiled.

'Ask the horseman,' I pointed to Peter.

Jack pushed a banknote into Peter's hand and winked.

'Reserve it for me.'

Peter looked down at the folded note and then at me. 'A tenner,' he mouthed round-eyed. What on earth could Jack the Pat want with the pony and cart? Still, a tenner was a lot of money and it was all going to charity so I shrugged and took myself off to the quoits final. Baz, watched by his adoring wife, lobbed some elegant rings. They sliced into the freshly puddled mud not a finger's width from the pin. Susan gave a little clap and beamed at Baz. It needed a ringer now to beat him and she could, she admitted, see the traditional copper kettle prize already in their hearth.

Little Petal carried Gunnar on her hip. She was feeling the heat but she had taken her white sun hat off and buried the baby's head in it; the baby, hard asleep, clung to her like a crab, oblivious to the jolting of the ample hip.

'Had your fortune told yet?' I asked her, nodding to where Nellie May sat in a tent, a teapot at her elbow and a pack of cards in front of her.

'Don't believe in it,' Petal replied a bit sharply. 'Nothing she told me last year at your place happened. Tall dark stranger indeed; she never told me about the little blonde one.' She hoisted the child in front of her and then rolled her fat arms up over her huge bosom, her lips searching across the baby's stomach. 'No, she never told me about you, my little precious,' she mumbled happily.

I left her sitting on the grass, her legs, the heavy Rubens-type legs that Fiery worried about, wide apart, and her caftan draped over them. She kicked off her sandals and closing her eyes pulled the sleeping baby up to her face.

Peter couldn't wait to tell me his news. Jack the Pat had taken Canary Mary for a ride in the coup cart. 'He put his arm around her and made her laugh,' he told me in a concerned voice, 'made me lead them out over the common and down the lane. Giggling and cuddling they were.' He seemed a bit annoyed with his Aunty Mary.

'Anything, er, change hands. Anything like a small clock?' I asked him.

Peter thought carefully, biting his lip. 'She gave him a little parcel wrapped up in blue tissue.'

'The clock,' I said quietly and with feeling. 'The sod's got the clock.'

Rabbit, contrary to expectations, wasn't drunk at three o'clock. He wasn't drunk at four o'clock either; a little unsteady, but not drunk, as he wrote out his estimate of the number of peas in the jar. '3,643 exactly,' he said, making the leg of the last three so emphatically that the lead in his pencil broke. Miss Wells smiled and screwed the sharpener with an elegant turn of her wrist. Rabbit was counting on winning the pea guessing for Baz had just pipped him in the quoits match, the potatoes and eggs he'd filched from the Colonel's garden had failed to win a place in the produce section, and the dressed stick he'd entered had been disqualified. Totty had recognised it as one of his he'd lost on the fell two summers ago. If the peas didn't come through he'd leave the field without a sneck lifter and, as he'd told an incredulous Ted, 'he'd die of starvation before he'd cadge beer'.

Cousin Leopold won the dressed stick competition and Belgiana had so many prizes for her jams and chutneys that Mucky Marion could only bring herself to give her the most cursory of nods.

'Wattery jam, any bugger can mek wattery jam, my fatless sponge should a' won, damned judges didn't even taste it,' complained Marion, biting off a mitten and flinging it into her pram. 'Don't know why I bothered, it's all a fiddle.'

Fiddle or not, she bought a handful of tickets for the Tombola. 'Might win a bottle to assuage me sorrows, eh,' she said, looking up at me and unable to keep a smile from her brown face.

Baz, smocked and official looking, rang a hand bell at the tent flap. 'Sale starts in five minutes!' he bellowed, as he silenced the last humming tones of the bell with a big thumb.

Sam had partaken his fair share of the bottle. The rickety card table sagged under the weight of his arms, and his hat, pushed to the back of his head, revealed a white and perspiring brow. 'Come on John, let's get the show on the road.'

Long John tied the tent flaps back and gave a hand shielded bellow. 'Come on! Bargains galore.' The bell clashed its harsh tongue again. 'Come on, roll up, bargain time.'

Sam closed his eyes and with an effort raised an arm. 'John, John that's enough wi' the bloody bell. They'll come, they'll come.'

Come they did, they left side shows and Tombola, left guess this and guess that and crowded into the tent. I caught Long John's arm. 'Go to twenty-five quid on the bike for me.'

Mr Martin stood alone behind the Tombola, arms folded and his takings stacked in neat piles in an open toffee tin. The sago had fled and so had many a tin but the two port bottles still rose above the flotsam of packets and jars. They were, the labels proclaimed and the white frosty stencilling confirmed, vintages. Good names, good years.

'A pound's worth, please.' Mr Martin spun the drum. Nothing. 'Go on give us another quid's worth.'

Mr Martin like most bank managers is suspicious of spontaneity, and more than a little perturbed when that spontaneity concerns money. 'You sure?' he asked, arching his brows. I got two fives in my second pile of tickets: a tin of custard powder and a bottle of port. I looked carefully at the seal, it looked all right but then Long John is a very crafty man.

Vicky dug me in the ribs. 'So this is what you were after,' she said, picking up the port.

'Careful with that, it's cost me a fortune,' I whispered, as we walked hand in hand up to the auction tent.

The shop had done nothing she told me sadly. 'Might as well not have bothered.'

Sam was in good form as the bellows of laughter showed. He was just selling 'Kaiser Bill's overcoat' – a herringbone raglan of enormous size and weight. Billy Potts had tried it on and, as he'd told Ted, 'It fit near enough.'

'It's a gentleman's coat Billy,' his cousin had said knowingly. 'Wear that down in the land of my fathers an' them Welshmen'll be throwin' old ewes into thi' wagon for nowt.'

'A pound Billy, give us a pound,' urged Sam.

Billy offered a pound and Mrs Lewis, seeing in it a good cover to keep the frost from the potatoes stacked in the out-house, fluttered her hand and bid one pound fifty. Billy clenched his teeth, spread his knees wide to the consternation and discomfort of the two elderly women who flanked him in the front row, and gave a growl. 'Two quid.'

'Two quid.' Sam beamed and rapped his cane. 'It'll last thee out Billy.'

The new owner of the overcoat did not seem too pleased. 'This isn't the place for a poor man,' he muttered, shaking his head.

'Come on now Billy. If tha' gets a snizey lambing time tha' can wrap half the flock up in that.' Sam laughed. Billy smiled up at him as he took the massive coat from Long John.

I eased the bottle of port out of my pocket and looked at it again, making Vicky tap my arm and whisper, 'Put it away. People'll think your an – well, you know, alcoholic.'

I ignored her, and ran my finger around the seal for the umpteenth time until a haughty and withering look from Mrs Smythe-Robinson made me re-pocket the bottle quickly.

Long John wheeled the bicycle in front of Sam, he squeezed each brake then rang its bell. 'Damned good bike Sam,' he said, loudly, for the benefit of the crowd.

Sam wiped his brow. 'From a good stable, this steed – a tenner anybody.'

Long John waited a second or two then offered a fiver on, I believed, my behalf. The bidding was slow. A stiflingly hot afternoon is not the best time to sell bicycles, especially heavy, well-made machines.

Sam's cane rose to his shoulder. 'Eleven pounds. Seems cheap.'

Stephanie's half-strangled cry turned heads and arrested the cane mid-flight. 'No! No! That's the Reverend Sidney's you can't sell that.'

Sam blew out his cheeks. 'Entry form states . . . ' He shook open his spectacles and nosed them on, 'property of Sidney Murray, no reserve.' He waved the chitty aloft as if that action confirmed beyond all doubt both ownership and intent. 'I'm instructed to sell madam, and my bid is here, eleven pounds.'

Stephanie pushed between me and Vicky. 'Twelve pounds I'll give you twelve pounds,' she said. Then, turning to Vicky, 'There must be some mistake. Sidney's very fond of that machine.'

Long John nodded a bid, and kept on nodding long after my twenty-five pound limit was passed. Stephanie wrung her hands. I think she didn't realise, or had forgotten, it was a fifty–fifty auction and she would get half the money back or she would not have shaken her head and strode off so angrily

323

when the bike was knocked down to Long John for thirty-five pounds.

Vicky and I walked to the top of the field hand in hand. The Colonel was supervising the laying of white tapes and pacing out with military strides some things that needed to be paced out. Ted, his face as red as a turkey cock, searched the hedge bottom for my cannonballs and The Ship's tug-of-war team, having lost to the Fighting Cocks, had consoled themselves with a drink or two. They lay under the sycamore, a semi-circle of white legs and vested chests interspersed with empty bottles and discarded t-shirts.

Little Petal and Fiery plodded back to their van, the baby locked in Fiery's arms yawning a closed-eye, wriggle-mouthed yawn. The debris of the day cluttered around the legs of abandoned tables and little groups of villagers bent heads together that were heavy with gossip.

I lifted the children on to the coup cart and then handed Vicky in and led the pony down the field, steadying her as she pushed her round rump into the breeching.

Mucky Marion jostled her pram towards the gate. She stopped and raised a bottle to her lips, then wiped them with the back of a mitten and grinned up at my cart load.

'It's only tonic wine. If it wor' sherry I could a' done summat wi' it – but I'll just 'ev to sup it.' She let go of her pram handle staggered back three paces and broke out into a raucous laugh.

Miss Wells was at the gate. She darted her thin body at me. 'Well done,' she cried, pushing the red card and a fifty pence piece into my hand. 'No one's ever beaten the Colonel's eggs before.'

Fiery honked his horn and waved goodbye and a happy Reverend Sidney told a puzzled Rabbit that he hadn't won the 'guess the peas' competition. 'You see Rabbit, nobody's daft enough to count them, we just think of a number.'

I led a tired Topic out on to the road and like most ponies when they know they're stable-bound she quickened her pace.

Long John, his brown smock flying, rang a continuous carillon on the bicycle's bell as he careered down the field, described a wide arc across the road which nearly brought him to grief on the pub steps, and then taking advantage of his momentum, pedalled furiously up the green. He gripped the side of the cart with a big sunburnt hand and winked at the children.

'Who's a lucky man?' he grinned.

'I see you got the bike, John,' I said, leaning on Topic. He breathed another grinful of fumes into my face.

'No! I bought it for thee. I know tha' said twenty-five but I thought, it's a damned good bike, he'd want me to go on.'

'Thirty-five quid,' I said, slowly turning the fifty pence piece in my hand. 'Thirty-five quid and I've had to buy back half my belongings, and they've lost my cannonballs.'

Long John lifted the port bottle half out of my pocket. 'Hey, you got the Lightning,' he laughed. 'Thar' a lucky bugger.'

Ted passed us half-hiding the fish vase under his jumper. Old Mr Hall stopped to pat Topic and tell her she was doing all right. Miss Wells waved from the bottom of the green and Baz and Susan strolled up arm in arm clutching a shiny copper kettle between them.

Charlie propped the door of The Ship open and smiled a welcome to Rabbit who had just pushed a laughing Mucky Marion home in her pram and had been rewarded with a 'sneck lifter'.

Mrs Smythe-Robinson ignored her nervous husband and,

head held well back, pointed their massive car between the gateposts and followed the Reverend Sidney's Morris Minor down the washfold track, creeping dangerously near as he stopped to wave goodbye to his hated bicycle.

My cocks crowed and were answered by the Colonel's and Starlight Ramsthwaite Beauty whinnied from the apple house making the mare stir and prick her ears.

'Yes John, the luck of a Countryman.'

Also from Sphere, more of Max Hardcastle's
Tales from the Dales

A COUNTRYMAN'S LOT

April 2011

The first instalment of Max Hardcastle's *Tales from the Dales* series.

Max and his wife Vicky have a daydream. One day, they'll sell their cramped city-centre antiques shop and the overflowing upstairs flat and relocate to the beautiful Yorkshire Dales. If they could only find the perfect place to house both family and business, then that fantasy might become a reality . . .

When a smallholding in a remote Dales village comes on the market, it seems like the answer to their prayers. Bullpen Farm might need 'some renovation', but it has an orchard, outbuildings and all the charm they've dreamt of. Before long, the Hardcastles find themselves the proud owners of a collection of ramshackle buildings and the newest members of a close-knit community which seems to have more than its fair share of eccentrics.

From the antics of the antiques trade to the uproarious incidents of village life, it turns out that rural living isn't quite as tranquil as they'd imagined!

978-0-7515-4419-0

THIS COUNTRY BUSINESS

March 2012

In this third volume of *Tales from the Dales*, the Hardcastle family continue their life among the colourful inhabitants of Ramsthwaite. Whilst village characters, such as Canary Mary and Fiery Frank, divert them with a variety of bizarre adventures, Max and Vicky are still facing challenges on their smallholding. Their antiques business, on the other hand, is thriving, and attracts as many curios as ever, such as crystal balls, a station clock and a locked safe.

As the year proceeds towards the annual Hound Trail, the village enjoys its customary ups and downs – events brought beautifully to life by Max Hardcastle in this warmly engaging memoir.

978-0-7515-4429-9

Other titles available by mail

☐ A Countryman's Lot   Max Hardcastle   £7.99

The prices shown above are correct at time of going to press. However, the publishers reserve the right to increase prices on covers from those previously advertised, without further notice.

──────────────────── sphere ────────────────────

Please allow for postage and packing: **Free UK delivery.**
Europe: add 25% of retail price; Rest of World: 45% of retail price.

To order any of the above or any other Sphere titles, please call our credit card orderline or fill in this coupon and send/fax it to:

Sphere, PO Box 121, Kettering, Northants NN14 4ZQ
Fax: 01832 733076   Tel: 01832 737526
Email: aspenhouse@FSBDial.co.uk

☐ I enclose a UK bank cheque made payable to Sphere for £ . . . .
☐ Please charge £ . . . . . . to my Visa/Delta/Maestro

☐☐☐☐☐☐☐☐☐☐☐☐☐☐☐☐☐☐☐

Expiry Date ☐☐☐☐   Maestro Issue No. ☐☐

NAME (BLOCK LETTERS please) . . . .

ADDRESS . . . .

. . . .

. . . .

Postcode . . . . Telephone . . . .

Signature . . . .

Please allow 28 days for delivery within the UK. Offer subject to price and availability.